ECOLOGIES OF ARTISTIC PRACTICE

Leonardo

Seán Cubitt, Editor-in-Chief

Social Media Archeology and Poetics, edited by Judy Malloy, 2016
Practicable: From Participation to Interaction in Contemporary Art, edited by Samuel Bianchini and Erik Verhagen, 2016
Machine Art in the Twentieth Century, Andreas Broeckmann, 2016
Here/There: Telepresence, Touch, and Art at the Interface, Kris Paulsen, 2017
Voicetracks: Attuning to Voice in Media and the Arts, Norie Neumark, 2017
Ecstatic Worlds: Media, Utopias, Ecologies, Janine Marchessault, 2017
Fred Forest's Utopia: Media Art and Activism, Michael F. Leruth, 2017
Making Sense: Cognition, Computing, Art, and Embodiment, Simon Penny, 2017
Weather as Medium: Toward a Meteorological Art, Janine Randerson, 2018
Laboratory Lifestyles: The Construction of Scientific Fictions, edited by Sandra Kaji-O'Grady, Chris L. Smith, and Russell Hughes, 2018
Invisible Colors: The Arts of the Atomic Age, Gabrielle Decamous, 2018
Virtual Menageries: Animals as Mediators in Network Cultures, Jody Berland, 2019
From Fingers to Digits: An Artificial Aesthetic, Margaret A. Boden and Ernest A. Edmonds, 2019
MATERIAL WITNESS: Media, Forensics, Evidence, Susan Schuppli, 2020
Tactics of Interfacing: Encoding Affect in Art and Technology, Ksenia Fedorova, 2020
Giving Bodies Back to Data: Image Makers, Bricolage, and Reinvention in Magnetic Resonance Technology, Silvia Casini, 2021
A Biography of the Pixel, Alvy Ray Smith, 2021
Living Books: Experiments in the Posthumanities, Janneke Adema, 2021
Art in the Age of Machine Learning, Sofian Audry, 2021
Design in Motion: Film Experiments at the Bauhaus, Laura Frahm, 2022
Northern Sparks: Innovation, Technology Policy, and the Arts in Canada from Expo 67 to the Internet Age, Michael Century, 2022
Christa Sommerer & Laurent Mignonneau: The Artwork as a Living System 1992–2022, edited by Karin Ohlenschläger, Peter Weibel, and Alfred Weidinger, 2023

Computational Formalism: Art History and Machine Learning, Amanda Wasielewski, 2023
Picture Research: The Work of Intermediation from Pre-Photography to Post-Digitization, Nina Lager Vestberg, 2023
Art + DIY Electronics, Garnet Hertz, 2023
Voidopolis, Kat Mustatea, 2023
After Eating: Metabolizing the Arts, Lindsay Kelley, 2023
Tactical Publishing: Using Senses, Software, and Archives in the Twenty-First Century, Alessandro Ludovico, 2023
The Future Is Present: Art, Technology, and the Work of Mobile Image, Philip Glahn and Cary Levine, 2024
Living Surfaces: Images, Plants, and Environments of Media, Abelardo Gil-Fournier and Jussi Parikka, 2024
Heartbeat Art, Claudia Arozqueta, 2025
Ecologies of Artistic Practice: Rethinking Cultural Economies through Art and Technology, Ashley Lee Wong, 2025

See http://mitpress.mit.edu for a complete list of titles in this series.

ECOLOGIES OF ARTISTIC PRACTICE

RETHINKING CULTURAL ECONOMIES THROUGH ART AND TECHNOLOGY

ASHLEY LEE WONG

THE MIT PRESS
CAMBRIDGE, MASSACHUSETTS
LONDON, ENGLAND

The MIT Press
Massachusetts Institute of Technology
77 Massachusetts Avenue, Cambridge, MA 02139
mitpress.mit.edu

The MIT Press would like to thank the anonymous peer reviewers who provided comments on drafts of this book. The generous work of academic experts is essential for establishing the authority and quality of our publications. We acknowledge with gratitude the contributions of these otherwise uncredited readers.

This publication has been supported by the MIT Press Grant Program for Diverse Voices.

This book was set in Arnhem Pro and Frank New by Westchester Publishing Services. Printed and bound in the United States of America.

Library of Congress Cataloging-in-Publication Data

Names: Wong, Ashley Lee, author.
Title: Ecologies of artistic practice : rethinking cultural economies through art and technology / Ashley Lee Wong.
Description: Cambridge, Massachusetts : The MIT Press, [2025] | Series: Leonardo | Includes bibliographical references and index.
Identifiers: LCCN 2024032019 (print) | LCCN 2024032020 (ebook) | ISBN 9780262552165 (paperback) | ISBN 9780262382755 (pdf) | ISBN 9780262382762 (epub)
Subjects: LCSH: Art—Economic aspects. | Artists—Social networks. | Art and technology.
Classification: LCC N8600 .W65 2025 (print) | LCC N8600 (ebook) | DDC 338.4/77—dc23/eng/20241230
LC record available at https://lccn.loc.gov/2024032019
LC ebook record available at https://lccn.loc.gov/2024032020

10 9 8 7 6 5 4 3 2 1

EU product safety and compliance information contact is:
mitp-eu-gpsr@mit.edu

For Finley

CONTENTS

SERIES FOREWORD

Leonardo, the International Society for the Arts, Sciences, and Technology, fosters transformation at the nexus of art, science, and technology because complex problems require creative solutions. The Leonardo book series shares these aims of artistic and scientific experimentation, and publishes books to define problems and discover solutions, to critique old knowledge and create the new.

In the early twentieth century, the arts and sciences seemed to interact instinctively. Modern art and modern poetry were automatically associated with relativity and quantum physics, as if the two were expressions of a single zeitgeist. At the end of the Second World War, once again it seemed perfectly clear that avant-garde artists, architects, and social planners would join cyberneticists and information theorists to address the problems of the new world order and to create new ways of depicting and understanding its complexity through shared experiences of elegance and experiment. Throughout the twentieth century, the modern constantly mixed art and science.

In the twenty-first century, though, we are no longer modern but contemporary, and now the wedge between art and science that C. P. Snow saw emerging in the 1950s has turned into a culture war. Governments prefer science to arts education, yet they stand accused of ignoring or manipulating science. The arts struggle to justify themselves in terms of economic or communicative efficiency that devalues their highest aspirations. And yet never before have artists, scientists, and technologists worked together so closely to create individual and collective works of cultural power and intellectual grace. Leonardo looks beyond predicting dangers and challenges, beyond even planning for the unpredictable. The series publishes books that are both timely and of enduring value—books that address the perils of our time, while also exploring new forms of beauty and understanding.

Seán Cubitt, Editor-in-Chief, Leonardo Book Series

ACKNOWLEDGMENTS

This book is the result of over fifteen years of practice and research in the field of art and technology, where text and ideas have gone through many iterations. This latest version has been pared down and reformulated to provide a glimpse into a rapidly changing field. It is important to note that the bulk of the research was conducted prior to the COVID-19 pandemic and the advent of NFTs (non-fungible tokens). I have made some effort to update the text, though I hope the practices and ideas continue to resonate regardless of time and context to pave new ways forward.

I would like to thank my peers and colleagues at the School of Creative Media, City University of Hong Kong, who provided the support to develop the research in this book, particularly my supervisors Damien Charrieras and Linda Lai for their comments and support during the development of the research. I would like to thank Yuk Hui who provided me support during the writing of this book, and opportunities to work with the Research Network for Philosophy and Technology and the journal *Technophany*. I value the new colleagues and institutional support from the Department of Cultural and Religious Studies at the Chinese University of Hong Kong, particularly Pang Laikwan and Benny Lim, for providing opportunities to further my teaching and research stemming from this book. Thanks also to Peichi Chung and Katrien Jacobs for their support and guidance in navigating academia. I would like to acknowledge the support of Christopher Salter and Matthew Fuller during my undergraduate and graduate studies, whose early guidance and inspiration led me to the place where I am now.

I am grateful for all the conversations and encounters with artists and practitioners in the book, and with those who are not mentioned who may have fed directly or indirectly to this research. Beside those featured in the book, I'd like to thank Genoa Mungin, Claudia Hart, Paolo Cirio, Mattia Casalegno, Mat Spisbah, and Edwin Lo, and many others for discussions over the years about art and practice. Thanks to those I met during a two-month research trip to California including Tom Leeser, Ed Shanken, and Samantha Culp. I value the team at Sedition, which includes Rory Blain, Vilius Paulauskas, and Estela Oliva, who shaped my experience there. I appreciate the conversations with Julia Kaganskiy, formerly of New Inc, the museum-led incubator for art, technology, and design in New York; Kay Vasey from MeshMinds, a nonprofit foundation and creative technology studio in Singapore, for sharing their work; and Alana Kushni, for inviting us to participate in the Serpentine Gallery's Legal Lab. While some of these projects are not discussed in the book, they form part of a wider discussion on the ecosystems for supporting art and technology.

In addition, I would like to thank Emily Verla Bovino for our ongoing conversations on art, theory, research, and writing, and Ryo Ikeshiro and my sister, Tiffany, for reviewing and commenting on early versions of chapters of this book. Many thanks to Emily Doucet for her thoughtful editorial support and guidance in shaping the framework for the book. Finally, I am grateful for the support of my parents for trusting me in my academic and artistic endeavors. Forever thanks to my partner in life and with MetaObjects, Andrew Crowe, who contributed his insight and support throughout the editorial process, and for providing me with the strength and encouragement to embark on this exciting journey together.

INTRODUCTION: THINKING ECONOMIES ECOLOGICALLY

In 2017, upon returning to Hong Kong after nearly a decade in the UK, I started a studio called MetaObjects with my partner Andrew Crowe. One of our first collaborations was with the artist Samson Young, working on a 3D printed sculpture. Following this first 3D printing project, Young invested in a large-format 3D printer to continue to work in the medium. We agreed to help facilitate production for him on the machine. When the printer arrived from Europe, we discovered it couldn't fit in the lift of his studio building. As a result, Young had to get a separate small studio space nearby, just for the printer. Due to the high cost of property in Hong Kong, we suggested that Young share the expense of renting the space with MetaObjects. We would then use the studio as our own production space. This unexpected event ultimately acted as a steppingstone for us to get our own space in Hong Kong, a difficult proposition in a city with high rents. Through this arrangement, we had the opportunity to allow other artists to use the printer while MetaObjects facilitated the production, while also continuing to produce works for Young. While we could have simply retained the printer for Young's use, we saw the opportunity to enable other artists to use the printer as a shared resource as a response to limited access to such technologies. In doing so, our practice opens possibilities for the practices of others via community support where artists are given reduced rates to use the printers. We understand the economic situation in Hong Kong and the struggles artists face concerning space and access to resources. From this one project, our work with Young has evolved into a long-term collaboration founded upon a trust-based relationship in which we mutually support each other by sharing knowledge and resources. By thinking of ourselves as part of a network of interdependence, we have shifted our role as practitioners to one in which we collectively foster the material conditions that enable art to exist.

Working across virtual reality (VR), 3D printing, motion capture, audiovisual production, and web development, MetaObjects encourages knowledge sharing about new digital tools and processes through a collective and collaborative process of learning through doing. We have developed collaborations with artists and cultural institutions to enable a deeper understanding of the possibilities of advanced technologies. In this sense, our work with MetaObjects does not start with a predefined idea. Through an immanent practice of engaging within daily realities, we open the possibility for the invention of new practices and relational possibilities with and among others in the community. Through this open-ended approach, we began to carve out a role through the diverse collaborations across disciplines and sectors, mediating between sectors of art, technology, and academia. In the course of our work, I began to see how creative practices are contingent, emerging in response to the environment, rather than as something that can be planned and strategically mobilized. In particular, I began to observe how practices engaging with art and technology have renegotiated the meaning and value of art. Just as the size of Young's printer initiated an agreement for resource sharing and collaboration for our studio, economies are the social and material relations that provide the conditions of possibility for artistic practice.

Shifting away from a human-centered approach to economics, which places *Homo economicus*[1] as the rational and self-interested "man" at the center of "the economy" as a singular, grand, and universal concept, I propose thinking of "economies" (plural) as multiple, diverse, and consisting of interconnected networks of collaborators and institutions engaged in a process of circulation and exchange. *Economies* are both social, consisting of humans interacting with each other and generating meaning and value through shared practices, and material, consisting of the technologies, space, and monetary means to produce and circulate art. These practices are emergent as they respond to dynamic technological, economic, social, and cultural environments.

The etymology of the word "economy" derives from the Greek term *oikos* (οἶκος), meaning management of the "household," environment, habitat, or milieu in which we are embedded. Matthew Fuller and Olga Goriunova remark on the link between "economy" and "ecology" as words both containing the prefix "eco-": "Oikos unites the economic and ecological activities of the household. It is hard to disentangle shelter and value; it is tragic that it is hard to disentangle ecology and economy."[2] Through this book, I suggest thinking about economies *ecologically*.[3] This is not necessarily to think only of our natural environment, but to think of *cultural* ecologies[4] as the relationships that connect us with other living and nonliving things, and to consider the processes of knowledge production and meaning making as part of our social and technological environments. To think of cultural economies in ecological terms is to consider other people, organizations, and technologies as constitutive of our everyday environments. Rather than looking at artworks as stand-alone objects separated from their context, I look at artistic *practices* in situated contexts. The term *ecosystems* has the potential to be understood both in terms of ecological and economic systems. Informed by a systems-thinking approach,[5] I look at diverse communities in the cultural economy from art markets, and online digital cultures, to design industries, in relation to larger systems of the financial, technology, and academic sectors, and consider how these different systems interact as part of a larger whole. Practices within these systems evolve in relationship to each other, for instance alongside technological advancements, economic developments, or artistic movements. On an individual level, thinking ecologically involves thinking about how we are connected as part of a shared cultural milieu, through networks of collaborations, congregating around shared resources. An ecological perspective represents artistic practice as the result of collective interdependencies that evolve over time, thereby necessitating a broader view of economies beyond simply observing the units of exchange.

BEYOND PRECARITY AND CONDITIONS OF DISEMPOWERMENT

This book emerged through a process of grappling with the material conditions of, and discourses around, precarity that have become pervasive in the cultural field. Historically, the image of the "starving artist" has been used to describe the precarious position of artists. In his book *Why Are Artists Poor?*, Hans Abbing details the impoverished living conditions of artists, a trend that began largely in the nineteenth century as artists became more autonomous and moved away from dependent relationships with aristocratic wealth. More recently, the notion of precarity has been widely discussed as a symptom of post-industrial capitalism and an economy based upon flexibility and freelance and project-based work.[6] Precarity becomes a persisting condition where there is reduced social welfare, while full-time salaried positions are replaced by temporary and short-term contracts. The growth of this economy is marked by the rise of digital technologies, as a global and networked economy founded upon the sharing of knowledge and information, intellectual property, and a service-based economy. Art and technology are necessarily swept up in these transformations in larger economic systems, including the intersections of the art market, technology, and finance industries.

Artists and practitioners struggle with financial insecurity, despite the growing importance of culture and creativity to the global economy. They are forced to become more entrepreneurial in a highly competitive market economy. New forms of exploitation emerge, particularly in the creative industries, with a rise in short-term contracts and unpaid internships. Forms of free labor and self-exploitation become a norm, born from the desire to "do what you love."[7] Silvio Lorusso uses the term "entreprecariat"[8] to describe the precarious conditions of entrepreneurs who are left to bear the risks of running their own business. The rising cost of rent in major cities also means many artists need to juggle multiple jobs to sustain their lives. The contemporary condition is characterized by its liquidity, its "fragility, temporariness, vulnerability and inclination to constant change,"[9] which presents a highly destabilizing existence. In this context, artists and cultural workers are left disempowered and precarious, in the throes of the market. Capitalism can be viewed as an all-encompassing reality, which continually adapts, capturing all forms of life to the degree that it becomes impossible to imagine anything beyond it.

While academic research in the humanities and social sciences tends to focus on alternative economic models such as platform cooperatives, social enterprise, and peer-to-peer,[10] to name a few, these practices often remain small-scale, marginalized, and utopian. While some may imagine artists in opposition to the market, there has long been an economic necessity for artists to engage with the market. Even the noncommercial sector feeds the dominant art market, what Gregory Sholette calls the "*dark matter*"[11] of the art market. Forms of resistance and efforts to escape the market are rendered impotent when these communities are either left on the fringes of society or complicit in perpetuating the economies they seek to undermine.[12] There continues to be contradiction between resisting market forces and being coopted by them. The focus on noncommercial and alternative practices often ignores broader research into the commercial sector.

The processes of making a living and making art, however, do not need to be diametrically opposed. As stated by Andrew Barry and Don Slater, "Instead of viewing economics as a bad science it would be better to view economics as a set of technical practices."[13] Taking up this idea, this book examines economies as social and material processes in order to imagine how shifting these techniques might create new forms of relations and systems of value. Rather than critiquing artists engaging with capitalist cultural economies or dwelling on the debates around precarious labor, I examine how artists are engaging with different cultural economies *in practice*. By suspending critique of the economy to examine the relationship between artistic practice and the economic relationships that provide the material resources necessary to sustain it, I argue that a more holistic and multilayered view of economies as dynamic processes is necessary for the reorientation of practice toward more meaningful and sustainable ways of engaging with contemporary art, design, and technology, and the markets surrounding the sectors.

At the same time, today's cultural economies and the art market continue to be haunted by modernist values and conceptions of art grounded in authenticity, uniqueness, and originality. The art market as understood in European history rose during the Renaissance and Early Modern period in the fifteenth century in Belgium and Italy.[14] Like museums dedicated to the collection and preservation of art, the art market valorizes material authenticity. These institutions enforce values of uniqueness and originality that emerged from the Enlightenment and the Romantic ideal of the artist as genius.[15] The market fixes an object as a finite and collectable entity just as museological practices of preservation are mechanisms that capture and fix a work of art within history and time. Here, artists are original authors of finite objects and commodities for trade, rather than actors within dynamic temporal and collective processes as some Chinese conceptions of art may suggest.[16] According to philosopher Byung-Chul Han, "Chinese thought distrusts fixed, invariable essences or principals,"[17] favoring instead a vision of nature where everything is constantly in flux in infinite variability and change. Throughout this book, I attempt to approach an understanding of cultural economies as variable and diverse, and constituted through dynamic processes of creation and circulation. These processes are enacted and reenacted in time, where art objects do not exist in and of themselves, but rather need to be placed into circulation in order to remain in our shared consciousness. In this sense, it may be possible to consider a temporal conception of artworks sustained through a collective effort. By shifting away from the hegemonic logics of authorship and ownership that structure the art market, we can identify different practices that may produce different, and potentially more equitable, economies.

Over the years, I found myself playing a role in the creative economy, contributing value as a practitioner yet also feeling exploited by precarious labor conditions of increasingly neoliberal economic regimes. I began my journey as an independent cultural worker in do-it-yourself (DIY) music communities. Following art school, my practice evolved to working with video and time-based media. I saw organizing events as part of my own artistic practice.[18] I did not curate exhibitions, but facilitated events, and later publications and discursive platforms.[19] However, these projects were hardly sustainable. These early experiences supporting artists and enabling experimentation continue to inform my thinking on art and artistic practice as shared temporal experiences. I did not start from curating objects displayed in white cube gallery spaces as the practices that

I was interested in did not sit comfortably in the traditional gallery, museum, or art market system.[20] Creating new platforms for diverse forms of art was a way of creating an environment and space for art and culture to exist. This seems to be characteristic of works employing different forms of technology, where the medium itself is the message (as Marshall McLuhan might say[21]), dictating the meaning of a work, its circulation, reception, and existence in the world. The unification of art and technology, as suggested by the Ancient Greek term *tékhnē* embodies both meanings of art and craft, and implies the creation of new cultural milieus where artists and practitioners adapt their environments to create new spaces for art that transcend the boundaries of museums and galleries.[22] Such ephemeral practices extend beyond the established traditions of the art market. Without a clear economic model for sustaining this type of work, artists and cultural workers are faced with a precarious situation.

Fresh out of grad school during the global economic crisis of 2008, I needed to reconsider my practice and how I was going to make a living. I began working at Sedition (to be discussed at greater length in chapter 3), an online marketplace based in London that specialized in the sales of limited-edition videos and images by contemporary artists seeking to create a new marketplace for digital art.[23] I worked with Sedition from 2012 to 2017, during which time I began discovering ways of experimenting and intervening with art markets from within. The experience at Sedition marked a shift in my own work, which took many more years of reading and reflecting to fully understand. I have come to see it as a shift in my own thinking and practice from modes of critique[24] toward an *affirmative practice*. As Braidotti writes: "The praxis of affirmative ethics actualizes virtual possibilities and therefore constructs possible futures starting from the here and now. This constructive approach transforms the negative conditions of the present into productive conditions for affirmative practice."[25] Rather than dwelling on negative conditions such as the lack of resources, an affirmative practice seeks to make positive impacts, however small they may be. This might include identifying opportunities to share resources and open opportunities for other artists, as in the case of MetaObject's collaboration with Samson Young. From working at Sedition as a means to escape precarity, I gained insight into the commercial gallery world, and the diverse economies, cultures, and communities in which forms of art and technology circulate. This intimate understanding of the art market allowed me to understand my own role and relations with artists as a process that is much broader than my job to sell art. Through the knowledge I gained from working at Sedition, I began to see the possibilities for rethinking my engagement in the field as a shifting in my ethical and political perspective. I saw ways to enable and support artistic practices through this experience, which also carried me through to new projects and initiatives with MetaObjects.

While most studies on art and economics tend to focus on modern and contemporary art markets, or the relationship between art and labor, I look specifically at artists and organizations working with technology operating within the contemporary art field, whose practices overlap with artists in general, but also extend beyond to the wider creative industries through interdisciplinary practices straddling art, design, science, sound, and music. This book examines the economies of individual artistic practices as they evolve in time through their projects. By analyzing a constellation of practices, this research makes visible the diverse economies with the potential for rethinking the relationship of art and the market. In the field of cultural economics, there is a tendency to study art and culture through the frameworks of functional economies,[26] where art is continuously rationalized in economic terms and treated as an "exceptional economy," as in not fitting the frames of traditional neoclassical market mechanisms.[27] Instead, this book presents what might be considered an unorthodox study of cultural economies as a diverse set of systems and practices. The study of art and technology requires a broader scope, understanding contemporary practices as part of diverse creative economies in what we might consider an expanded art market.

As an embedded practitioner, I too am *becoming-with* the artists and organizations that I encounter in the field through lived experiences of engaging within economies, where we mutually negotiate a role and practice. To understand the efficacy of an economic system is to understand pragmatically "what works"[28] for whom and in what ways, and the emerging meanings and values of art. Rather than reflecting on the economy from the outside in opposition to the market, it is my intention to operate immanently from within to identify the sites for potential intervention or change. The constant negotiation of a means to create work may be described as a process of "making do," which in the common definition refers to making the most of scant resources. However, in Michel de Certeau's use of the term, it reflects a mode of practice that has potential to subvert and transform daily practices.[29] Making do with what you have involves creative invention, but also connotes a politics of shifting tactics and uses of things beyond calculated strategic practices. These dynamic practices are "ways of operating" or "modalities of action," which can be critical, experimental, artistic, and subversive.[30] There are a multiplicity of ways of moving, operating, and acting that are presented in the process of "making do" to open up possibilities for the future. A move away from a mode of critique is to avoid dwelling on the criticisms of the economy at the expense of addressing the very real need to adapt to current conditions. At the same time, it is not a celebration of the "irrational exuberance"[31] surrounding innovation, creativity, and technological advances, but rather, taking a neutral position to recognize the necessity of engaging within contemporary cultural economies while opening up new relational possibilities.

DIVERSE ECONOMIES OF ART AND TECHNOLOGY

The concept of the creative economy emerged as a product of neoliberalism and globalization in the 1980s. These developments in the global economy, led by political leaders such as Ronald Reagan, Margaret Thatcher, and in some respects, Deng Xiaopeng, led to a shift from Fordism, an economy based on industrial labor, to post-Fordism, an economy based on intellectual labor, while factories were relocated to emerging economies like China.[32] The notion of the creative economy first appeared in British cultural policy in the late 1990s, detailing the key role played by art and culture in neoliberal agenda. Tony Blair's New Labour policies sought to promote the UK through its cultural exports, which has become the model for countries around the world. Following the 2008 economic crisis, there was a further restructuring of the global economy placing the creative industries at the center of the UK economy. These developments have led to increasing privatization of the arts and cultural sectors, where in the UK, Arts Council England has faced widespread and continuous defunding over the past decade.[33] Aligning with policies around the creative economy, cities and countries worldwide have sought to place culture as a key driver of growth, a practice that continues to this day. Examples include Singapore, which was named UNESCO's Creative City of Design in 2015,[34] while Changsha was designated China's Creative City of Media Arts[35] in 2017. The Art Tech initiative announced in the Hong Kong government's 2020 Policy Address[36] aims to fund art and innovation across educational, business, and cultural sectors in order to remain globally competitive. Art engaging with advanced technologies such as artificial intelligence (AI), virtual reality (VR) and augmented reality (AR), motion capture, and 3D animation are used to brand cities as modern and sophisticated. While these kinds of art and technology initiatives fulfill the creative economy agenda, they also engage with the art market, which present tensions with mass market economies and the creative industries.

In the 1950s and 1960s, the rise of mass media and popular culture prompted art to merge with the culture industry. Artists like Andy Warhol blurred the boundaries between high and low art. Bohemianism became conflated with a new bourgeois lifestyle. The postwar period also saw a rise of government funding of the arts, leading to an increasing professionalization of the field engendered by MFA programs, art prizes, and cultural institutions. Since the 1980s, corporations and the private sector have played a larger role in the economies of art as part of increasing privatization, which has been discussed by writers and scholars such as Chin-Tao Wu, Isabelle Graw, and Martha Buskirk.[37] In developed economies, the late 1990s saw the birth of the "creative entrepreneur" as described by author and literary critic William Deresiewicz in his essay and book *The Death of the Artist*.[38] Rather than reject the market, twenty-first-century artists have become creative entrepreneurs, necessarily engaging in self-employment and juggling multiple jobs. Artists participate in activities of brand building, social networking, and commodity production. Narratives around the creative economy present grand visions for artists and cultural workers; however, the realities rarely add up. Today's hyper-commercialized and technologically accelerated environment raises questions for artists and practitioners on how to renegotiate a practice within it.

The field of art and technology is a largely undefined and contentious space situated between sectors and disciplines, converging with the art market, technological innovation, and creative industries. The practices of artists and organizations working with art and technology present a unique area of study to understand the diversification and convergences of contemporary cultural economies, partly perpetuated and enabled by technological advancements. Between nonprofit forms of funding such as grants, commercial economies of the art market, and corporate collaborations with brands, economies are understood as layered and coexisting simultaneously with one another. Artists engaged in art and technology necessarily navigate diverse systems and economies to sustain their practices, within which an understanding of the complex field of art and technology emerges through the dynamic negotiations of the means to create and circulate art.

In the 1980s and 1990s, the term "new media art" was used to describe forms of art and technology, as consumer technologies become more widely available. Centered on artistic experimentations with technology, new media art has traditionally remained on the fringes of what Edward Shanken has called the "mainstream contemporary art" (MCA) world.[39] This marginal position is due in part to media art's technical complexity, relationship to entertainment, commercial graphic design, and spectacular forms of art. Media art and early forms of internet art remained difficult to sell due to challenges of preservation and maintenance, as well as its unfamiliar digital aesthetics, technical complexity, and ephemeral nature. Mark Tribe, founder of Rhizome, and art critic Reena Jana describe the anti-establishment spirit of early new media artists and how they often operated without institutional support, outside of and against the market through self-organized networks, email lists, websites, and online forums.[40] Media artists often resisted notions of individual authorship and the commodification of art in support of a hacker ethics of decentralization, open access, and networked collaboration, aspects of which share the countercultural spirit and libertarianism of the tech industry.[41]

As a form of art and technology and an artistic movement responding to our digital condition, post-internet art emerged in the mid-2000s, characterized as work by the first generation of artists to grow up with the internet. As a result, these artists create works through the lens, techniques, and aesthetics of digital and networked technologies, while ironically appropriating practices of the creative entrepreneur. As coined by Marisa Olson and elaborated on by Artie Vierkant, post-internet artists employ digital technologies that are intrinsic to our contemporary mediated lives.[42] Having lived through the 2008 economic crisis, post-internet artists are responding to an increasingly neoliberal, hyper-mediated, and marketized economy. Many of these artists embrace the market partly as a means of survival and nihilistic acceleration. They simultaneously employ subtle forms of subversion through ironic use of corporate aesthetics, while actively exploiting market mechanisms for their work through an affirmative approach. Rather than critiquing capitalism, many post-internet artists appropriate the logic, language, and aesthetics of markets in ways that could be seen as complicit to it. The cultural shift within the political orientation of artists toward the market marks a move from the margins to the mainstream to explore new possibilities for artistic practice. Through an intimate look at the practices of artists and organizations, I begin to map in this book a partial perspective of the economies of art and technology. I say "partial" so as not to claim to present a complete reality, acknowledging instead that there are infinite possibilities and variations of relational arrangements.

By examining these diverse economies[43] through the practices of artists and organizations, we can understand how artworks are constituted via their circulation, where meaning and value of art shifts and transfigures in the process. There is a need to attend to the meaning emerging from every relation and process of exchange. In what Benjamin Lee and Edward LiPuma call the "cultures of circulation," a cultural form, such as an artwork, is understood as a cultural phenomenon as it circulates in an economy. Artworks, and the communities engaged in the process of circulating them, are co-constituted via the performativity of the market. Lee and LiPuma propose that circulation is a "cultural process with its own forms of abstraction, evaluation, and constraint, created by the interactions between specific types of circulating forms and the interpretive communities built around them."[44] Within this conception, artworks acquire meaning and value through their circulation in diverse economies of the art world through exhibitions, events, and online communities of the art world. Rather than follow fixed notions of commodities circulating in prefigured systems of production and distribution, as in neoclassical economics, artworks and their markets are produced in the process of circulation. In this dynamic process, ways of exhibiting and selling conceptual and post-media artworks in an interdisciplinary context where works are not defined by their medium, are constantly being negotiated and invented. Art does not somehow operate outside of social and economic systems; it is embedded within them, enabling its production and role within society. Artworks are social *things* and cannot be separated from the economies in which they are circulated because they are constituted by them.[45]

ECOLOGIES OF ARTISTIC PRACTICE

Rather than studying the practices of individual artists working alone in their studio or studying artworks at the end of production, this book contextualizes the work of artists in terms of the collaborators that help put their work into circulation or, that co-produce the artworks. These relationships are constantly renegotiated and are open to different possibilities for the creation and circulation of art. Relationships include those with galleries, curators, collectors, corporations, and fabricators who provide material resources, such as funding, equipment, skills, and space to create art.

Together these diverse relationships constitute what Isabelle Stengers has called an "ecology of practices." For Stengers, an ecology of practices allows for the emergence of new practices through the evolution of complex relationships that allow for an inner necessity to propel a shift toward change. She writes, "The problem for each practice is how to foster its own force, make present what causes practitioners to think and feel and act. But it is a problem which may also produce an experimental togetherness among practices, a dynamic of pragmatic learning of what works and how. This is the kind of active, fostering *milieu* that practices need in order to be able to answer challenges and experiment changes, that is, to unfold their own force."[46] For instance, the necessity to find a new space for the 3D printer with Young initiated a process of collaboration in the mutual desire to find a means to create art. By engaging in the practical realities of the lack of affordable space in this instance, we experimented with an arrangement to share the space and the resource as a means of creating an environment that can enable others to engage with technology. Within the chapters, I examine how in the process of negotiating a means to create work, circulating artworks online and offline, and creating work in collaboration with corporations and artists-as-corporations, these diverse relations begin to unfold new practices. Rather than practices being dictated from without, artists discover new ways for their art to exist in the world. In this way, practices are not predetermined and diverge from the narratives presented by public policy, or practices laid out by the industry. Throughout the book we may gain a nuanced perspective of the kinds of practices that matter for artists.

The artists and organizations selected here are entry points to a complex field. Despite their similarities in their engagement with forms of art and technology, their practices span diverse perspectives in relation to the art market and contemporary cultural economies, from which I illuminate only a few. The purpose is not to grasp a complete conception of the whole of the creative economy, but rather get a sense of the diversity of practices and possibilities within it. As mentioned, I focus on commercial economies as a means to finding a way of engaging within a hypermarketized space. By considering mid-career artists, we can understand how the economies for sustaining their practices have evolved over time.[47] The cases are geographically spread across North America, Europe, and East Asia (connected to my own orientation within the field), yet they are also interlinked and circulated as part of a globalized economy. At the same time, the cases contain their own regional specificities in which they are situated, where the diversities of practice are also presented, requiring analysis on a case-by-case basis. The intention is not to produce generalizations, but rather to explore possible ways of thinking of our diverse economic relationships to inform the future.

To begin, consider the case of Lorna Mills, an artist who works with video and internet based in Toronto, Canada. She has largely sustained her artistic practice through working in game development and video production. Since the 1990s, she has worked with videos and animated GIFs (an image format widely used in internet art) as part of her art and has found affinity among a generation of post-internet artists, a movement of artists producing works in context of social media and our digitally mediated condition. The images for her works are appropriated from notoriously transgressive sources across the web, including 4Chan, porn sites, and a range of Russian, American, and British domains. She studied digital media and has worked in film, video, painting, and photography in her artistic career. Lorna Mills is represented by TRANSFER Gallery in the United States, in various locations in New York, Miami and Los Angeles, and DAM Gallery in Berlin.

Founded by Kelani Nichole in 2013, TRANSFER Gallery (now simply known as TRANSFER following the COVID-19 pandemic as their activities moved online) was among a few commercial galleries (at the time) dedicated to promoting and selling "born-digital" artworks or works created and sold in the digital medium. As suggested by the name, TRANSFER alludes to a mode of circulation of digital files through a network. The gallery specializes in VR, AR, video, GIF animations, and installations that focus on artists making computer-based artworks and forms of networked and experimental media art practices. With TRANSFER, Mills circulates her artworks online for free while also selling her works as video installations to galleries and museums. At times contradictions are produced between digital economies valuing free distribution versus the economies of the art market valuing scarcity and uniqueness of the object. Mills has experimented with different formats for distributing her work such as videos installations, animated GIFs freely circulated on the internet, licensed videos for display on media facades, and as NFTs (non-fungible tokens). TRANSFER experiments with formats to enable the circulation of immersive artworks such as VR, simulations, and games, including the TRANSFER Download, which allows works to be presented in exhibitions as three-channel video installations. The gallery pays close attention to documentation and licensing of digital artworks that are sold in the art market to encourage appropriate care and stewardship. Like with conceptual art, digital art does not have a fixed materiality, but is rather sold with documentation, instructions for restaging an artwork, sets of materials, a license agreement, and at times, a certificate of authenticity. In this way, the conceptualization of the artwork changes in the diverse ways it is sold and circulated both online and offline, requiring experimentation in the methods of presentation and distribution.

onformative is a digital art and design studio founded in 2010 by Julia Laub and Cedric Kiefer and based in Berlin. The studio works across art, design, and technology, creating generative art installations as part of their commercial work for clients. Their artistic practice spans data visualizations, generative design, and audiovisual, interactive, and kinetic installations. Alongside their commercial design practice, they also create artworks to experiment with new technologies, which also acts as a form of research and development (R&D) for their commercial projects. By promoting their self-initiated unpaid artistic projects, they have attracted the interest of corporate clients, who allow them to experiment with new technologies and develop unique collaborations with musicians and sound designers through their commercial work. Blurring the boundaries of art and design, onformative has developed a practice that can sustain experimental practices through commercial design. The structure of their studio is also renegotiated through their projects spanning artwork and commissions with corporations like Dolby Laboratories, where in the process, onformative redefines what it means to be a studio.

New York-based duo LoVid was formed by Tali Hinkis and Kyle Lapidus in 2001. LoVid's art practice employs analogue and digital technologies and craft and code to create immersive installations, audiovisual performances, videos, textiles, synthesizer sculptures, and participatory projects, and stems largely from LoVid's engagement in the DIY experimental music community. Hinkus and Lapidus have previously supported their practice through a mix of touring, talks and screenings, teaching, and grants, and they now develop large-scale projects with a wide range of collaborators and partnerships with universities across art and science. They sell their works as both physical and digital editions, which are the primary means for sustaining their practice. These different economies place different kinds of constraints on their practice, which begin to shape the organization of their time and labor and the resulting work itself.

Desmond Leung is an artist based in Hong Kong who works across video, painting, VR, and AR. Leung started his career working in the multimedia production industry as a creative director. In his work, Leung produces large-scale video installations and interactive works influenced by an interest in mindfulness and spirituality explored through motifs and abstractions found in water and nature. He has always had an interest in Chinese painting, and eventually developed a technique for creating moving-image ink paintings. The technique involves filming the process of painting in a tray of water, where the movement and splashes of the ink are video-captured to create a flowing moving-image work. His work in the industry gave him deeper knowledge of video production and screen technologies that informs his practice. Leung has collaborated with CHANEL, the fashion brand, to create new artworks for display on their facades and shop interiors. He notes that commissions in public space allow for broader awareness that connects people in cities and provide him with opportunities to develop new artworks, which are different from licensing or releasing digital editions on the online platform Sedition, as private displays often do not initiate a creative process. Leung and several other artists discussed in this book including LoVid and onformative have worked with Sedition to release their works as digital limited editions and as commissioned and licensed artworks for public displays.

Founded in 2011 in London, Sedition distributes digital limited editions by contemporary artists. The platform seeks to create a new way to collect art in the digital age (prior to the emergence of NFTs). While there was a need to create a sense of value by creating artificial scarcity of infinitely reproducible digital objects, there was simultaneously a desire to promote the artworks on social media contradicting its model of uniqueness. For Leung, Sedition presents a curated platform to share his work with a network of art collectors internationally but provides little in terms of income to support his practice. Such contradictions are seemingly resolved with NFTs where artworks are allowed to circulate as memes and go viral, contributing to their market value. NFTs in this way render artworks into financial assets, where there is an abstraction from the object and its ownership that began with licensing and the certificate of authenticity.

Jacqueline Kiyomi Gork, a Los Angeles–based artist who works across sound, performance, textiles, and installations. Gork grew up in the San Francisco Bay Area and has been involved in the DIY art and music community there. She is represented by Empty Gallery in Hong Kong, which has a strong interest in supporting experimental practices. Founded in Hong Kong in 2016 by Stephen Cheng, with director and curator Alexander Lau, Empty Gallery is designed as a black space: no natural light, black painted walls, and soundproofing create an immersive environment for sound and moving images, performances, sculptures, and installations. Working with Gork to sell conceptual and ephemeral sound installations requires inventing formats for their sale including packaging for materials, digital files, and instructions for restaging artworks like *The Lab Box: Inside You Is Me* (2016). Gork explores material forms of textiles by using absorptive materials that also act as sound insulation in her installations. Artists explore material forms for their work as a means to engage the art market centered on selling unique material objects. There is an experimental process involved in the selling of conceptual artworks and complex installations, whereby the artwork can materialize in diverse forms in future restagings. Gork has also received sponsorship from Meyer Sound, which produces loudspeakers and audio systems that have been loaned in-kind for her exhibitions. Sponsorship as an economic relationship with the artist materially shapes the form of the artwork and conditions what is possible for the artist to create. In exchange, Meyer Sounds receives credit in the promotional material of the exhibition.

Samson Young, mentioned at the beginning of this introduction, is a Hong Kong artist who works across sound, video, drawing, sculpture, and installation. After completing a PhD in music composition from Princeton University, he came back to Hong Kong and began teaching at the School of Creative Media, City University of Hong Kong. He has since left his teaching position to pursue his artistic career full time, having reached a point where he was getting more opportunities to present in major exhibitions, such as winning the first BMW Art Journey Award in 2015 and representing Hong Kong in the 57th Venice Biennale in 2017.

At MetaObjects we have allowed our practice to evolve through our collaborations with artists (such as Young) and cultural institutions. By taking an open-ended approach to our studio, we can play a role in mediating between sectors and disciplines to nurture and foster the possibilities for artists to engage more closely with advanced technologies. To think of our studio practice ecologically, it has allowed for mutually beneficial long-term relationships to emerge that support a process of knowledge and resource sharing. As such we carve out a role in the artistic community, which is also subject to change as we find new opportunities to engage in the field. These opportunities include developing speculative projects with blockchain technologies, such as the decentralized autonomous organization *Ensembl* (2021).

The Thoughtworks Arts program, which included the Thoughtworks Arts Residency, Art-A-Hack™ and Hardware Hack Lab events, was founded in 2016 in New York by Andrew McWilliams, a British artist, software engineer, and lead technologist at Thoughtworks, and artist and scholar Ellen Pearlman. It was hosted by Thoughtworks, a multinational technology company founded in 1993 and headquartered in Chicago, that specializes in software design, development, and IT consultancy. At the time of writing, the company has forty-eight offices in nineteen countries, with over ten thousand employees. The Thoughtworks Arts program was based in New York City, which fulfilled the company's mission for social justice, and enabled employees to participate in projects to develop their skills and knowledge. The residency played a role in corporate social responsibility, where social impact initiatives also helped the company attract new clients. At the same time, artists gained access to corporate resources to create new work. The relationship with the corporation was negotiated to create a mutually beneficial collaboration with artists. The program was led by individuals who were able to negotiate the relationship between the corporation and artists in a sustainable way. By leveraging resources through their positions within corporations, McWilliams and Pearlman helped create new spaces for the development of art and technology. Unfortunately, following the COVID-19 pandemic and lackluster growth, the company laid off 4 percent of its workforce including cutting the Thoughtworks Arts program entirely.[48] Long-term sustainability of these collaborations is dependent on a corporation's dedication to the arts and their ultimate priorities. In situations where cuts need to be made, the arts are among the first to go as an investment with little direct financial return.

The artist, curator, and entrepreneur Xu Zhen has played a key role in fostering the local art scene in Shanghai. His own conceptual art practice self-consciously interrogates representations and aesthetics of power in the art market, institutions, consumerism, and advertising, where he has launched several businesses and organizations both as functioning companies and as art. In 2009, Xu Zhen launched MadeIn Company as an art production company, to create artworks as products and to inadvertently hide behind the brand. He then plays with identity and branding by creating the XU ZHEN® brand under which he produces artworks. In 2014, he founded the MadeIn Gallery to present exhibitions by emerging artists in Shanghai. Having gained commercial success with his art and business-as-art, he has also come to play a key role in fostering the art community and generating discourse in the art scene. To think of the corporate entity as a medium for artistic intervention is to also challenge or raise questions toward the normative practices in the commercial sector. Through irony and forms of institutional critique, Xu Zhen's practice creates an ambiguity that opens new aesthetic possibilities for art to circulate in contemporary systems of production. To think of corporations as organizations ecologically is to see how they respond to the needs of a community, inventing practices that contribute to creating an environment where other artistic practices can thrive.

teamLab is an international art collective founded in 2001 in Tokyo by Toshiyuki Inoko along with four university friends. They have now grown to be an interdisciplinary collective including artists, programmers, engineers, CG animators, mathematicians, and architects. They work as a team of individuals with different specializations to allow for collective experimentation with technology as a tool to create artworks. Working with technology requires diverse skillsets beyond the capacities of one person. Similar to onformative operating as a production studio to sustain their art practice, teamLab managed to work at a large scale by creating highly popular large-scale immersive installations around the world. This unique practice has paved the way for them into the art world, where they are represented by Pace Gallery, Martin Browne Contemporary, and Ikkan Art. Their internal organization allows for open-ended interdisciplinary collaboration in teams, where their philosophy embraces creative process.

Looking at these diverse practices of artists and organizations, it becomes possible to see how contemporary art, as it exists as variable objects, poses unique questions for rethinking how cultural economies function today. By decentering cultural economies from the centrality of products, while gravitating toward process creation and circulation, we think less of exchange value and more of shared knowledge and experiences and the social role that art plays in society. Economies are not merely functions of buying and selling, but practices that can generate new relationships and aesthetic possibilities. This creates a larger conception of cultural economies that embodies all of the processes involved in bringing art into the world and allowing it to endure in our collective memories of experience. Artworks do not exist in and of themselves but are part of an ecology of artistic practice in which the artist is no longer entirely in control, challenging notions of individual authorship. This creates an understanding of the field in which art exists fundamentally as something that is shared rather than owned.

PROCESSES OF MAKING, CIRCULATING, AND ORGANIZING

Rather than follow artworks as discrete objects circulating in an economy, the following chapters examine creative economies as a set of dynamic, changing processes. The intention is not to propose "best practices" or strategies, in which every practice is contingent, situated, and subject to constant renegotiation, but rather a way of thinking and doing that opens toward new practices and relations with others. By surveying a diverse range of artistic practices, I present new possibilities for practitioners engaging in their own unique creative ecologies.

In chapter 1, artworks are understood in relation to the processes of negotiating time and space to create art, such as between forms of paid labor and often unpaid artistic labor. Here, I examine the different kinds of paid labor that artists undertake in order to secure the means to sustain their artistic practices. I consider how specific skills acquired through these practices expand the boundaries between paid labor and often unpaid artistic practice and the ways it shapes the work produced by these artists. Additionally, I look at the ways in which the different economies that artists engage in to support their artistic practices—from grants to developing collaborations with scientific institutions to performing and touring to working with commercial galleries to physical artworks and NFTs—begin to dictate the organization of their time and labor and shape the kinds of work produced by imposing requirements to fit various commercial or government agendas. As economies play an increasing role in how artworks come into being, this raises the question of how they can be considered as part of the artistic process itself.

Chapter 2 bridges the connection between conceptual and digital art, both considered a part of contemporary art in general. With the rise of conceptualism, contemporary art is no longer defined by specific medium, like painting or sculpture, but engages diverse medias and forms. Contemporary artworks are circulated as high-value objects in galleries, where methods are invented for their sale on the art market. Galleries participate in conceptualizing the artwork and how it can be packaged and sold with a license agreement, certificate of authenticity, documentation and instructions, along with materials including digital files. The artworks have a variable materiality in which different restagings of the work can take different material forms and arrangements. Artworks are staged as site-specific installations in exhibitions, where galleries and curators play a role in the spatial design and arrangement of the artwork in space, contributing to the creative process. Licensing and the certificate of authenticity separate a work's ownership from the object of art, where there are possibilities to consider licensing as a rental contract. Licensing is more commonly used in the media industries and presents unique considerations for artists to retain control of their artworks. As rental contracts, artworks can circulate as temporary displays beyond an economy of sales. Thinking of art less as a finite object and instead as processes of staging and restaging artworks in exhibitions, we can reimagine contemporary art markets around temporary exhibitions where artworks exist in permutation and variation. Licensing plays a role in defining what constitutes the work of art and how it is to be restaged in the future. In this way, licensing can be approached creatively as it contributes to what the artwork is and how it will exist in the world.

Building on the discussion on licensing in chapter 2, chapter 3 looks at the economies of selling art in a digital format, both online and offline and in open and closed systems of distribution. These modes of circulation bring different kinds of meaning and value to the artwork, where the artwork *transfigures*[49] as it circulates in diverse economies. Digital art, due to its infinite reproducibility, poses challenges for its sale in an art market that values unique objects. Through the work of Lorna Mills, by selling art in a gallery as editions and installations, while allowing the images to circulate freely on the internet, artworks acquire different meanings and values. For Sedition, at times there are tensions between circulating artworks online on social media and the need to create a sense of scarcity and uniqueness through digital limited editions. Between the promotional economies of our digital age and the art market of unique objects, artworks circulate in different systems of value and appreciation that coexist. Artworks are understood and valued as viral images on social media and as high-value objects of ownership. NFTs, as an application of blockchain technologies, emerged to create unique digital objects that can be bought and sold, which essentially act as a licensing agreement and certificate of authenticity. While artworks are already conceived of as financial investments, NFTs take financialization to its next logical conclusion, foregrounding its form as a financial object that can be bought and sold digitally. In the increasing financialization of art, with NFTs, ownership is separated from the object, where smart contracts serve as a license and certificate of authenticity. NFTs have contributed to the sustainability of certain artists working with software or generative art, whose work was not previously widely circulating in the traditional art market and galleries. However, the rampant speculation around NFTs and their design as a system for financialization leaves little value to be gleaned beyond purely private interest and profit.

In chapter 4, moving on from the financialized digital economies, I look at the ways in which corporations have been playing a larger role in the economies of artists working with technology. Through different mechanisms of corporate patronage, such as licensing for media facades, commissions, and artist residencies, it becomes possible to see how these collaborations shape artistic production. By analyzing different kinds of corporate patronage, I demonstrate how the meaning and form of artworks are transformed in the process to serve particular corporate agendas. I also consider the types of relationships that are valued by artists to approach an understanding of art as processes of creation that need to be sustained in time and space. Licensing as rental contracts for the display of video artworks for media facades becomes a means for artists to distribute their artworks beyond the gallery space. However, these displays require little creative input from the artist and serve primarily as extra income. Commissions more often include a production budget, and in this sense initiate a process of creation, allowing artists to continue this work. However, many companies who are commissioning artists for their brand seek to employ the arts in their marketing strategies, where the distinction between art and advertising is blurred. This also happens on media facades as artworks are displayed on public screens in cities that normally are reserved for advertisements. To allow an artwork to circulate in contexts where it can be appreciated as art requires the care of curators as context creators. In other ways, technology companies are supporting artists to create works by supporting access to tools, resources, and spaces through artist residencies. As part of corporate social responsibility agendas, corporations promote the arts to demonstrate their engagement with social issues. While corporations can provide important access to resources for artists, the low priority given to the arts means these initiatives are often short lived. Creating mutually beneficial relationships between corporations and artists requires internal stakeholders who are able to accommodate the interests of both parties. Artist residencies emphasize a process of creation without necessarily producing a product, like with a commission. A corporate artist residency sustains a process of experimenting with technology and knowledge sharing with employees of the company.

Chapter 5 extends the discussion of corporations, but rather than as patrons: artists themselves are registering as brands and commercial entities. Through a discussion on forms of institutional critique and corporate aesthetics within art, I raise possibilities for thinking of organizing and forming a company as part of an artistic process. It becomes possible to appropriate the forms of commercial enterprises without necessarily following their logic of profit. Or rather following their logic mockingly, as in the case of Xu Zhen, to subvert or obscure the corporate form. The ways in which companies are organized internally can also be approached creatively to support experimentation and open-ended collaboration. Organizations as a concept and form can be experimented with even in the roles that they play in the community, where they can be mobilized to support others. At times, in places like China and Hong Kong, the company as a legal entity has more power in the eyes of the government, which can afford more access to resources that can then be channeled to the community. These are just some suggestions for the ways commercial entities can serve as a conduit to enable artistic practice and possibilities in the community by bridging gaps in knowledge and also navigating freely between different sectors and disciplines. To play with conventions and to liberate practices from them allows us to find new ways for artworks to exist in the world within our highly commercialized cultural economies.

Bringing together the various practices and collaborations discussed in this book, I develop a more complex view of art and technology as they exist within diverse cultural economies. I challenge modernist conceptions of the art market, to reorient values around shared processes of creation and circulation of art, rather than exchange value. Throughout the book, I examine diverse perspectives that open to new spaces and possibilities for art and technology to exist in the world, despite the commercialized environments in which we live. By understanding art as collective processes, I argue that we can reformulate the cultural economy around mutually supportive ecologies of artistic practice that can endure in time as iterations of our shared contributions.

1

THE MEANS TO MAKE

As contemporary artists engage diverse media in their practices, they necessarily participate in multiple income streams to sustain their work. Practices are multilayered and coexist as artists engage diverse art forms simultaneously. Economies begin to shape the experience of time and labor through the constraints and affordances experienced in the environment. Practices produce boundaries between nonartistic paid labor and art making, by creating separations in time and space, or by blurring them together by allowing them to feed into each other. In each project the meaning and form of the work, role of the artist, and role of technology are defined in different ways. I examine economies as organizational practices that condition how artists create work and argue that the process of securing the means to make creative work should be considered a part of the artistic process itself. By understanding economies in this way, I demonstrate how each project is constituted by a different set of relations, emerging through diverse social and material practices. Rather than thinking of art simply in terms of its finished product, I suggest that the economic and relational context of the artwork's creation conditions the meaning and form of the work.

In this chapter, I discuss the work of Lorna Mills, an artist who created a separation between paid labor and art making. By maximizing the time to make art, through high-paid, low-effort work, she created an environment in which she could concentrate on developing a labor-intensive practice. In contrast, onformative as an art and design studio attempts to bring together their commercial work and their artistic practice, creating a self-sustaining environment, in which their commercial clients become more open to artistic experimentation. Finally, I turn to LoVid, a duo that has worked across diverse media and contexts to understand how grants, commercial galleries, and touring have shaped their workflow. Working across disciplines, LoVid's collaboration with universities and scientific institutions through their adjacent work in psychology has enabled them to develop new experiments with haptic technologies. Each of these three examples offers a different insight into how an artist organizes their time and labor in order to secure the means to create art.

Through the efforts of these artists to sustain their practice through other forms of work, we can see how the different forms of work that artists do alongside their artistic practices contribute directly or indirectly to their art. Artists working with technology acquire and hone technical skills to create work, or otherwise find a means to collaborate with people with diverse skillsets. Due to the rapidly changing technological landscape there is a constant need to develop new skills and engage with new advancements in technology. By taking into account the various income streams that contribute to sustaining artistic practices, this chapter considers the knowledge and skills artists acquire in their nonartistic paid labor as an analytical component critical to understanding the artworks that these artists produce. These are the beneficial impacts other sectors may have on the arts. This has been termed "overflow" or "spillover" of "ideas, skills, knowledge, and . . . capital"[1] when discussing the social and economic impact of the creative industries in the wider economy and in cultural policy. However, this is too often framed as a spilling outward to the wider economy, rather than an inward motion benefiting the arts and cultural sector.

Practices are constantly being renegotiated in an open-ended relationship to the future. What emerges as important for an artist evolves as artists engage different economies in their practices. The issues experienced in this chapter are situated in time and place and are not representative of the infinite diversity of possible practices. Rather than fixing a practice as a model to follow, the intention is to demonstrate how practices change over time and are contingent on their social, economic, and technological environments.

As I outlined in the introduction, to think about economies ecologically suggests developing a sensitivity to the inherent possibilities emerging in a situation. As these case studies demonstrate, economies are sociomaterial entanglements consisting of social practices (such as writing grants, working with commercial galleries, or performing and touring) and material arrangements (such as a studio space and working with technologies), which acquire meaning and are co-constituted in the process of negotiating a practice. Artists respond dynamically to shifting environments, which condition their practice. Practices evolve with the constraints and affordances encountered in the environment, for instance, restrictions of resources, space, and time to create work. Practices also shift over an artist's career and an artist engages in different economic activities to sustain their work. Such a relationship to the environment suggests an ecological perspective, where "affordances of the environment are what it *offers* the animal"[2] and values and meanings evolve as one creates a livable habitat for existence. It suggests how we may create an environment to better sustain artistic practices. In order to map several examples of these economies, this chapter situates artworks in relation to the processes undertaken to accrue the material resources required to make them, as opposed to understanding them primarily as finite objects.

LORNA MILLS: THE SEPARATION OF "ART" AND "WORK"

Mills is an artist who works across video and installation using found images and animated GIFs as an image format that enables short moving image sequences, sourced across the darknet and porn sites (see figure 1.1). In the past, Mills sustained her practice by developing children's games using Flash. However, Flash eventually became obsolete for Mills's purposes, and she spent a significant amount of time learning new skills. Mills struggled over her career due to technologies becoming obsolete and changing trends in the field. "Part of me is a little tired of it because over the years I've wasted so much time on new software and new skills

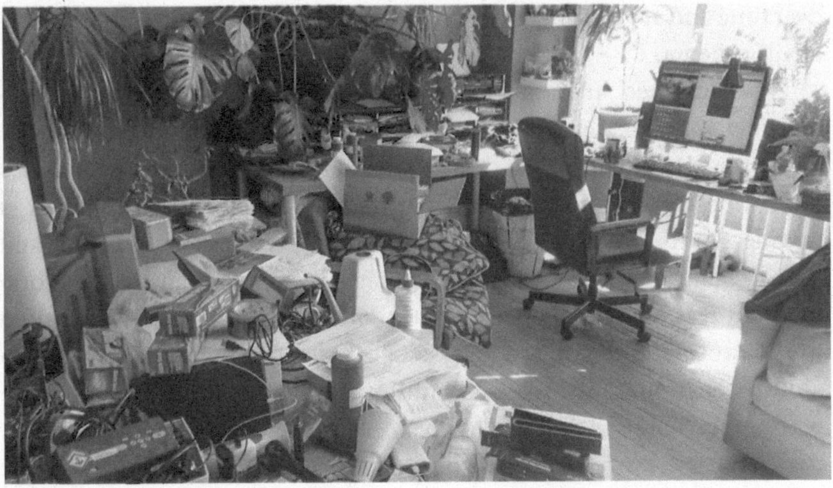

that became redundant really quickly. . . . Especially doing it on your own time picking up new software for a job that you may get or may not, or then it becomes suddenly irrelevant in six months—I don't want to waste my time that way anymore."[3] The landscape of technologies falling out of use and the shifting availability of work impacted her work and her available time for making artwork. Mills felt a constant need to reskill and upskill, which consumed her time for art making and, more generally, reflects the ways in which artists are not entirely in control of their labor conditions.

Working with technology presents the challenge of constantly learning and maintaining skills, which may be supported by work in other fields. Learning often requires an investment of time as a form of unpaid labor, which poses challenges to work and practice in an economy of rapid

1.1

Lorna Mills's studio in Toronto, 2016. Courtesy of the artist.

technological innovation. Bernard Stiegler would deem this loss of knowledge as part of the process of "proletarianization"[4] that is short-circuited by an accelerated economy that seeks constant renewal. To be able to develop a practice over time and to share a common practice over time and over generations is to create "long circuits" of knowledge.[5] An economy driven by innovation changes the demand in the job market for different skills, where certain jobs requiring skilled labor are devalued through the rise of outsourcing and are increasingly replaced with AI. Through her experiences working with new technologies in her profession and encountering challenges in the job market due to the potential eventual obsolescence of those skills, Mills viewed learning new skills as a burden. Technology becomes a matter of concern in her practice, where with its rapid advancement new skills were required to maintain a steady income.

Mills's artistic practice was also dependent on her means of sustaining a living wage. Her strategy was to make her commercial work as easy to execute as possible, using technologies that are less at risk of obsolescence so she could focus more time and energy on her art. By selectively seeking high-paying commercial video production jobs that require a relatively low investment of time and energy, she was able to pursue her artistic projects more freely without the pressure for her artwork to be self-sustainable. Mills left herself time to develop her practice freely, as she intentionally minimized her time spent on paid work. The temporalities of work change over time as the intensities of projects categorized between commercial work and art making ebb and flow. There is a "flow of agency"[6] in the ongoing negotiation of a practice, which is dependent on the availability of work as well as the opportunities for an artist's practice to generate income under changing economic conditions. It is important for Mills to have the freedom to create work without limitations, where she has developed a practice that engages with pornographic imagery and other kinds of explicit online content. By separating her artistic practice from paid labor, she was able to explore forms of internet culture and aesthetics that would likely not sit well with clients. Keeping her practice in the realm of art allowed her artistic freedom to develop more challenging forms of art.

For Mills, art in this instance is kept separate from the need to make a living. Art market scholar Olav Velthuis draws on the work of sociologist

Viviana Zelizer to describe how art may be kept sacred, separated from the "hostile worlds"[7] of the market, as in the case of Lorna Mills. This strategy has allowed Mills to develop a more labor-intensive technique in her work involving many hours searching the internet for animated GIFs and then collaging them together in video-editing software, reflecting how the organization of her time affects her artistic practice. Mills values the time and freedom granted by the clear division between her paid work and her artistic practice. By creating a boundary around her commercial video work, she gave herself more free time to focus on art making. This may be similar to how individuals attempt to strike a work-life balance; however, artistic practice becomes another mode of work in order to develop into a career that also requires time to nurture and hone a particular technique or explore new ones, find opportunities to exhibit a work or plan and execute exhibitions.

For instance, in terms of new techniques, Mills's interest in short animations has led her to work with lenticular prints as a materialization of her videos. In one instance, she was commissioned by contemporary art center Mercer Union in Toronto to create a large-postcard-size lenticular artwork that was distributed as an exclusive gift to members. The 400 members of the center are a selective audience who understand the nuances and intentional provocations of art. In this instance, Mills was able to select a rude image for art audiences who may be more open to obscenities in art. The cost of printing lenticulars is high because the primary clients are advertisers and corporations with large budgets. In this case, these were ten-frame lenticulars versus the three- or four-frame lenticulars. Lenticulars allow Mills's work to circulate in other material and analogue forms. Additionally, Mills will often show her works as video installations in galleries (like *Double Unicorn* at Import Projects, Berlin, 2013; see figure 1.2), on outdoor media facades, and through online distribution (as discussed in chapters 3 and 4). Such public displays are less open to showing explicit content. Mills is represented by TRANSFER Gallery in the United States and DAM Gallery in Berlin, which offer opportunities to exhibit and present her work internationally.

Art lacks an instrumental value that cannot be remunerated in the same way as commercially paid production work, which is valued based on Mills's skilled labor and time. However, if the artwork is then sold or

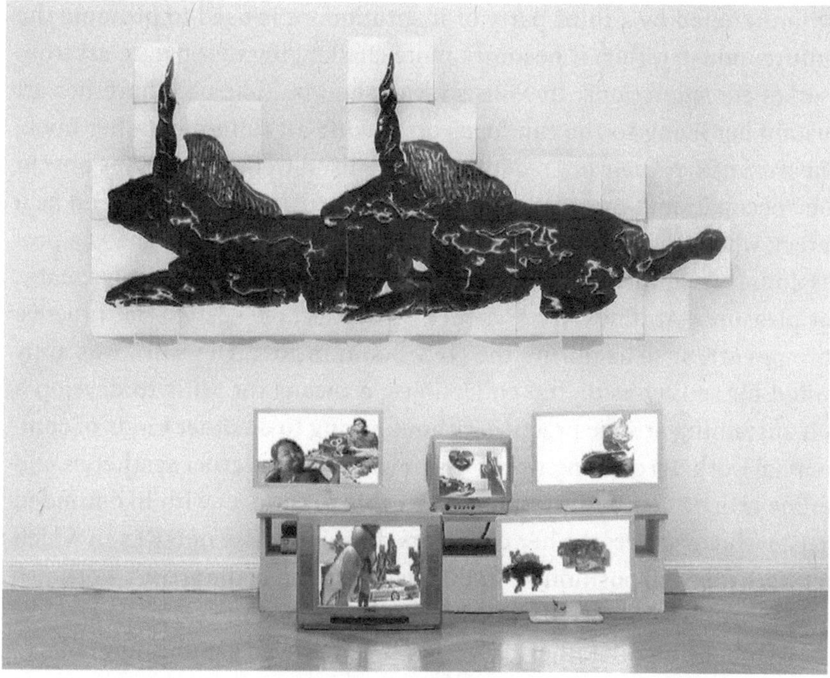

1.2

Lorna Mills, *Double Unicorn*, animated GIFs and glazed digital prints, installation view, Import Projects, Berlin, 2013. Courtesy of the artist.

commissioned by a third party or institution, or is used to promote the culture industry, then it becomes more challenging to separate art from market considerations. In Mills's ideal, she would be able have her art sustain her living so she can focus on making art full-time. In her book, *The Work of Art: Value in Creative Careers*, Alison Gerber describes how in the "occupational turn" of the arts, where artistic practice is seen as a career, where to be considered a "full-time" artist suggests one is a professional artist, in contrast to a hobbyist or amateur who simply creates for pleasure.[8] At times in her career, Mills was able sustain her practice through art, such as during the NFT boom in 2021. Her work was aptly suited for selling as digital collectibles, a means for Mills to develop a self-sustaining artistic practice without having to do other kinds of commercial work. By creating works that engage with internet aesthetics and online artistic communities, Mills was able to connect with like-minded artists who also became her collectors during the rise of NFTs in which her work was well positioned. In this way, the form of the artist's work also shapes the possibilities for art to circulate in different economies.

At other times in Mills's career, she had received significant grants to sustain her practice. In Canada, where Mills is based, the Canada Council offers grants to support the projects of established artists who have a track record in their practice. Mills has also received some grants to support her work, but it took her twenty-five years of developing her practice before she could apply for larger, longer-term grants. More recently, she received a two-year Canada Council grant as well as the Chalmers Foundation grant,[9] which supported her work for a year. At times, Mills had enough commercial work to support her practice and therefore did not apply for grants. She believes it is morally responsible to keep public funding available to those who are most in need. In this way, she balances both commercial and nonprofit funding streams to support her practice, where there is a shifting over time between different modes of practice from working full-time on art to working full-time on commercial work.

Generally, grants are beneficial on a project basis, but do not often provide long-term support. To challenge these principles is to reconsider the design of grants and funding mechanisms in ways that are less rigid and limiting to the creative process, and also to consider the long-term sustainability of artists. Examples of alternatives include cases such as the Nordic granting system that in the 1970s began offering a guaranteed income for artists, an amount adjusted according to other income the artist was receiving.[10] The scheme was later replaced in 2013 with a ten-year artist grant with the possibility for renewal.[11] There are various other kinds of long-term organizational or research funding such as the one- and three-year grants to local arts organizations offered by the Hong Kong Arts Development Council[12] and larger project grants offered by Creative Capital[13] in the United States. It raises questions about how grants could be considered to enable long-term support for artists, but also support forms of collaborative and process-based practices that may not have clear outcomes.

Mills's time/work organization contrasts with the approach of onformative, as a studio that seeks to bring their artistic work and commercial work closer together. Zelizer uses the term "nothing but" in contrast to "hostile worlds," which assumes there is outside of the market, and it is impossible to separate the spheres of the market with other sacred spheres of, for instance, non-economic form of artistic pursuit. This can be seen in the practices of onformative described in the next section of this chapter, though there are tensions between the separation and unity of their artistic practice with their commercial work. How boundaries are made and not made also has an effect on artistic practice, allowing Mills, for example, to develop a practice involving explicit content that also paved the way for her participation in the NFT market, to be discussed at greater length in chapter 3.

ONFORMATIVE: CARVING OUT A PRACTICE BETWEEN ART AND DESIGN

onformative is a digital art and design studio founded by Julia Laub and Cedric Kiefer based in Berlin, working across generative art and design, audiovisual production, data visualizations, and kinetic installations. The studio combines the production of commissioned work for clients like Samsung, Nike, and Porsche, and what Laub and Kiefer call "self-initiated projects" as self-funded experimental and research-based artistic projects.

onformative's founders started their studio after graduating from design school in Germany and after discovering each other's work online.

After working remotely together, they moved to Berlin to consolidate their work as a studio. In the beginning, they had trouble defining what they did and felt torn between disciplines of art and design, as Kiefer explains: "It's also not that you necessarily have to separate these things so clearly. It's not either one thing or the other. It's not art or design . . . If we have to position ourselves, it's definitely that we are a design studio with a strong artistic focus."[14] Kiefer's explanation shows how the process of negotiating a practice is inherently unstable, where there are ambiguities and possibilities to enact practices differently.

To produce commercial design projects for large clients, onformative's core team consists of nine staff members: designers, coders, project managers, and a communications manager, alongside freelancers who are brought in to work on specific projects. Working with technology on large commercial projects necessitates diverse collaborators with different skills. Operating as a studio means the identity of individual artists is subsumed under the company name as a collective and as paid employees of the business, some of whose employees may be considered "non-artists." While onformative differentiates between their paid "commercial work" and unpaid "self-initiated" art projects, there is a desire to bring these categories closer together and blur the distinctions between them. At the beginning there was a clear separation between their commercial work, where they cared less about the creative aspect of the work to focus on simply sustaining the studio. Now their art projects are supported by the commercial design work they do, and they produce artworks in their free time as a means to experiment and learn new technological skills and techniques.

An example of their audiovisual works is *Meandering River*, a study of the landscapes of rivers fluctuating rhythmically in real time AI-generated audio and data-driven visualizations (see figure 1.3). Presented as a multiscreen installation, the work produces unpredictable patterns reflecting on the natural processes of erosion through the studying of satellite imagery. onformative's artistic process in this case involves research into natural phenomena and producing studies and experiments using generative music and visuals. While artistic labor can indeed become a form of unpaid or "free labor"[15] contributing value to the economy as human capital,[16] the skills acquired through onformative's artistic practice

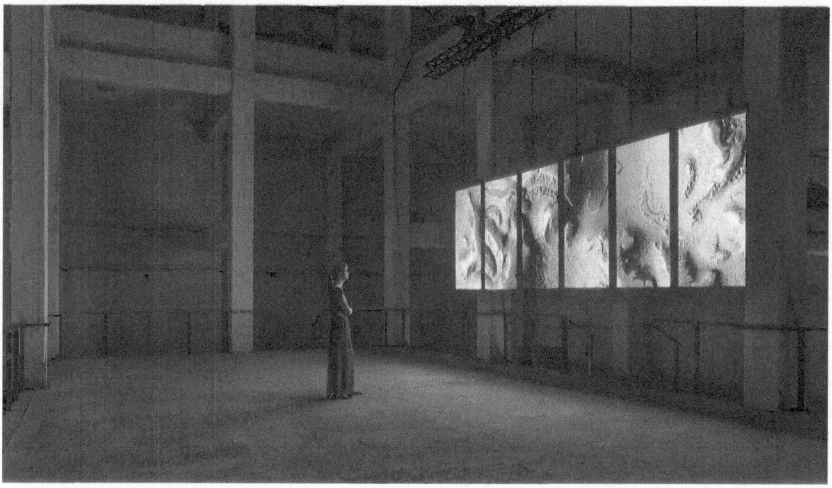

subsequently benefit their commercial work. This form of unpaid labor is made productive within the economy, opening questions regarding how this kind of work should be remunerated.

As onformative made their own artistic projects and promoted them online, they started to get more inquiries about their artworks, leading to commercial projects that allowed them to develop their artistic techniques (figure 1.4). The unintended consequence of creating art and releasing it for free was promotion for their studio and the type of work they would ideally like to create. In the immanent process of developing their practice, they discovered a means to bridge their commercial work and artistic practice. To maintain a meaningful practice, they prefer to continue their self-initiated projects and not only focus on commercial work. Kiefer explains, "If you get a lot of projects and if you start to make

1.3

onformative, *Meandering River*, audiovisual installation, Funkhaus, Berlin, 2018. Courtesy of onformative.com.

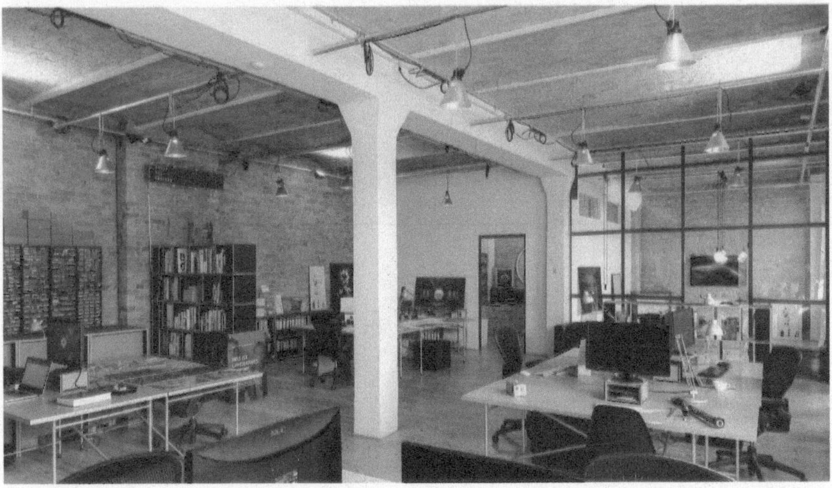

some money, in the end finally, after several years, you start to forget the reason why you actually do what you do, and you have to be careful that you don't miss that point."[17]

While onformative's commercial work takes precedence, this priority makes it difficult for the team to complete and release their artworks in a timely manner. At times, they have dropped artistic projects after losing interest, or the technology has moved on, or other people have released similar projects. Their goal is to get their art projects out faster to avoid such scenarios. The challenges of balancing commercial work and art practice requires onformative to make sacrifices on their commercial work in order to complete their artistic projects. Their open-ended artistic process means sometimes they may never get to a point where a project is considered complete. At some point they have to decide when to say "stop" on a project when they collectively feel the idea is not going anywhere or

1.4

onformative's studio space in Berlin. Photo: Kerstin Müller. Courtesy of onformative.com.

the concept or technology is no longer relevant. Ideally, onformative prefers to work without constraint on their artistic projects, enabling more experimental approaches not restricted by budgets or timelines.

Rather than repeating the same process for their clients, onformative takes each commercial commission as an opportunity to try something new. onformative differs from other design studios, which may repeat the same type of work because it can be lucrative to do so, but for onformative this approach would quickly become repetitive and mundane. Despite being able to make more money by repeating familiar processes, they would rather take each project as an opportunity to learn. As a result, onformative does not specialize in one area, but prefers to keep exploring new creative challenges. This introduces the difficulty of learning and experimenting into the process, on top of the need to maintain high-quality work for clients. Self-initiated projects become an important means to expand knowledge and conduct research. If onformative can learn and experiment through their paid work, then it is ideal: "If somebody asks us to actually create something similar, we always try to create something new because we try to use this opportunity to develop ourselves further, but we also don't want to deliver the client just the same thing, a copy of what we already did."[18]

For artists working between art and design, creative studios or agencies become a form of enabling commercial collaborations with brands. These commercial projects in turn help fund artistic practice. FIELD, fuse*, and Zeitguised are examples of studios who work in this way.[19] While some studios prefer to keep their commercial work separate from their art practice—Zeitguised, for instance, branched out to create Zeitguised Studio and FYI Henriksson[20] as separate commercial entities—others find it more difficult to make clear distinctions between their commercial and artistic work. Such artists and designers might treat their artistic projects as a form of R&D to test new ideas, aesthetics, and technologies. Working commercially enables the studios to work more freely on projects that potentially require larger teams and budgets. Working with technology suggests one has technical skills to also work commercially in creative industries or implies a necessity to collaborate with others with complementary skills. We begin to see artistic practice as consisting of not just individual artists, but also studios with multiple collaborators.

onformative made a different decision; rather than pursue art full-time, they found a way to integrate their artistic practice into their work in commercial design. Kiefer explains, "If you want to be an artist and only be seen as an artist, I think you have to stop working on commercial jobs. Otherwise, you're probably not making it in the art world, but that was never really appealing to us . . . although we are still interested in actual platforms and opportunities where our work could be shown."[21] These diverse practices and strategies have different effects on an artist's practice. In onformative's efforts to bring their art and work together, they forego their reliance on art market economies and their recognition and validation in the art world. Despite occasionally being shown in museums, galleries, and festivals, their visibility in the art world remains peripheral to their commercial design practice. While their work involves experimenting with new technologies, their visual aesthetic is that of a commercial design studio, which hinders their presence in the contemporary art world that may dismiss their work as purely visual and technical rather than conceptually grounded.

onformative's understanding of their practice emerges through the ways they have negotiated between art and design, producing unstable boundaries that are open to renegotiation. This process of defining a practice by creating separations (or not) is one of "carving out" a practice. Design is differentiated from art in that it serves a utilitarian function, although these distinctions have been blurred, such as in the case of movements and schools like the Bauhaus,[22] the digital design aesthetic of onformative's work means that it does not fit in certain art contexts. To carve out a practice, as the term suggests, means to also create or bring into existence a practice in the relation between form and matter,[23] where form emerges from a dynamic sociomaterial process. onformative can be considered as an art-led design studio, while there remains a divide between their commercial work and self-initiated artistic projects. With a team of employees and salaries to support, the studio necessarily has to take on highly paid commercial work to sustain their practice.

For onformative, their clients' interest in their artworks allowed their commercial work to become closer to art commissions, wherein they are able to work with a high degree of creative autonomy yet continue to be paid at commercial rates. Kiefer elaborates, "The main goal should be to actually merge them to come closer together, so that the commercial work becomes more and more artistic, or you get paid for your personal work better. I mean I'm still realistic. I know that there's always a separation between your own work and the commercial work."[24] There is an indeterminism on whether to join commercial work and artistic practice or keep them separated. There are instabilities in every practice of boundary making, which can be merged or separated depending on the situation. At times, different practices of commercial work and artistic work are brought together. Other times they are made distinct, often when, ultimately, there is a desire to be paid commercially for an artistic practice. The performativity of economies means that there is potential for practices to be enacted differently in every instance.

For onformative, there are affordances in operating as a commercial studio where they are able to self-fund their artistic projects with a team of collaborators. Whether to combine or separate their commercial design practice and their artistic practice is also an aesthetic choice, which has different effects on their practice. Such consequences may include the confusion between client work and artistic work if they are to be viewed together as part of a studio's practice, and whether the artistic practice is developed enough to stand on its own as a producer of works of art without the design practice informing it. These are the inclusions and exclusions created in the boundary-making process of developing a practice.

onformative's artists and designers do not engage with the art market, but rather the commercial design industry, though its members have tried to apply for grant funding in the past, but found that grants are insufficient in supporting larger collaborative projects developed over longer periods of time. The grants that onformative was eligible for normally ranged from €5,000 to €20,000 at most, which may be enough for an individual artist, but can only support the studio as a team for about a month. The granting structure limits onformative's artistic practice by requiring a set budget and timeline, restricting their more open-ended creative process. Just as forms of commercial work present constraints on a practice, grants also require a clear vision of the end result, which does not allow for a more exploratory mode of practice. Such grants are designed for individual artists but do not enable larger-scale collaborative works.

Working commercially has enabled onformative to develop complex collaborative and experimental works with technology. Their works employ a digital design aesthetic in contrast to the crude and low-resolution aesthetics of Lorna Mills's works. Where onformative values learning and experimentation in the production process, Mills disliked the need to constantly develop new skills in her paid work, creating instability. Rather, onformative seeks to create time and space to allow for experimentation and research with new technologies that have also become part of their client work. Bringing together their commercial design work with their artistic practice means onformative has less of a presence in the art world, where there is less recognition for their work as art. In this sense, economies shape the meaning and form of their work in the context of the processes that enable forms of art to exist.

LOVID: SHAPING THE ORGANIZATION OF TIME AND LABOR

Practices are constantly renegotiated and shift alongside changes in the cultural, economic, and technological environments. The New York–based duo LoVid, formed by Tali Hinkis and Kyle Lapidus, has maintained an interest in lo-fi aesthetics using both digital and analog technology (see figure 1.5). Their work spans material practices of textiles and prints to time-based media, including performances, videos, and NFTs. Over twenty years and more, their practice has evolved from engaging with grants, collaborating with scientific institutions, and touring to engaging more with commercial art markets. LoVid's practice engages diverse economies that condition the organization of their time and labor, which also shape the meaning and form of their works.

In the beginning, LoVid's practice was supported primarily through grants and in-kind support. Hinkis and Lapidus did not invest significant amounts of money, other than space and free time, in their work. LoVid's artists have received many grants of varying amounts over the course of their career. As New York–based artists, their opportunities to apply for grants are partially limited by grants available at the city, state, or national level. Every grant has its own regional specifications where government funding in particular is often reserved for local residents.

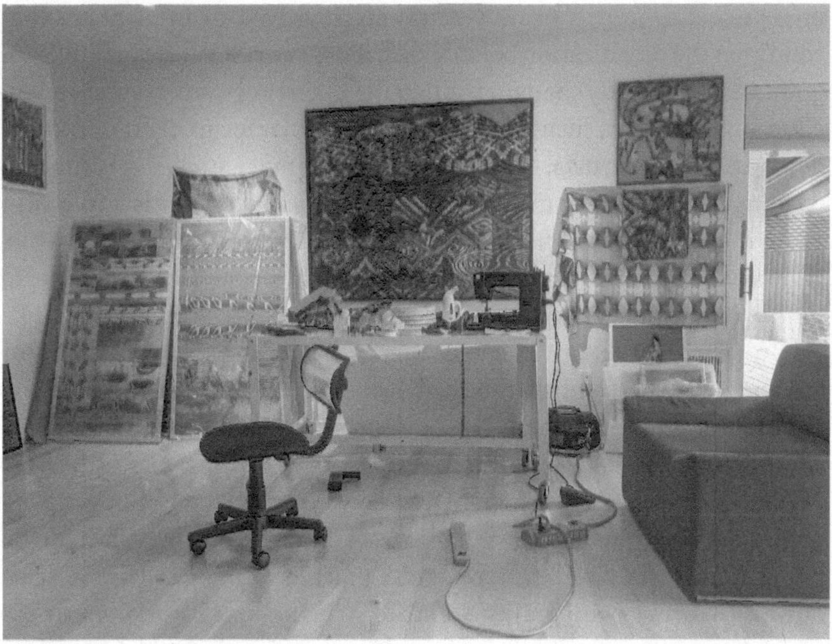

Grant funding presents constraints on practices, conditioning how artists make work.

From the mid-2000s, LoVid worked with such organizations as Eyebeam, the National Endowment for the Arts, New York State Council on the Arts, and Experimental Television Center. Hinkis and Lapidus received several regranting opportunities, which for a time provided them with additional, substantial support. In most cases, artists can only receive the same grant once, but regrants allow artists to receive funding multiple times, which is important for artists who require external support over the course of their careers. Working with grants creates a model of working

1.5

LoVid's studio in New York, 2021. Photo by LoVid. Courtesy of LoVid.

on a project-by-project basis. Grants can be viewed as mechanisms that condition the organization of labor of artists. The rules and availability of grants are constantly changing, reflecting different governmental and institutional agendas, such as supporting particular forms of art or specific demographics of artists. Such agendas also influence what gets funded, creating boundaries of inclusion and exclusion, where artists may also adapt their practices to fit the requirements of a particular grant. While grants certainly enable certain kinds of artists and practices, they can also inhibit others depending on their scope.

In a single year, LoVid could often get one larger project grant for $10,000 to $20,000 and then one or two smaller grants of about $2,000 to $4,000. Significant time is typically spent on grant writing, which has conditioned LoVid's working process. Hinkis explains, "I feel like for over ten years working with grants, I've always worked on a budget. So, I know how much income I have, and I base my time and my project on the budget I have. If I have less money, the practice is going to have to scale down."[25] Working with grants begins to structure one's working process around particular deadlines, requiring management of budgets and reporting of the project to funders. As artistic practices become entwined with economic systems, so do grants begin to shape workflow, and the organization of time to make art. However, rather than thinking of grant systems as fixed structures, we understand they exist in a diversity, where practices differ, for instance, by region or may change over time. Grants may be viewed as a technology for funding artistic projects, but as a concept they are malleable and may be restructured to better support artists. As a generalization, it can be said that many grants operate in this way of overdetermining the artistic process by requiring a clear project outline and outcome defined in the proposal.

Particularly for mid-career artists,[26] an early dependency on grants can later create a period of impasse; after getting all the grants they can get, they lose their means to make work, while also looking to engage other income streams to support more ambitious work not enabled by the limited budgets of grants. LoVid have discussed the challenges of being mid-career artists,[27] with particular regard to the tendency for art grants and funding opportunities to support young artists while celebrating established ones. Grants enable artists early in their careers, but this quickly diminishes in time for mid-career artists. Practices are enabled and hindered at different stages of a career by different funding structures. Such a shift in time requires the constant negotiation of an artistic practice throughout one's career as an ongoing process of reflection on the meaning of our work and life's necessities.

With Lapidus's academic background and profession in neuroscience, LoVid have also found opportunities to develop their work through collaborations and residencies with scientific institutions, such as at the Science Gallery Dublin, the New York Hall of Science, and the Re-Touch Lab at University of California Santa Barbara. Through these collaborations, they are able to develop the aspects of their practice that explore environmental data, haptics, and wearable technologies. There is a flow of knowledge and resources from science and research institutions to support the economies of art and technology. Forms of agency emerge through the embodied forms of knowledge acquired through various experiences in the field of work, where knowledge begins to flow from other fields and sectors to support an artistic practice.

Examples of LoVid's work include their collaboration with scientific researcher and electrical engineer Sean Montgomery at Harvestworks Electronic Arts Center to create a work called *Telephone Rewired* (2013),[28] which involved the use of electroencephalography (EEG) monitors on participants to create an audiovisual installation based on modulating neuronal oscillations and creating a feedback loop where the experience would alter the participants' cognitive function.[29] The project was part of the Creativity + Technology = Enterprise Residency program in collaboration with the Industrial and Technology Assistance Corporation (ITAC), a nonprofit organization that helps early-stage technology firms. While we can understand how knowledge-transfer schemes are largely designed to extract knowledge from the creative research sector, we can also find spaces where knowledge transfer may be designed to inversely support artistic experimentation. It becomes possible to imagine how we may take a model and subvert its logic, where it's no longer about *what* method is used to direct knowledge, but *how* and to what ends.

Working commercially presents a different mode of practice than working with grants or nonprofit institutions. LoVid are now engaging more with the commercial art world to evolve their artistic practice. Hinkis explains, "I think the way the market is right now, if you do not dip your toes in this mainstream commercial art world, it would be harder for you to achieve bigger goals."[30] A shift from the marginalization of media artists in relation to the contemporary art world can be seen following the emergence of the post-internet generation in the 2010s, who take an affirmative approach to the market. By working indiscriminately across traditional art forms of painting and sculpture alongside digital practices, such as videos and NFTs, artists are able to engage different income streams to sustain their practices. Working with commercial galleries presents a very different way of working than with grants. After successfully getting most of the grants they could get, LoVid shifted to a studio practice. In contrast to grant writing, a studio practice requires making an initial monetary investment on materials to make work rather than spending time applying for grants before beginning production, which in turn changes the workflow. Hinkis explains, "I think it does affect the way you work in the long run. It affects your rhythm, and it affects the way you approach your work."[31]

While artists may feel a desire to be paid and remunerated for work to resist forms of (self-)exploitation and "free labor,"[32] LoVid also recognizes the greater meaning of making art as extending beyond the economic expectations of return. Hinkis explains, "As an art person, I worked a lot for no money and I think it's one of the best things I've done. You have to figure out the money, there's no way around it. You figure it out."[33] Inspired by the work of Dan Sandin, a pioneer of video and computer art who also gave them the schematics for his instruments for free, LoVid artists feel indebted to this culture based on the gift economy,[34] which can be thought of as a social responsibility to contribute back to an artistic community as a continuation of a longer lineage of work. Says Hinkis, "Sometimes when you do this kind of work, there's certain things that you have full ownership on and there's some things where you're just continuing where someone left off."[35] Artistic labor takes on different meanings in different contexts. At times there is an expectation of return, while at other times art making belongs to a greater social and cultural purpose. As Abbing states, "Most artists are situated in-between; they are neither totally commercial nor totally selfless."[36]

Previously, LoVid's practice involved extensive performing with lo-fi video and noisy electronics. From 2003 to 2010, LoVid would tour several times per year, but this arrangement involved extensive time on the road, waking up early, and driving during the day to perform a show in the evening. Early in the artists' careers, they could survive off small budgets and even managed to tour with children, securing additional funding from presenting talks at universities. They were able to keep their costs low by striking a balance between periods of intense travel and time spent at home, in the changing temporalities of a practice. The LoVid duo is no longer able to travel so freely, and their kids have grown older. Thus, LoVid began to shift their practice away from performing to a studio practice and can no longer take extensive time away. This choice is a shifting of temporality, spatial movement, and rhythm in the organization of their practice. Different artistic practices such as performing arts shape the organization of life and labor. While touring can be fun and exhilarating for a period of time, it often becomes unsustainable over the long term, whereas being in one place allows an artist to develop a studio-based practice.

Coming from a background in DIY music and art, LoVid continues to be inspired by practices of independent distribution, which promotes a culture of sharing through informal and mutually supportive communities of artists who become collectors of each other's works. Technological advancements have made it easier to self-distribute through online platforms. LoVid was engaged in DIY communities through an arts and craft fair called La Superette, which they organized over a ten-year period ranging from the late 1990s to the mid-2000s.

Following their interest in DIY culture, LoVid more recently began selling limited-edition scarves based on their video works. The images for the scarves are taken from their glitched video artworks and digitally printed onto fabrics, engaging both physical and digital processes in their production. Their videos are generated using analog video and audio techniques, which are then transformed back into a material object by printing the patterns from the videos onto scarves, which reflects the variable materialities in which contemporary artworks exist. Each material form of artwork also engages a different economy for its circulation, from performances to galleries, to online platforms.

These scarves evolved from LoVid's earlier work with textiles and wearable technologies that they would perform in, such as in their work *VideoWear* (2005) (figure 1.6). The work features LCD screens and speakers that were stitched together using their printed textiles, prior to the

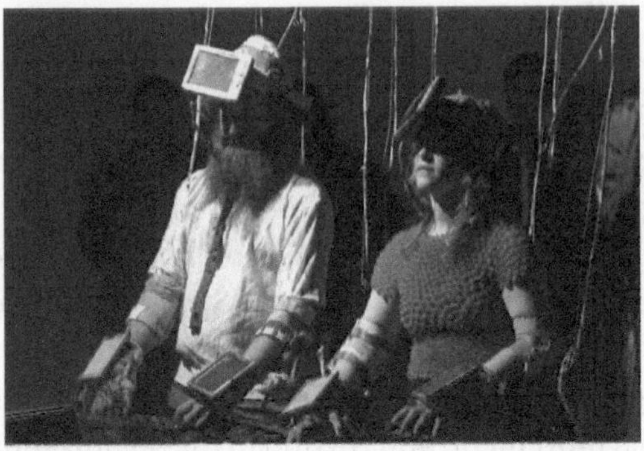

widespread use of smartphones.[37] In addition to the performances, the works would also be displayed in galleries as video installations that bring together analog and digital techniques. The scarves are printed on silk and synthetic materials (figure 1.7) through widely available online textile printing services. Initially, LoVid didn't intend to sell their textiles as products, but after a few inquiries to buy them, they warmed to the idea and began selling them as limited editions.

LoVid attributes this career shift to changes in the social, technological, and economic environments, where they felt they needed to engage more with the commercial market. They also faced issues of sustainability and the internal contradictions of self-organization.[38] The rise of online distribution with platforms such as Etsy and an increasingly competitive environment have encouraged many artists to turn toward more viable income streams through the sales of products. In an entrepreneurial society, there is pressure for artists to build their brand. LoVid began selling their scarves as artist-designed items to also reach new audiences for their work. Having not sold many artworks in commercial galleries,

1.6

LoVid, *VideoWear* performance, Living Arts, Tulsa, Oklahoma, 2005. Photo by Living Arts Tulsa. Courtesy of LoVid and Living Arts Tulsa.

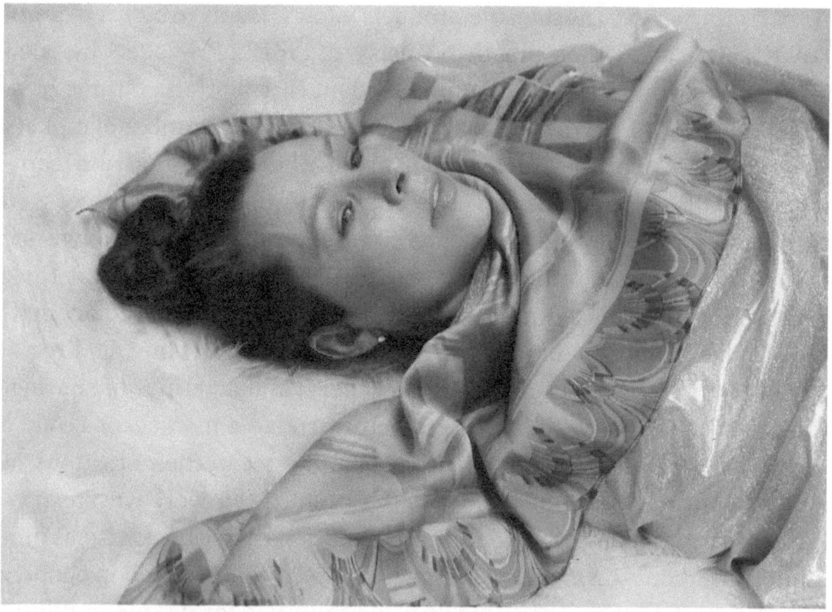

LoVid explores different ways of circulating their works in contexts that are less elitist and more accessible to wider audiences. Being based in the suburban milieu of Long Island, many of their friends and neighbors are not familiar with art and find a means to engage with LoVid's work through their products. Artworks circulate among different communities, including non-art audiences, gaining another meaning and value for art as artist-designed goods. For LoVid, selling scarves becomes a means of connecting to the non-artist community around them. Artworks have become a means to build conversations with those who may not be familiar with art and collecting.

1.7

LoVid, *Aluminism*, limited-edition scarf/ wearable artwork, 2019. Photo: Styled and produced by Zhuoyuan li and Kaiqi Cai. Model: Kylin O'Brien. Courtesy of LoVid.

Creating scarves as saleable products allows people to own a piece of LoVid's work when their practice consists of difficult-to-collect installations and performances. While independent distribution cultures have largely moved online, there has also been a rise in the number of makers as a movement of people interested in making their own things and learning new skills through tinkering. The maker movement's wider access to digital tools and technologies means cultural production is no longer be reserved for niche communities.[39] LoVid values being able to share their work with wider communities, rather than engaging with elite art markets. They embrace a culture of circulation that supports buying directly from the artist (rather than through a gallery) and an ethics of sharing. The practice of selling their scarves helped create a market for LoVid's work where they learned about the value and price of their creations in a type of art market beyond the gallery system. Their work with textiles exists as material objects sold as limited-edition scarves, but also as animations sold on a USB or NFTs. However, NFTs (as discussed in chapter 3) engage different mechanisms and communities for its sale in digital economies, which rely less on gallery exhibitions and face-to-face interactions with collectors.

LoVid engages both digital and physical economies simultaneously as demonstrated in a solo exhibition *Hold On* (2022) at Postmasters Gallery in New York (see figure 1.8).[40] The exhibition features a series of digital tapestries as still images of their video works printed on canvas that are embroidered and patched together as a collage. Alongside the tapestries are NFTs as part of the *Hugs on Tape* series. The series features short videos of people hugging drawn from twenty years of collected footage processed using LoVid's distinctive analog audiovisual technique. Distributing works as NFTs creates a means for artists to sell their works digitally in a medium that has been traditionally hard to sell in a physical art market. NFTs have enabled artists like LoVid to engage more with commercial galleries and the art market where they can explore both digital and physical economies for their work. Additionally, an NFT from this series, *Hugs on Tape (Beals)* (2021) is in the Whitney Museum of American Art collection.[41] NFTs have created a new market for digital artworks that run parallel with and as part of the economies of commercial galleries and museums.

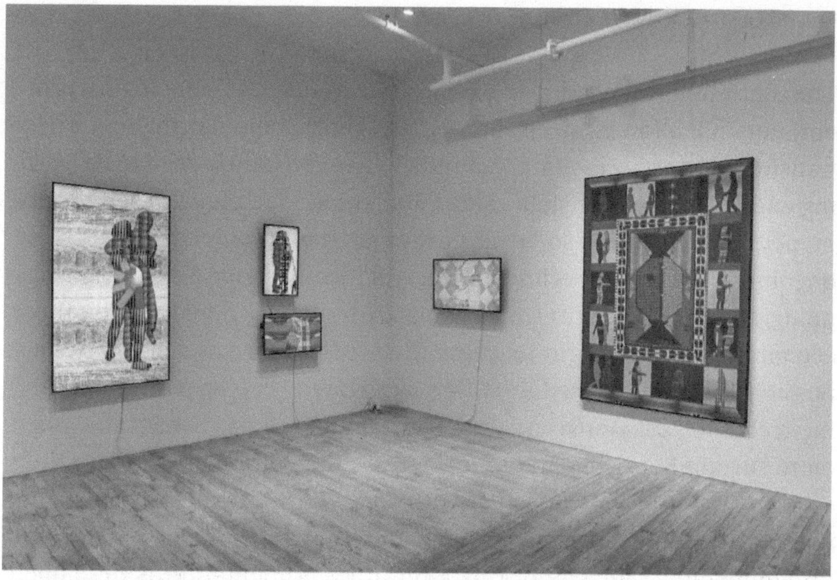

The conventions of exhibiting in galleries and online as NFTs means artists begin to shift their practice to accommodate different contexts and platforms for their work—for instance, creating well-crafted objects that are more easily saleable in galleries or a short series of videos to be sold online as NFTs. While different material forms are present in the artist's practice, there is a process in which artworks are transfigured to better fit the context in which they are presented. With new formats and platforms for the distribution and sale of artworks, artists necessarily engage diverse media and forms in their artistic practices, which evolve alongside changes in the environment.

1.8

Installation view of tapestries and digital video on screens from LoVid, *Hold On*, solo exhibition, Postmasters Gallery, New York, 2022. Photo by Postmasters Gallery. Courtesy of Postmasters Gallery and LoVid.

FACILITATING KNOWLEDGE FLOWS

The continuous innovation that characterizes today's technological economy does not allow for deep and sustained engagement with tools. These transformations necessitate that individuals constantly need to be learning and updating their skills. Skills and knowledge may be used to earn money, but they can also be applied to an artistic process as part of an ongoing process of experimentation and learning. However, as the technological milieu dictates which tools are available to make work, these economic relations begin to shape what forms of art and aesthetics are possible. This is reflected in Mills's struggle to keep up with the changing technological landscape after Flash fell out of use, which she relied on to sustain her living and onformative's integration of R&D into their self-initiated projects, as well as with commercial projects when clients are more open to experimentation. Often this time for trial and error is unremunerated. For LoVid, this kind of experimentation is developed in collaboration with universities that have the resources to sustain research and innovation with technology. Each of these practices prompts questions about how we can better support sustained engagement with advanced technologies and facilitate ongoing learning and knowledge exchange for artistic ends.

Different funding models, such as artist grants, working with commercial galleries, or touring presents different constraints on practice. These practices condition the organization of the artist's time and labor (the "workflow") and have an impact on the form of the work produced. In this way, economies are the social and material processes that enable artworks to exist in the world. But just as importantly, the nonartistic work that artists do to support their living indirectly or directly contributes to their artistic practices. Ideas, knowledge, and connections overflow from other sectors to shape the artist's practice either by providing technical skills, conceptual knowledge, or access to resources to create work. For instance, Mills's skills in video production are also employed in her own artistic practice; for onformative, there is a fluid exchange between their artistic practice and commercial work, where knowledge from their commercial work and artistic practice feed into each other; and for LoVid, their knowledge of the sciences and academic field, and allows them to work more closely with scientific institutions and universities to develop their work in new directions involving haptic technologies.

To think of artistic practices temporally is to understand how they shift in time over the course of a career and to consider the changing social, technological, and economic environments. When presenting a comparison between different practices, it appears they are spatially fixed, yet Henri Bergson reminds us of the often-forgotten temporal dimension. This dimension is notably recognized in Bergson's "lump of sugar" example, in which sugar can be seen as differing in degree from other objects in space while forgetting its potential to dissolve in time as a difference in kind.[42] Artistic practices in this sense are never fixed and are in a constant process of becoming. This openness to the future does not fix a relationship to the economy, but rather leaves it open for new relational possibilities to emerge.

In chapter 2 I will look more closely at the different ways artworks circulate in contemporary art markets in diverse material forms. By conforming to conventions of the art market, artists and galleries engage in a process of redefining what constitutes the artwork to make a digital or conceptual artwork ownable, where the meaning and form of the artwork may also shift.

2

CIRCULATING IN POST-MEDIA ART MARKETS

In the process of selling post-media artworks, the object of ownership becomes the documentation, certificates of authenticity, or licensing agreements validating its originality. While these instruments help enact a shared understanding of a work, as well as create a sense of its value and authenticity, they can also vary widely, as different works are understood differently in different contexts. Conceptual and digital artworks take on variable forms in each restaging since the materiality of the art object is not fixed. Here, the word "variable" is used to describe the various forms of material and media that make up the same artwork in its different instantiations. The artwork exists in multiple forms and contexts in its circulation. Different materialities of art offer different possibilities for circulation in different economies both online and offline. Conversely, economies evolve and adapt to accommodate new forms of art, where practices, values, and conceptions of art shift over time. In this way, art cannot be conceived independently from the economies in which it is embedded and through which it is circulated. To examine economies as the dynamic process of bringing artworks into the world, in this chapter I focus on how conceptual and digital artworks are presented and sold in commercial galleries. In chapter 3, I will contrast these practices with online modes of circulation and digital economies. The focus on conceptual and digital art is intended to challenge epistemologies of art as fixed material objects, and opens to diverse practices and arrangements of the art market. The intention is to move toward a conception of art as constituted in temporal processes of creation, which allows us to consider how artistic practices may be sustained *in time*.

To illustrate the ways in which conceptual and digital artworks circulate in the commercial art market, I look at two cases from TRANSFER Gallery (who now simply go by TRANSFER to accommodate a broader virtual practice beyond the physical space) and Empty Gallery, two spaces whose curatorial focus is on forms of immersive media and VR (TRANSFER) and on sound and experimental practice (Empty Gallery). Both galleries have developed practices for exhibitions that challenge traditional notions of the white cube gallery and invent new practices for the art market. The license agreement, certificate of authenticity, and documentation and instructions for displaying the artwork become the qualifiers of the artwork itself. The galleries engage in a creative process of conceptualizing and packaging the artwork for its future restaging, requiring different technical and material supports for its display in site-specific exhibitions. Through this practice, galleries help make the artwork comprehensible as a unique object of ownership, shaping how the artwork is experienced in space, and also how it is able to be owned and appreciated in the future. The artwork's existence is brought about collectively by the artist, gallery, technology, collectors, and curators via its circulation in the economies of the contemporary art market. In this way, galleries participate in the creation of artworks as they help design the ways in which the artworks are sold and presented in exhibitions, processes that contribute to artworks' circulation and existence in the world.

When art is no longer defined by its medium as a finite object, licensing is employed as a legal instrument to facilitate the sale of artworks. Licensing also enables a rental economy for temporary displays for art beyond sales, where the artist retains the rights and control over their work. It shifts the art market toward different models of circulation, rather than a linear transactional relationship of buying and selling. Licensing enables the artwork to exist in multiple forms according to the terms of use as stipulated in the agreement. Contemporary artworks exist in multiple forms and media and circulate in diverse economies. By following the movement of objects, this chapter makes visible the economic practices that constitute an artwork. Licensing allows for artworks to exist in various material forms, wherein with the emergence of conceptual art, contemporary art was no longer defined by a fixed material object, a quality shared with digital art.

The post-medium condition emerged along with conceptualism in the 1960s with the "dematerialization of the art object" as described by Lucy Lippard, where artworks are no longer defined by mastery of a particular artistic medium and in which the concept takes precedence.[1] The concept of the "post-medium condition," as described by Rosalind Krauss, challenged modernist critic Clement Greenberg's notion of "medium specificity" by resisting the reduction of the medium to its physical properties and specific techniques and formalist practices.[2] As such, contemporary artists explore diverse medias in their practice in an interdisciplinary context. What Peter Weibel called the "post-media condition"[3] places old and new media on equal grounds beyond hierarchies between fine arts and technical arts. In an age where digital media usage has become universal, where all artistic disciplines require some form of technical mediation or support, art is considered part of the already mediated world where all artists are, in a sense, media artists. The prevalence of digital media also saw rising interest in "immaterial" forms of art; art based on ideas, process, interaction, communication, and information as temporal flows, and art forms proliferated to include installations, performances and media technologies.[4]

To discuss the "immateriality" of digital art can be misleading as it suggests digital objects do not have a material existence, when they do exist as electrons, undersea cables, computers and screens. I use the term "material" to discuss the modern conception of artworks as fixed and unique objects that can be bought and sold on the art market, whereas digital and conceptual objects share a variable materiality, where they need to be staged and executed in context in order for them to exist. For instance, conceptual art often comes with a set of instructions for executing the work, such as Yoko Ono's *Instruction Paintings*,[5] while digital art often exists as files or packages of code that need hardware to execute and display the artwork. Digital artworks are made of executable files where the artwork exists when the "algorithms act" or respond to input.[6] Digital files are essentially algorithms that need to be opened up and run on a computer where the artwork is generated and may be executed differently each time. The running of the algorithm is the artwork in action. Conceptual and generative forms of digital art mark the difference between *autographic* artworks, which are unique instantiations with finite objects such as paintings, and *allographic* artworks, which are informational, such as a musical score or software code which can be performed or staged with variations.[7] To allow these allographic artworks to exist in the future is to initiate possibilities for their circulation in various restagings and in other media and forms as events existing in time. Rather than focusing on preserving a unique material object, as with conventional conservation methods, contemporary artworks persist as they are practiced, performed, and restaged in the future as living processes. Making is at once a process of conserving art as embodied knowledge and experience. Art in this sense is not held in inanimate objects, but rather as social and material practices and events that take place in time and space. In consideration of digital art, this is not only computers or screens as objects, but also the digital files as executables that interact with or are experienced by audiences as an event.

In his book *On the Existence of Digital Objects*, Yuk Hui develops an understanding of digital media as relational objects. Digital objects (e.g., online video, images, and/or text files) do not exist in and of themselves, but are constituted through a web of relations as we engage with them as part of ubiquitous media environments and platforms such as social media.[8] Digital objects, which include digital artworks (such as digital images, video, sound, software) are constituted through their circulation online and in exhibitions in different social and material practices. Digital art historian Christiane Paul uses the term "neomateriality" where digital objects are defined as part of social and cultural processes along with data, systems, and machines.[9] Rather than considering artworks as discrete objects, artworks are understood as relational objects via their circulation as dynamic social and material practices.

Artists have long questioned the validity of the artwork as a unique material object, where there are historical links between conceptual art and technological art with artworks featuring audience interaction, feedback from the environment, and information networks. This connection has been elucidated by art historian Edward Shanken. His essay "Art in the Information Age" draws a link between conceptual art, the curatorial work of Jack Burnham, and the influence of technology and cybernetics. Conceptual artists like Les Levine, Hans Haacke, and Joseph Kosuth demonstrate an interest in systems thinking in which art is not understood as a finite object, but instead constituted via dynamic processes and information flows.[10] Conceptual art's engagement with technology contributed to a way of thinking about art as processes over products, where we can align the flow of thoughts and ideas, with the flow of data and information. While there continues to be value in original, unique, and scarce objects in the art market, these economic arrangements exist concurrently with conceptions of art as practices and processes. However, as described by writer Melissa Gronlund on Burnham's conclusion, we continue to be "thinking in objects yet living in systems."[11] The art market of unique objects continues to persist, despite the long engagement of artists in more conceptual and ephemeral practices. In order to understand the layered complexities of contemporary economies, this chapter focuses less on *what* these economies are and instead examines *how* they are enacted in specific instances that can enable and sustain artistic practices beyond a logic of pure exchange and profit.

Beyond a fixed materiality of the art object, contemporary art, including conceptual and digital art, can take multiple forms, where the artwork's materiality becomes secondary to its concept; the focus is no longer on the objects but the ideas. In the post-media condition as described by Weibel, artists embrace a wide range of media removing the distinctions between traditional media (paintings and sculptures) and those formerly called "new media."[12] Contemporary art is considered part of the already mediated and technological world where all artists are, in a sense, media artists. At the same time, according to Krauss, it is no longer necessary to identify media art by its medium, as all forms of art become more broadly part of contemporary art in the post-medium condition. What is often referred to as the "online art market" primarily pertains to material artworks sold through online platforms. I differentiate digital art as "born-digital" works created for their experience online and on screens and devices. While digital art also includes physical objects such as 3D printed sculptures created using digital processes, when I discuss digital art here, I am primarily referring to their existence as electronic systems, including computer, software, apps, websites, and more.[13] Returning to

Lee and LiPuma's "cultures of circulation," where the artwork is understood via its circulation, economies and their objects are co-constituted in the process of trading, selling or collecting art. In the contemporary condition, artworks take multiple forms; they engage economies of material objects, such as painting and sculptures, but they also exist as conceptual objects, for example, installations and performances; as well as digital objects, such as digital files for videos, sound, VR, AR, MR, robotics, and internet artworks. The conception of the work of art may shift as it circulates in different forms and contexts for its reception.

Throughout this chapter and chapter 3, we zoom in and out from following the artwork as it circulates through galleries and online platforms and through different cultures of circulation. The contemporary condition enables art to exist and be valued in multiple ways economically, socially, and culturally, each contributing to the sustainability of art and artists.

EMPTY GALLERY: THE VARIABLE MATERIALITIES OF CONCEPTUAL ART

Empty Gallery is designed as a black cube gallery to support experimental practices with sound and video. The space becomes part of the aesthetic experience of the artworks, where the gallery pays particular attention to the spatial design of each exhibition. Black boxes, as opposed to the white cube, are used more broadly for cinema experiences beyond the art context and can also employ the cinematic model of ticketed access and large audiences. Brian O'Doherty recognizes the white cube as a modernist construction of the 1920s that is specific to the art world, where the black box of the movie theater is associated with mass culture.[14] As time-based art entered museums and galleries, it challenged its association with forms of mass culture, enabling art to engage another economy and context for its reception. Black boxes create more of a sense of immersion particularly for practices with sound requiring less engagement with vision. Exhibition making becomes a process of inventing a means to present works in different material arrangements in different spaces, contributing to the ways in which works are collectively experienced and valued as part of an aesthetic practice.

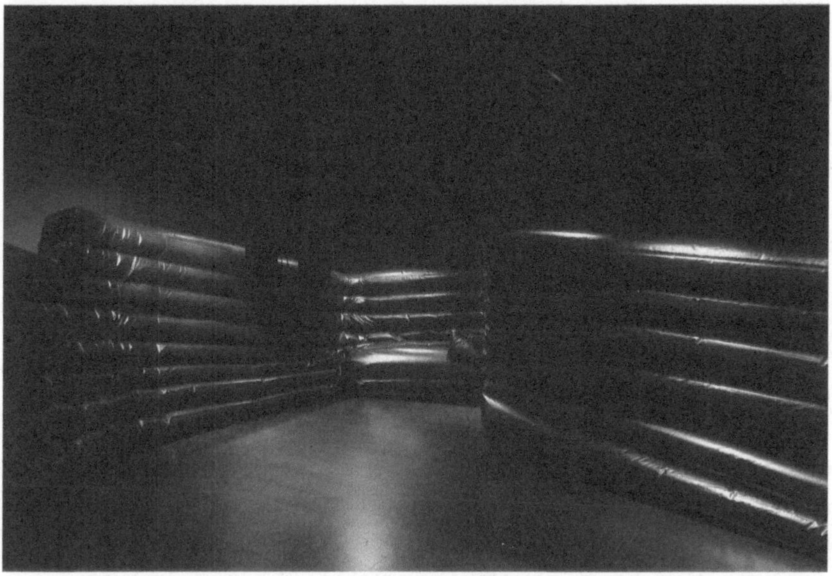

Jacqueline Kiyomi Gork's *Catchy* (2017) is an example of an Empty Gallery exhibition featuring an inflatable maze (figure 2.1) in which visitors were drawn through a dimly lit environment by sound cues, the entire space becoming a unified experience, with sculptural and textile works found throughout the exhibition. The sound cues shift and fluctuate as visitors move through the space, and the volume and frequencies of the sounds are carefully tuned for the space. The inflatables and textiles also act as a means to modulate the sound within the space. The work becomes a sonic experience, allowing audiences to rely less on their visual perception and more on touch and sound.

In the case of Empty Gallery, *Catchy* was sold with contractual specifications stating that the artist must be physically present during the

2.1

Jacqueline Kiyomi Gork, *Catchy*, installation view, Empty Gallery, Hong Kong, 2017. © Jacqueline Kiyomi Gork. Courtesy of the artist and Empty Gallery, Hong Kong.

installation of the work to ensure the work sonically functions as intended within the space. The nature of her work requires Gork to carefully adjust the audio according to each space, which becomes a constraint on her practice. Concerns like these have limited the possibilities for her work to travel, as some international institutions may lack the requisite budget. Artists may be contracted to install the artworks as a "service provision" as Andrea Fraser would describe it, as a way of engaging artists in a labor process dependent on creative, skilled, and intellectual labor in a service economy. Restaging an artwork may involve labor contracts, which provide artists with a legal framework to defend their working conditions, rather than basing their income on abstract values of artworks. The cost of purchasing the entire installation would be a much higher price, where only a museum would have the expertise and resources to care for such a work, which leaves greater uncertainty for its sale and remuneration. It becomes possible to consider how artworks may be rented for temporary displays, rather than as objects of ownership.

To give an example, Gork's work *Inside You Is Me* (2016)[15] was developed during a residency at The Lab, a nonprofit experimental art space in San Francisco. The work is a performance environment, which took four years to produce, and was funded through grants. Presented as a sound sculpture and multichannel sound installation, the artist staged performances with local artists in the installation. As a temporary exhibition and series of performances, the work was then developed into an object that could be sold and collected as the material legacy of the work. *The Lab Box: Inside You Is Me* (2016), developed in collaboration with curator Dena Beard, is sold in an edition of five, with two artist prints as a box set (see figure 2.2). Inspired by the avant-garde practices of Fluxus Boxes, Merce Cunningham's Capsules, and Marcel Duchamp's *Boîte-en-valise*,[16] the work is transformed into mixed media boxes as original reproductions of an artist's work. The work comes with a set of instructions on how to restage the work and an artist agreement borrowed from a template provided by The Lab, which includes different spatial and material considerations. The box included a toolkit with materials, examples of performances, and loose instructions for thinking about sounds' texture, volume, and fluctuation of pitch. Gork did not

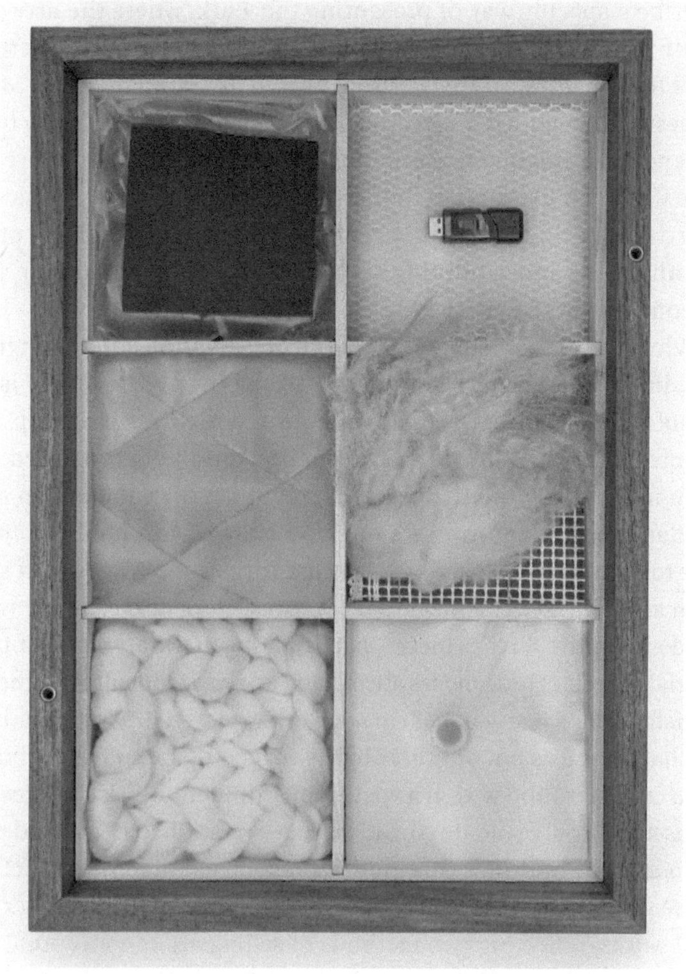

2.2

Jacqueline Kiyomi Gork, *Inside You Is Me* (without top), 2016; The Lab Box: urethane diffusion tile, walnut box, foam, fiberglass, felt, human hair, sheepskin, silicon, Universal Serial Bus stick (with 7 .mov, 47 .wav, 12 .tif, one .doc, and 5 Max MSP files), electrostatic prints, and ink on paper; collection SFMOMA, gift of Marjory Graue and Martin Bloes. © Jacqueline Kiyomi Gork. Photo: Don Ross. Courtesy of the artist and The Lab, San Francisco.

prescribe a specific way of presenting the work, where the artwork can take diverse forms in the various restagings of the work. Different materials for the physical installation, as well as sound files and MaxMSP patches were included on a USB stick in the box. It shifts away from dependency on a singular and original material object, where the restaging of the work can use similar, but different materials in accordance with the artist's specifications. It engenders a process of inventing practices for both selling and exhibiting art, which are contingent on the artwork and concerns of the artist.

While the precise challenges of the preservation and maintenance[17] of media artworks have been subject to ongoing debate due to issues of technological obsolescence, the variable materialities of conceptual and post-media artworks move away from the notion of art as fixed objects frozen in time as modern museums might suggest. Rather, an artwork is understood as requiring staging and restaging in public contexts in order to continue to exist as a living artwork as it engages with society.

In addition to her conceptual artworks, Gork also sells her works as sound-absorptive textiles pieces, participating in the art market of unique material objects. These pieces are created as a way to insulate sound within her installations. Early in her career, Gork explored different kinds of textiles that served as not only art objects that could be collected, but also a way to control sound within a spatial environment. Gork's interest in textiles as a material could be considered an evolution of her sound practice within an art world that continues to value fixed material objects above all else. Absorptive textiles become the aesthetic material of her sound-based works, reflecting two methods of selling art as conceptual objects and as material objects in the different and coexisting epistemologies of art. While sound artworks are difficult to sell in the art market, Gork's work shows they can exist as conceptual objects; as sets of documentation, instructions, and a contract. While there is a habit of selling conceptual art in a particular way, there is also an openness to experiment with new practices to enact different possibilities for what constitutes the artwork, and how it is sold and understood in an art market. As the artistic process is experimental and challenges conceptions of art itself, there is also an experimental process of engaging with markets to present what might be understood as a commodity for collection and acquisition.

While some works of conceptual art manage to gain value and prominence, many others may not. By employing the practices of Fluxus in the use of boxes of instructions, Gork allows her work to be understood and valued alongside particular canons of conceptual art. The process of evaluating conceptual art is a highly opaque process that is often only legitimated by insiders of the art world, who act as gatekeepers determining which artworks can and cannot circulate. While the variable materiality of conceptual and media-based artworks limits their sale on the art market, museums tend to play a large role in acquisitions of complex installation works. However, since documentation and licensing agreements dictate the artworks' sale and restaging, it raises the possibility of thinking of art beyond ownership and toward economic approaches that sustain practices as services, such as labor contracts that engage artists in the restaging of a work or as rental contracts for temporary displays of artworks. In the sale of an artwork, artists retain the copyright, but lose control over the work while the collector continues to earn profit from its loan and resale (unless otherwise stipulated). Licensing when serving as a rental contract allows artists to retain ownership and control over their work and continue to earn from the loan of their work for temporary displays.[18] Such legal arrangements may be designed to better accommodate artists.

While Gork works across diverse media in the post-media condition, she can also engage with textiles as a material practice through her work with sound, where she creates unique objects that can be sold more easily on the art market. Gork feels that, since different funding streams all have their pitfalls and challenges that begin to shape an artistic practice, it is necessary for artists to explore all the economies for their practice, particularly as grant funding is shrinking in the United States. She explains, "I feel like you kind of have to do all of it. Grants are going to be able to fund a certain type of work that commercials are not going to. And commercials are going to fund a certain type of work the grants are not going to."[19] As Abbing states, "Most artists are situated in-between; they are neither totally commercial nor totally selfless."[20] Artists necessarily explore multiple economies for their work, and also multiple forms from objects to installations and performances in other modes of practice. However, to shift the centrality of ownership in the art market, one must consider licensing as playing a larger role in today's creative economies.

LICENSING: TOWARD A PLURAL CONCEPTION OF THE ART OBJECT

A license agreement is a type of contract and legal instrument that governs relations between parties, and in the case of art and artists, act "as determinations of who/what constitutes persons and things."[21] While practices may exceed legal definitions and terms, they also help ensure that collectors or clients perform their duties, such as making timely payments to the artist. A license agreement helps create a common understanding of the artwork and its terms of use, such as duration of a display, specification of the artwork, and timelines and budgets for delivery. While licensing enables the sales of conceptual and digital forms of art, it also raises questions about when there is no longer a fixed object, whether a market centered on sales and ownership of artworks continues to make sense in today's economies. Beyond sales, licensing can also allow for the use, display, and modification of a work of intellectual property, where artworks exist in a multiplicity of forms and contexts.

Licensing provides permission for the reproduction of intellectual property, including patents and trademarks including on products like posters, T-shirts, or other merchandise. Licensing is also employed in the distribution of stock imagery and photography, where platforms like Getty Images, iStock, and Shutterstock provide the rights to use or reproduce images for design or journalistic purposes in print or online. Within the arts, Design and Artists Copyright Society (DACS), a nonprofit organization in the UK, is a company that specializes in handling licensing and resale rights for visual artists pertaining to the use of images of artworks. These reproductions are perceived as derivatives of original artworks rather than artworks themselves, yet they're more accessible to the everyday consumer in print media, or as mass-produced commodities. The process of licensing is attributed to the brand and production of mass commodities, where according to Celia Lury, brands are assemblages as an intensive process of assembling culture.[22] Artworks exist in a multiplicity of forms and contexts, circulating in diverse economies, which are no longer limited to unique and scarce objects of ownership.

Licensing is perhaps an under-regarded economy of art, in an art market centered on the sale of unique material objects. While licensing[23] is used to provide legal permission to use any kind of intellectual property, including artistic works, it is a method used to enable the distribution of film, video, and broadcast media. For instance, there are a number of historical nonprofit art organizations founded in the 1970s and 1980s that focus on archiving and distributing the films and videos of professional artists. These organizations include Electronic Arts Intermix in New York, Video Data Bank in Chicago, LUX in London, and Vtape in Toronto. In Asia, organizations like Videotage in Hong Kong and Video Bureau in Beijing archive and promote video works in the region. Many of these organizations license works for exhibitions and screenings and distribute works through film and media festivals.

However, with online media, this rental model is becoming obsolete. Erika Balsom, who has written on artist film and video distribution, sees both official channels and informal networks of sharing works online as coexistent and thinks that both methods contribute to a wider ecology of how media circulates today. She writes that "radically different forms of distribution compete and cooperate, from the sale of limited editions on the art market to authorized and unauthorized online distribution and the sale of mass-market DVDs and Blu-rays. Film and videos routinely circulate across these infrastructures, sometimes at the behest of their makers and sometimes as the result of unauthorized copying, existing simultaneously in multiple distribution models."[24] This layering of practices and methods of distribution regards both the formal and the informal economies. Within art, the practices are much less standardized than music or film, where art can take multiple forms, just as the contexts and use of the works can vary greatly.

Within art, licensing becomes a means to display and loan a work while also serving as a means to protect the terms of use and attribution of the work, as the artist retains the copyright. Licensing shifts away from treating art as a unique object, where the concept of ownership becomes a perpetual license, which grants the rights for an institution or collector to use and display the work in perpetuity. Licensing has affordances as a legal contract, mediating the relations between artist, collector, and artwork and dictating how these economies are enacted. While practices may not follow the contract exactly, they help ensure a mutual understanding of the artwork. A contract delineates the boundaries of subjects (the artist and client) and objects (artworks or media files). At the same time, contracts become necessary for markets to be enacted in a particular way as the means for artists to control the distribution of their work and define the terms of use and remuneration. Legal frameworks such as licensing agreements, service agreements, and artist contracts can be taken as a medium for experimentation[25] in that they contribute to how economies are enacted, which in turn effects the collective production of the market.

For instance, Serpentine Galleries has initiated an R&D Platform on Future Art Ecosystems including the Legal Lab,[26] exploring new infrastructures for enabling art and technology collaborations. Legal design as a practice promoted by agencies like Amurabi in France can be more than simply the aesthetics of legal contracts, but rather looks at how they participate in creating the world through language and how it is enacted in practice. Since legal language is often complex, few artists are equipped to read and tailor contracts and agreements to their needs without hiring legal consultants. By using simplified language and visual design to clearly present legal concepts, it aids in the process for designing legal contracts and agreements both visually and in practice. However, to consider the conceptual form of the law also challenges philosophically the language for what constitutes personhood, ownership, and intellectual property, where such concepts are artificial constructions that have been normalized. Art critic Sven Lütticken in his essay "Legal Forms, Value-Forms, Forms of Resistance"[27] suggests how we might reclaim notions of personhood to appropriate meanings and terminologies as an artistic practice, which are in fact abstract concepts. Beyond an economy of ownership, licensing has become a means to empower artists to consider the terms of their labor and temporary uses of their art, shifting away from economic practices centered on financial speculation and accumulation. Licensing allows art to exist in multiple and diverse forms and media, where art may evolve as it circulates in different contexts. Art is thus sustained through its future restagings, as collective and shared experiences.

Due to the often informal nature of the art world based on close personal contacts, artworks are often sold without a contract. However, conceptual artworks lack a fixed materiality, and media-based works in their infinite reproducibility necessitate a contract to dictate what constitutes the artwork and terms of how it is to be displayed, loaned, and sold. As observed by media art collector Alain Servais,[28] clear rights and standards should be required for the distribution of video and media artworks, as the ambiguity of the object makes these works challenging to own and collect. Servais proposes that when a work is purchased the agreements should specify the exhibition rights, resale rights, reproduction rights, morals rights, and requirements for maintenance and repair of the work. No regulation exists on how such works are collected and sold, while the variability of the object poses challenges for its collection within the art market. Licenses establish concretely what counts about the artwork in its status as an object to be owned, circulated, and resold. A license enables a work's circulation within the art market, in which fluid objects can be collectively understood. Having multiple and varying contracts with different rights and legal bearings creates challenges for the sale and resale of conceptual and post-media artworks. The fact that licensed artwork may exist in multiple formats and edition sizes—as high-priced artworks but also on hard drives and USBs as digital files, or as streamed videos online—compromises the value of a work in the art market. However, licensing also enables forms of distribution without the necessity of owning and maintaining the works. It enables artists to retain control and ownership of their work, beyond economies oriented around sales to collectors who become the primary benefactors of future sales of the work.

TRANSFER: EXPERIMENTS WITH DISTRIBUTION FORMATS FOR IMMERSIVE MEDIA

TRANSFER is described as "an exhibition space that explores the friction of virtual studio practice and its physical instantiation."[29] The gallery experiments with ways of presenting digital and time-based media works within the commercial gallery context, where space becomes an extension of the work itself. TRANSFER artists greatly value the experience and interaction with the artwork when engaging in the exhibition-making process. TRANSFER seeks to provide a curated context for showcasing work in diverse media and formats. There is a desire to stick "true to the medium" to exhibit and sell works in their original media, which is normally virtual reality (VR) artworks or other kinds of software or internet-based artworks, despite the difficulties that can arise when selling these forms of art. Rather than conforming to an object-based economy of paintings and sculptures, TRANSFER seeks to develop a market for digital art while experimenting with methods for its presentation and distribution in the art market. By resisting falling back on material forms to make them more saleable on the art market, TRANSFER's dedication to the digital medium, such as VR artworks, necessitates inventing a means for artworks to be sold and valued in the art market and museums.

When TRANSFER Gallery sells work as digital objects, the sale is documented and prepared with a set of instructions on how to install and present the work as the artist intended along with a contract to delimit the terms of the work and its use. The documentation,[30] which is considered part of the purchase, may include specifications for any necessary equipment, and list available services of a technician who can help install the work. Each instantiation of the work is site-specific, as the artists are usually involved in the restaging process to ensure the appropriate presentation of the work. This falls in line with conceptual art practices, such as art curator and dealer Seth Siegelaub creating *The Artist's Reserved Rights Transfer and Sale Agreement* in 1971.[31] In it, he attempted to develop a standard for sales of conceptual works, giving artists rights to determine where their artwork can be exhibited, and also specifying that they are to receive 15 percent of resale revenue. As part of the sale of the conceptual object, the contract acts as a license to allow the exhibition of the work, which is a practice more common within media industries. While the licensing standard of resale rights was not widely adopted by galleries at the time, licensing became a part of a means to sell conceptual and digital artworks.

Agreements help artists, artworks, and collectors enact the market in a particular way, dictating the terms of use and resale of a work. Contemporary art is not defined by a fixed materiality or a stable object, but may take different forms and arrangements in future exhibitions. In addition to the license agreement, TRANSFER Gallery founder Nichole also helps to create a set of formats and arrangements according to which the work can be presented. While these practices of documentation and the contract may sound similar to the process of selling a conceptual object, there are specific material considerations such as technical support, maintenance, equipment, and copying and sharing of files to take into account. Digital objects are considered both as part of conceptual art, but also independently, given their particular material concerns.

At times, artworks engaging with technology circulate as contemporary artworks, where the use of media in the artwork is secondary to the concept or ideas explored in the work. Technology is merely a means to communicate ideas, though as we find with Marshall McLuhan's suggestion "the medium is the message," it becomes difficult to ignore that the form of the artwork and the means of transmission are contributing to the meaning of the work itself. In other instances, artworks explore the medium itself and its creative and aesthetic possibilities. The artwork is about the aesthetic qualities of the medium and the skills of the artist to use it. The focus on the medium and form of the artwork itself is a more limited understanding of art, where artworks engaging with technology can also explore the role of technology in society and raise critical questions and debates around it. The relationship of form and content with contemporary art is where content takes precedence over an emphasis on the use of technology itself. However, there is also a challenge in the fetishization of technology in today's economies, which makes it difficult to escape the definition of art by its medium.

While contemporary art wants to avoid the question of media specificity, there continues to be questions around how to exhibit and sell digital artworks in the traditional art market and white cube galleries. It requires inventing techniques and practices for selling forms of digital art, and a language and community for its appreciation. It also requires experimenting with spatial arrangements of the gallery setting suitable for media-based works. For instance, for virtual reality (VR) artworks, Nichole considers transforming the work into an immersive installation within a space. Nichole is responding in particular to the constraint of the individualized experience of the VR artwork from within a VR headset. Creating an installation around the VR artwork allows for visitors who are not wearing the headset to have an experience of it as an installation. Nichole explains: "What I am commissioning is actually the installation design around the VR work. How does that come into the space? How does that ease the sense of embodiment for a work, and how can that lead to more critical dialogue and conversation around a work? Otherwise, virtual reality can be quite isolating."[32] Nichole's investment in the exhibition design helps contextualize the work within a space for audiences to experience it. VR work becomes an installation rather than a standalone VR piece, where audiences also become part of the mise-en-scène. In each instantiation, the work is presented differently, depending on the equipment and space available. Nichole seeks to create an environment in which visitors can have a shared experience of a work. In this way, the context and circumstances in which people encounter the work becomes part of the artwork itself. The exhibition becomes a temporal experience, where art is not about objects in space, but a collective immersive experience. Exhibiting new forms of art and technology requires experimentation in practice.

For instance, Rosa Menkman's exhibition *Behind White Shadows* (2017) presents artwork both as a VR experience and as a physical sculptural work with projection.[33] While one person views the VR work titled *DCT:SYPHONING. The 1000000th (64th) Interval*, other audience members can explore the environment and installation (see figure 2.3). In preparation for the exhibition, a geometric structure called *Spomenik* was built using 3D projection mapping software to create a spatialized representation of the digital forms in the VR version. The work transfigures into new material forms as it is presented in gallery spaces. The exhibition becomes a temporal experience, in which audiences are embedded. The work bridges digital and physical environments, creating a hybrid space, which is less about the individual VR artwork and more focused on the entirety of the installation and experience.

The form of the work influences the practices of exhibition making and design of a space. These practices are also constrained by the space and availability of equipment, which may also in turn influence the form of the work. In this way, works are contingent on the materiality of the space and its available technological supports in a two-way relationship between the artwork and its milieu as the exhibition and institutional space, as well as the desire for shared artistic experiences. The materiality of the works influences the design of the space and begins to form different systems for the work's valuation and appreciation. Objects displayed in space are no longer central to the exhibition, but rather are valued as one aspect of a shared experience. Such an approach opens

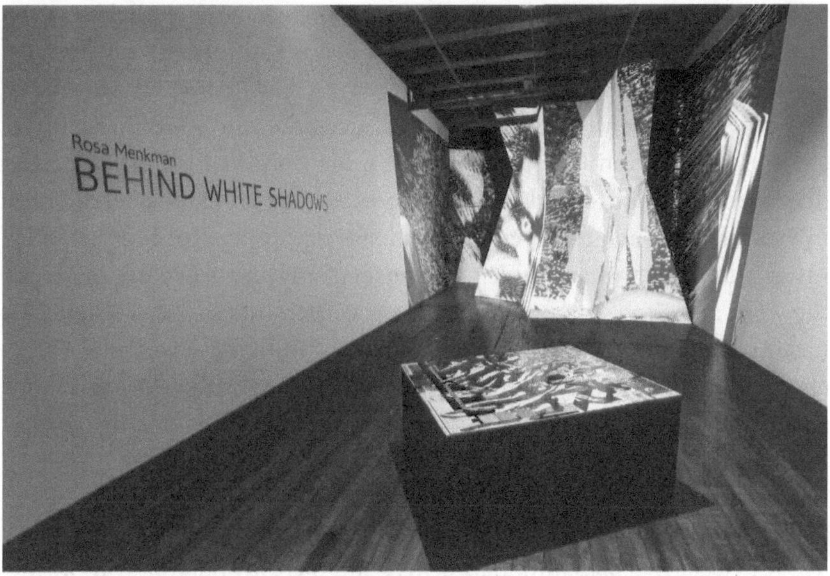

the proliferation of practices, including different arrangements of space, art, audiences, and supporting economies. Exhibition making and gallery practices necessarily evolve with the variable forms of the artworks they feature, opening to the potential emergence of new contexts and economies for art. The exhibition becomes a shared experience, which is then sold as a set of instructions for its future restaging. Collectors own the rights to display and loan the artwork for future exhibitions, where galleries invent formats and practices for collecting immersive media installations in the art market.

2.3

Rosa Menkman, *Spomenik*, with a VR installation of *DCT SYPHONING. The 1000000th (64th) Interval* on custom-built project wall presented in the solo exhibition *Behind White Shadows*, TRANSFER, New York, 2017. Photo: Tracie Williams. Courtesy of the artist.

In order to enable artworks to travel more easily, Nichole has developed the TRANSFER Download, which is a set of formats for presenting VR or other immersive media artworks. The TRANSFER Download was initially conceived as a series of VR artworks converted into a three-channel installation format to provide more options for the work to be displayed and distributed in exhibitions. VR artworks pose challenges in exhibitions, such as access to expensive equipment and the need for invigilation. Without multiple VR headsets, only one user can experience the work at a time. In response to these constraints of VR, TRANSFER has invented a new format for the display of immersive works as three-channel video installations. The TRANSFER Download seeks to allow for a shared experience of the work as an installation, while making it easier to exhibit and tour.

Both TRANSFER Gallery and Empty Gallery develop techniques to facilitate the circulation of artworks in exhibitions and as ownable artworks in ways that accommodate artists' interests in ephemeral art forms. Empty Gallery's curatorial approach engages less with digital media and advanced technologies. They follow a lineage of conceptual, intermedia, and experimental art practices, including analog film and audio, painting, and sculpture, alongside digital sound and video. While TRANSFER also sells digital artworks as physical installations, their interest lies primarily in supporting born-digital artworks to circulate.

The TRANSFER Download installation comes with a tablet with a playlist for selecting and playing the works, and a computer system to display the work on three synchronized projectors in a room. The three-channel video is a relatively easy way to create an immersive installation without requiring a VR headset or a powerful computer. Media artworks are often adapted to the space for each instantiation of the work, where the same work could be presented in multiple different ways. Using this method, different artworks originally created in a particular format, such as virtual or augmented reality, video games, generative artworks, simulations, or online artworks can all be reformatted to fit different spaces and environments. Nichole experiments with different formats for presenting the artworks to enable them to travel more easily, but only in ways that make sense for the individual work. For each artwork, different formats are developed in conversation with the artist to appropriately translate the

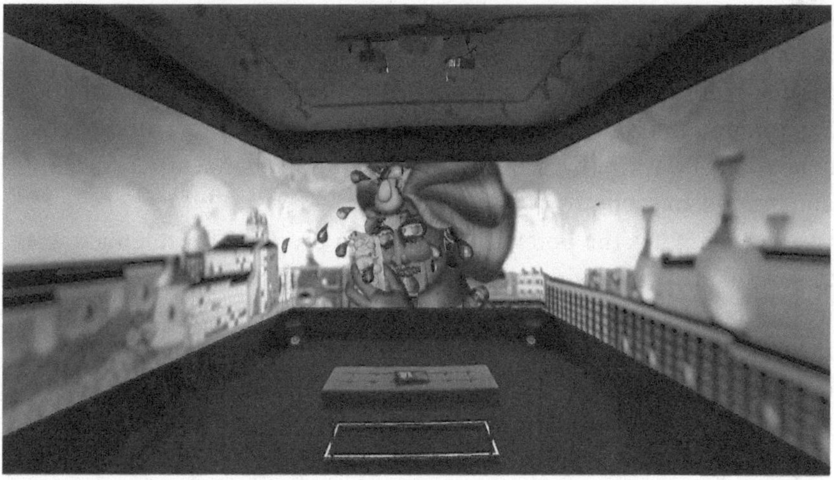

work into other spatial and media arrangements. TRANSFER Gallery is one of few galleries experimenting with methods to enable media art distribution. For the TRANSFER Download, Nichole has toured the works internationally as group exhibitions at Arebyte Gallery, London; Chronus Art Centre, Shanghai; Canal Street Gallery, New York; the Thomas Foundation, Santa Fe; and at SPRING/BREAK Art Show, Los Angeles (figure 2.4), enabling her represented works to reach wider audiences beyond her exhibition space.

The TRANSFER Download can be viewed as a touring screening program of three-channel artworks. Other immersive formats include 360-degree dome projections as a model for exhibiting immersive video works, such as in the *Immersion*[34] program series presented by Berliner Festspiele, which features a range of programs including temporal

2.4

Carla Gannis, *Portraits in Landscape, Sunrise*, TRANSFER Download, Installation view, Carl & Marilynn Thoma Foundation, Art House, Santa Fe, 2018. Courtesy of the artist and TRANSFER.

exhibition, mobile dome artist commissions, and VR artworks. Licensing and ticketed time-based experiences become a model better suited for media artworks than their sale as scarce objects within the art market. Experimentation with formats and licensing models allows for the reconsideration of ways for presenting and distributing digital artworks within and beyond an economy of sales of objects.

Licensing has the potential to enable a process of restaging a work to sustain artistic activities as a collective endeavor. Rather than collecting art to be held in vaults, art acquires cultural value when its appreciation is shared. Art collecting becomes meaningful for the collector when they participate in stewardship, in displaying the work in exhibitions, or in developing a long-term supportive relationship with artists. Artworks acquire significance via their circulation in their relational arrangements among artists, collectors, galleries, and audiences that enable them to exist in the world. Collecting art can be more than mere transactions, where the meaning and conception of art is constituted as relations between artist, collector, and milieu. To take care of how art exists in the world is to tend to these possible relations, constituting art and people and their roles and identities in the world.

FROM OWNERSHIP TO CIRCULATION

Selling conceptual and digital art requires an experimental process for defining the object that can be sold on the art market. Additionally, the ways in which the artworks are materialized in space requires a creative process that shapes the experience of the work. In this way, galleries contribute to the creation of the work, by defining the ways it circulates when it is purchased. Licensing agreements and instructions for restaging the artwork become the qualifier of the artwork that in and of itself lacks a fixed materiality. Artists like Gork engage diverse media where artworks are sold as conceptual objects that come with sample materials, a USB drive, and sets of instructions. The artist has also developed a material practice using textiles to serve as sound insulation for her installations. Working across media necessitates that artists engage in diverse economies to sustain their artistic practices, where artworks exist and circulate as conceptual, digital, and material objects.

For TRANSFER, the desire to work with born-digital artworks means the gallery also invent formats for exhibiting and touring VR and immersive artworks. The TRANSFER Download platform creates a format for experiencing VR artworks as a three-channel installation, where artworks can take multiple forms and be presented in different formats in different spaces and contexts. Moving away from understanding the artwork as a unique object in a specific medium such as VR, we observe how the work can evolve to create a shared experience as an immersive installation. This form of art is more conducive to economic models of ticketed events as can be seen with large-scale immersive experiences presented by collectives like teamLab (discussed in chapter 5). To shift away from an art market centered on unique material objects is to understand contemporary economies as collaborative processes with the galleries and others involved in staging and restaging artworks. These processes also include temporary displays supported by licensing as rental contracts that offer a model beyond that of private ownership. Each of these approaches requires a reconsideration of the art object, ownership, authorship, and the white cube as constructs that continue to persist despite the ephemerality of art in the post-media condition. Chapter 3 brings digital economies of viral media, social media promotion, and NFTs into conversation with the commercial gallery and licensing practices discussed in this chapter, to highlight the unique challenge of balancing scarcity and free circulation.

3

BETWEEN SCARCITY AND FREE CIRCULATION IN DIGITAL ECONOMIES

Art forms with variable materialities (such as conceptual and digital art) have the potential to engage practices beyond the sale of unique material objects. While chapter 2 discussed how practices and processes like events, rental contracts, and temporary displays have created novel economies to control the circulation of *material* instantiations of conceptual and digital art, this chapter examines how digital platforms have created new markets for digital and conceptual art. As this chapter will demonstrate, the shift toward a distributed and variable object departs from the modernist understanding of art as scarce, original, and finite objects. New practices have evolved in order for conceptual and digital artworks to be sold and collected in an art market. As suggested by philosopher Peter Osborne, multiple historical-temporal forms coexist, where contemporaneity is a *condition* of the "coming together of different but equally 'present' temporalities in temporarily totalized but disjunctive unities."[1] Conceptions of art as unique material objects of the modern era exist alongside conceptions of art in the digital era of social media and networked communication. At times these different conceptions of art create contradictions, or what Osborne describes as "disjunctive unities" between the logics of the art market valuing scarcity and uniqueness, and the online digital economies valuing the virality of media.[2] In this chapter, I will explore further the tensions between the logic of the art market and the promotional economies of online media. I discuss the cultivation of digital scarcity by examining Sedition, an online platform for selling digital limited editions, and the emergence of the non-fungible token market. The NFT market attempts to resolve the tensions between scarcity and free circulation through financialization, thereby creating an abstraction of the object of ownership.

Replication is inherent to digital objects. Digital art therefore challenges the epistemology of the art market that has long been centered on selling unique and scarce original objects. Douglas Davis explains that there is no distinction between copy and original in the digital object; each version of a digital file is virtually the same.[3] The copy is just as original as the original. The digital object enables infinite reproducibility. Every time a digital file such as an image is viewed on the internet, it creates a copy in the cached memory of a computer. Likewise, within Chinese culture, the concept of *shanzhai*[4] posits that there is no distinction between copy and original. For Byung-Chul Han, "the original is determined not by a unique act of creation, but by unending process, not by definitive identity but by constant change."[5] Reproductions are valued as equal to the original and copying is seen as an act of respect for the master. With open-source culture in software development, code is left open for modifications, where each developer builds on the work of others for the greater good, where there is less of a sense of ownership. Within generative art communities such as Processing,[6] artists are allowed to adapt or modify code and release it as their own artworks. While these are vastly different cultures, they all create a model of practice that allows for an open conception of art and its continuous iteration. I would argue that rather than having digital art conform to the outmoded epistemologies of the art market, priority should be placed on inventing new systems and practices for valuing and sharing art in its various forms in permutation and as collective and shared practices. All the cases in this chapter continue to reinforce the value of scarce ownable objects, either as installations sold in galleries such as TRANSFER, or as digital limited editions sold on platforms like Sedition, or as unique digital tokens like NFTs.

Efforts to control the mechanical reproduction of art in media like printmaking resulted in the creation of limited editions and certificates of authenticity as techniques to maintain a sense of scarcity and value for reproducible art. The artwork becomes an object that can be owned and protected through copyright. Limited editions were initially developed to "democratize" art through the production of multiples, making art available at a lower cost. In *The Consumer Society*, Jean Baudrillard recognizes the devaluation of art by creating multiples through its association with mass culture.[7] However, with the infinite reproducibility of digital files, the concept of limited editions does not apply, unless artificially enforced by forms of digital rights management (DRM). However, as artworks are allowed to circulate freely online, they maintain two existences: as high-value artworks and as free culture on the internet. The artworks' free circulation on social media compromises their uniqueness as digital limited editions on Sedition, where there is a desire to simultaneously promote the artworks while restricting access to them. Sedition as an online platform seeks to create artificial scarcity of digital videos and images using forms of DRM that provide limited access to streamed artworks.

Though technology has made it easier to remix and share creative works online, copyright has been used to protect the interests of corporations and major record labels. Creative Commons, a flexible copyright license, was created by intellectual property lawyer Lawrence Lessig[8] in order to empower artists to have more control over the use of their works by corporations, while also allowing for the use of their work by other creators.[9] Internet memes as a part of digital culture reflect a collective creativity based upon permutation and appropriation of found images, operating with disregard for copyrights, often on the terms of fair use and satire, just as forms of appropriation[10] are justified within the context of art. Meaning transforms through its circulation in different cultural contexts. An example is the Pepe the Frog meme (figure 3.1), an innocent and nonpolitical comic character created by Matt Furie, which was subsequently co-opted by the alt-right in the United States as a hate symbol for white supremacist extremism. Pepe the Frog subsequently came to represent the pro-democracy movement in Hong Kong without protesters' knowledge of the character's right-wing association.[11] This demonstrates how cultural forms such as Pepe may take on vastly different and contradictory meanings through their circulation in diverse contexts. Artworks can equally undergo such a transformation. To understand art as a shared cultural process is to also acknowledge its ability to evolve and exist with and beyond concepts of intellectual property and copyright,

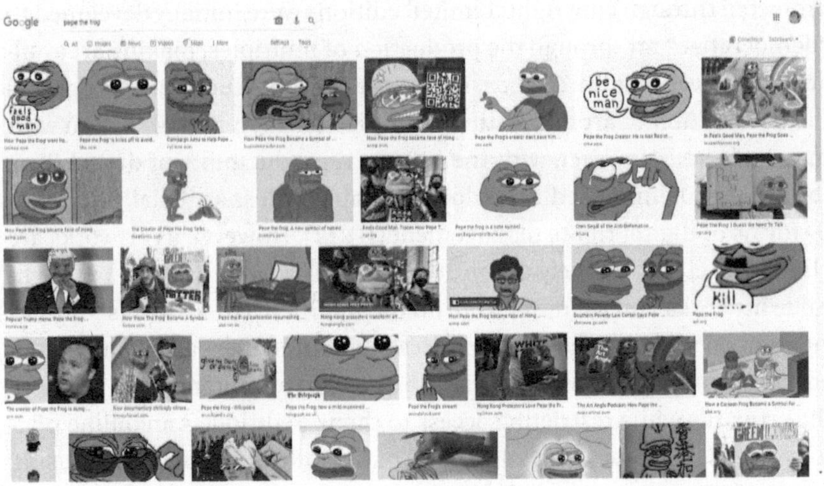

3.1

The Pepe the Frog meme, Google Images search result, screenshot, 2024.

and to ask how we might enable culture to thrive beyond notions of a finite art object. As will be discussed in this chapter, artists like Lorna Mills have created and shared artworks as animated GIFs online as part of their practice.

This tension between the scarcity of the limited edition and free circulation of the artwork online was somewhat resolved with the advent of NFTs, an application of blockchain technologies used for the sale of digital objects, which creates an abstraction with the object of ownership using financial technologies. A blockchain is a distributed, cryptographically immutable ledger, where transaction information is recorded and distributed across many computers, then verified without going through a centralized third party. Blockchains allow for the transaction history and provenance of an artwork to be recorded securely and permanently as NFTs of ownership, serving in a sense as a cryptographically enforced digital certificate of authenticity. The trading of NFTs is governed using smart contracts where protocols may be scripted as a form of licensing agreement. Through this process, artist royalties are programmed into smart contracts to ensure artists earn from secondary sales. However, due to NFT marketplaces not including royalty payments in smart contracts, artists have missed out on their earnings; for instance, the most popular creator-led platform OpenSea no longer offers mandatory collection of resale fees, demonstrating the failed efforts in supporting the interests of artists in the NFT space, which was viewed as part of the technology's greater potentials in the artistic community.[12] Additionally, upfront costs of minting NFTs at times posed challenges for artists, as well as concerns over energy consumption. Blockchain technologies emerged as a response following the economic crisis of 2008, decentralizing finance away from a centralized banking system.[13] At the same time, interest rose in managing art as a financial asset, just as the art market was realizing new profit records.[14] While the development of blockchain is connected to a libertarian ideal, both social and market libertarianism have come to inflect the digital art market since the advent of NFTs.

At the same time, the art market has grown alongside the financialization of the global economy since the 1990s.[15] Financialization creates an abstraction of a commodity that can be owned, traded, and speculated upon its future value. It further becomes removed from the object since the certificate of authenticity and licensing agreement relates directly to an object, whereas financial assets relate to its value. Nearly anything can be assigned a value and sold, even those artworks that have been destroyed (such as Banksy burning his own artwork after selling it as an NFT), with self-destructing NFTs becoming an issue in face of the immutability and permanence that blockchain offers.[16] Technological innovation of Silicon Valley is largely sustained by venture capital creating a culture of financial speculation and short-term gains around disruptive technologies and new business models. These diverse cultures come together through the social and material practices of selling NFTs. Bringing together the online economies of free circulation and offline economies of the art market founded upon scarcity, NFTs enable a work to be circulated online while simultaneously contributing the value of a work in the market as a financial asset.[17] The permutations of the artwork as part of internet culture no longer contradict its scarcity and ownership, however not without reducing art to a financial asset that can be speculated upon. The development of NFTs falls in line with the ideologies of innovation that surround blockchain technologies, with Sedition bolstering the elitism of the art market while seeking to engage online marketing strategies. Both speculative financial bubbles created by technological trends and the exclusionary politics of high-end art markets have their pitfalls, however. To understand them better, we can also identify the values within them that can be appropriated or reconfigured in other contexts. These values may include providing underacknowledged artists a curated platform to present their works to international collectors (in the case of Sedition, for Desmond Leung), or participating as a collector of NFTs as an artist while also discovering and supporting new artists in the process (in the case of Lorna Mills and her practice).

LORNA MILLS: GIFS AS POOR IMAGES AND HIGH ART

Through TRANSFER Gallery, Lorna Mills sells her works as video installations or animated GIFs as editions and unique works, while simultaneously allowing the images to circulate freely online as "poor images." Putting the work online promotes Mills's artwork while engaging with the online spaces from which the images originated. In the gallery, circulation is restricted where only a small number of people can purchase the artworks, creating tension if a collector finds the work circulated online.

With TRANSFER, Mills has sold her work in editions of three, with one artist proof, and also in larger installations as unique works (see figure 3.2). The animated GIF artworks are documented by TRANSFER in a catalogue by inserting each frame of the sequence into a spreadsheet. Collectors can then view the entire work as individual images. As stipulated in the contract for the artworks, the GIFs must be shown on a loop on a dedicated screen, rather than on a reel of different artworks. There are some collectors who buy digital art because it's affordable, making it possible to own a large number of artworks by artists for a low price. At this time prior to the NFT boom in 2021, Mills felt digital art was largely undervalued.[18]

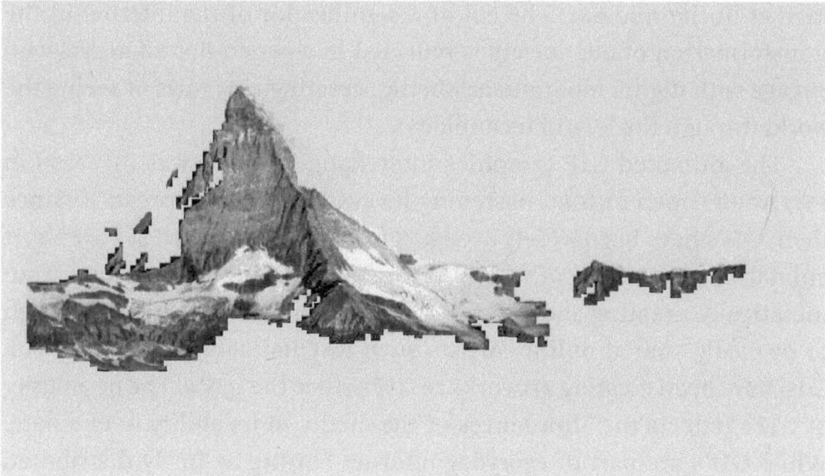

In the 2010s, the majority of digital works were valued considerably less than artworks produced using traditional media. A single-channel editioned animated GIF by Mills is $8,000, the highest price for this type of work sold by TRANSFER at the time of writing, while multi-channel installations are valued higher at $25,000 and up. The price is intended to align the value of art to that of luxury goods, such as a Louis Vuitton bag, but remains comparatively low in contrast to contemporary artworks, which rose to an average price of $25,000 in 2019.[19] What artworks carry that luxury items do not is "cultural and social prestige" and an "aura of cultural importance."[20] The relevance of a GIF to emerging internet cultures has given the work a higher value over time. The artist is attempting to raise the value of a GIF as a format by aligning the work as part of the post-internet movement, a strategy that gained prominence in the art

3.2

Lorna Mills, *Mountain/Light Time*, image still; animated GIF; and 1080p video, 1920x1080px, 2015. Edition of three and one artist proof. Courtesy of the artist and TRANSFER.

market in the mid-00s. The cultural significance of the internet in the transformation of our society is reflected in a generation of artists who engage with digital tools and aesthetics, creating new ways of seeing the world through the lens of technology.

The animated GIF (graphics interchange format) was invented in 1987 as an "open format, hastening its availability and spread."[21] Since then, GIFs have been widely used as a form of digital art. GIFs are short animations consisting of several static frames that play in sequence automatically, creating short moving images with file sizes small enough to be easily shared online. Artists such as Olia Lialina, Jodi, and Vuk Ćosi have been creating artworks as GIFs since the 1990s. The popularity of GIFs reflects the affordances of the media in its ability to circulate. While GIFs are part of everyday internet culture as freely distributed images anyone can create, Mills employs them as her artworks. When placed in the context of a gallery, a GIF's cultural significance in its association with internet art can raise its perception of value. However, the perception of animated GIFs and their value has changed dramatically with the advent of NFTs giving value to memes, generative art, and forms of internet culture. Mills actively participates in an online community of artists brought together by a common interest in internet art and aesthetics. Microblogging social media platforms such as Tumblr became a space for artists to share images and animated GIFs, creating a culture of sharing work. While many regarded these images as art, they were not easily monetized. NFTs emerged to enable the monetization of digital objects such as GIFs. To consider the negotiation of price and value in context of different art markets (the fine art market or the NFT market) becomes a dynamic process situated in time, as forms of art like GIFs allow for the emergence of the NFT market, which in turn transforms the possibilities for selling GIFs and digital objects in the future.

Pricing becomes a social process of understanding what a collector might pay for a video work, while raising the value of an artist's work in comparison to other artists. The perception of GIFs as a highly accessible format with a short duration and lo-fi quality becomes difficult to sell in the presence of higher-quality formats. Yet value lies also in the profile of the artist and the provenance of the artwork, as well as its cultural significance in the context of wider art history. Referring to sociologist Olav

Velthuis,[22] pricing and the valuing of artworks is socially and culturally constructed in the ongoing performativity of the art market by artists, collectors, and art dealers. Velthuis describes the ways in which prices are determined in the contemporary art market through "pricing scripts" as sets of routines that guide pricing decisions at different points of an artist's career.[23] Pricing is a dynamic process that is temporally emergent and negotiated as part of the interpretive communities of the art world, where pricing becomes "an art in itself."[24] It is a knowing through doing, where knowledge is gained on pricing practices in the art world, and collectively produced by its insiders. These practices include the valuation of artists based on their reputation, and on the size and complexity of a work.[25] The sizes of editions and consequent prices are constantly shifting; thus, there is no standardized practice of pricing. Pricing becomes a means of experimenting with the material-discursive practices of the art world to enable new forms of art to be sold and collected on the art market.

The practice of pricing GIFs seeks to give value to a format that can be infinitely reproduced and freely distributed online. GIFs sold at TRANSFER Gallery can range from under $100 to $8,000 depending on the work and artist. Mills sources many of the images for her animated GIF artworks from social media and platforms like GIPHY, and she also redistributes her work back on those same platforms. She attempts to return the images to their original sources in their authentic existence as images circulating online. For Mills, animated GIFs are intended to live online and circulate freely. She is not concerned over the authorship of the work, noting, "The strange thing about this format is how separated you can come from it, once the work is done. I don't have that weird sense of ownership."[26] At the same time, Mills is concerned about the value and perception of her work in the gallery context. There, works that are sold as high-quality video files and come with a certificate of authenticity, where lower-quality versions are circulated freely online as part of their conceptual existence. When her works exist online, she doesn't want to take claim for them, while she simultaneously insists on the value of her work and refuses to sell her work below a certain price point. Working with animated GIFs, Mills contends that it is essential for the work to also circulate online and to take on its own life; however, when presented as an artwork in a gallery, she thinks it should be treated and valued as such.

Lorna Mills's position echoes Hito Steyerl's essay "In Defense of the Poor Image," which describes the online circulation of low-quality and at times illicit pirated media. In different modes of circulation online, poor images can participate in economies of both "capitalist media assembly lines" of social media marketing, and "alternative audiovisual economies" of experimental art.[27] "The poor image is no longer about the real thing—the ordinary original. Instead, it is about its own real conditions of existence: about swarm circulation, digital dispersion, fractured and flexible temporalities."[28] The artwork as poor image takes on different meanings in the different contexts in which it circulates. Mills's work circulates in different cultures of circulation, both as poor images online and as high-value works in a gallery space.

Like readymades,[29] GIFs gain the status of an art object once placed in the context of a gallery. Circulation in the economy creates different meanings for art, with the potential to produce new unexpected relations. According to Artie Vierkant, with post-internet art, "the work of art lies equally in the version of the object one would encounter at a gallery or museum, the images and other representations disseminated through the Internet and print publications, bootleg images of the object or its representations, and variations on any of these as edited and recontextualized by any other author."[30] Beyond a fixed representational object, there is no reference to an original, just as Mills's work exists simultaneously in the gallery as a high-value artwork, and circulates freely beyond notions of ownership.

Mills encounters tensions and contradictions when she wants to promote her work by allowing her images to circulate freely online, while also refraining from sharing too much before a show. The conceptual notion that her works exist online as poor images contrasts with the pragmatic needs of promoting her exhibition. At the same time, TRANSFER doesn't see a conflict between releasing works online for free and selling them at a high price in a gallery. Nichole thinks that works that are created for online consumption are to be shared and experienced in this way, as freely circulating images, while to collect an artwork and to own it is to develop a culture of care in which an individual is invested in preserving the work over time. Nichole elaborates, "Collecting an artwork, it's an act of love, it's an object of affection. It's something that requires care and stewardship and that will always cost money and be expensive and be something that requires a dedicated individual to invest in, to preserve it through time."[31] Collectors of the artwork own the right to exhibit and loan the artwork, which is a different investment than someone who has downloaded the artwork for free. Creating a sense of value and scarcity for digital works and cultivating a culture of collecting new forms of art can be read as attempts to resolve the contradictions of selling internet art. However, an image's circulation plays another role in the economies of art contributing symbolic value and recognition of an artwork on social media. An artwork (or image) circulating online contributes to its value in the art market in today's promotional cultures,[32] in which it simultaneously exists as a scarce object and commodity.

When contrasting the cultures of circulation of the art market with the digital cultures of the internet, they present differing values and interests, which at times contradict each other. The artwork *transfigures*[33] in meaning and form as it circulates in diverse economies, for instance as high-value unique and scarce objects and as freely circulated images on the internet. In this way, artworks are polysemous, in that they acquire different meanings and states of being as they circulate in different cultures and contexts. It becomes possible to conceive of an artwork as "a fluid, shape-shifting, and name-changing object."[34] In his book *In The Flow*, art critic and media theorist Boris Groys describes the fluidization of the art object with regard to conceptual digital art in its different instantiations.[35] The forms of artworks are fluid and variable as the object is distributed in different forms and contexts. Artworks transfigure into another kind of object from ownable commodity to a meme that exists in permutation on the internet, when it is realized in different modes of circulation.

SEDITION: CREATING ARTIFICIAL SCARCITY

While Lorna Mills differentiates what is sold in the gallery from what is freely shared online, the challenge for the online platform Sedition, which seeks to create a model for the selling digital limited editions for display on screens and devices, is balancing the need to promote artworks on social media and selling a digital edition where there is little difference between what is owned and what is circulated freely.

Prior to the emergence of NFTs, Sedition attempted to invent a model for selling art in a digital format in an art market that was slow to adopt new technologies. Sedition wanted to establish value through scarcity. As a start-up, Sedition experimented with different models and had to invent practices, while building up and educating a community about how to collect and enjoy digital art. It was a challenge trying to explain to users what they were buying and how to use, trade, and display their artworks. To some artists and users, it was unintuitive and illogical and even futile given the reproducibility of digital media and the value of this reproducibility. To try to restrict the flow online was an impossible challenge, while trying to enforce a value in the scarcity and uniqueness of the digital artwork.

For Sedition, digital editions are seen as a natural evolution of an art multiple using mechanical print or chemical techniques such as etching, woodcut, or photography. Sedition sells works as limited-edition videos and images for display on TVs, tablets, and smartphones. Works cannot be downloaded but are held in the user's Sedition account in the "Vault," where the user can browse and create playlists of their purchased artworks. Purchased works come with a certificate of authenticity, with an edition number and artist signature viewable from the Vault. The certificate of authenticity participates in producing the semblance of originality by borrowing a practice of the material art world. However, the logic of scarcity and uniqueness runs counter to the nature of digital objects that circulate only through replication. As such, the certificate of authenticity as proof of ownership serves as the qualifying object of the work of art. Ownership becomes separated from the art object, which in fact exists as numerous files.

Early on, Sedition promoted works by prominent artists such as Tracey Emin, Bill Viola, Mat Collishaw, and Jenny Holzer[36] as a means to gain brand awareness. By aligning with high-profile artists in the art world, Sedition seeks to build a sense of cult value for the work sold on the site. New artworks and artists are launched on a weekly basis, where works sold on the site range from $5 to $1,500, from unique artworks to editions of 100, 500, and up to 5,000. The prices are low compared to works sold on the art market, thereby making art accessible to wider audiences. Creating a new marketplace requires experimenting with pricing and edition sizes in the creation of value for streamed digital objects, as well as cultivating a habit for collecting and viewing art on screens to build an audience for a new way of owning art.

Sedition reflects how art markets and systems of value are inherently unstable and invented in practice; they are constantly being made and remade through the performativity of the platform and the community of collectors. While initially the digital edition sizes were relatively large (in the hundreds or thousands) compared to most print editions runs (in the tens), Sedition also seeks to create value through scarcity. For example, associating with high-profile artists is intended to raise the value of their digital editions, while at the same time, the works are sold at relatively affordable prices to give wider access across an infinitely reproducible format. The practice of price setting and increased edition size becomes a means of negotiating supply, demand, and art value retention. Compared to artworks sold in the gallery, these artworks exist online on screens and devices, but Sedition's limited-access business model means only a fixed number of users can own the works.

On a technical level, Sedition operates as a form of digital rights management (DRM), where files are accessed and stored on Sedition servers. The digital objects are in fact multiple files, streamed from the cloud in a variety of sizes based on the size of the user's screen. Ownership becomes a form of license to access rather than possess a unique object, an effort to replicate the models of the physical art market in the digital realm. While the platform's digital editions were Sedition's primary model of circulating art online in a closed marketplace, Sedition also experimented with different practices for distributing art in a digital form.

Alongside the limited editions, Sedition has also developed the Art Stream, which allows users to subscribe for a monthly fee of $15 to gain access to stream any work on the site (except for the works that have sold out). This model provides an alternative to buying and owning individual artworks, following the Spotify or Netflix model for streaming content; however, the revenue for artists through such models is typically very low. Within the economic practices of Sedition alone, art exists in multiple types of relations: as owned access, as a tradable asset, and as a time-limited subscription. Art is streamed through the internet in a multiplicity of instances, where its contexts can vary widely. In its various modes of circulating art, Sedition creates a new mechanism for collecting digital works of art, while speculating on the future art market.

Sedition creates an economy for the sales of digital artworks in the art market, where artists can earn revenue from their work. Artists split sales revenue 50/50 with Sedition, which they can invoice on a quarterly basis. Since Sedition offers works at low prices, typically the revenue that artists receive from sales remains small; however, their works gain recognition and value though Sedition's presentation and promotion. The advent of the internet brought the phenomenon of "mass amateurization,"[37] where anyone could create and release work online through different platforms. The vastly increased number of artists creates a glut of content online, much of which is considered low-quality. Artists like Leung appreciate being presented online alongside some well-established contemporary artists. Leung explains: "This digital platform, it's really great for artists to help them to grow and to have exposures around the world. Even though the sales are not high, it's about the recognition of artists."[38] For artists, Sedition's curated online space showcases their work in the manner of a gallery. The notion of digital curation has become important in promoting high-quality artistic content.

Sedition necessarily extensively uses social media to promote artists and artworks and invests in online advertising. Typically, images of artworks shared on social media are low-resolution excerpts or still images from videos, with previews of artworks watermarked, in contrast to the full resolution of purchased editions. These techniques help preserve the value of the editions themselves, while also increasing visibility of the artworks online.

Even in the process of circulating artworks freely online, there are different meanings and intentions associated with the image object. In the case of Mills, she allows her artworks to exist freely online beyond ownership and attribution to her. In other instances, artworks are attributed to the artist and shared on official social media accounts or websites like Sedition, with details of the artwork information such as its description, year of creation, edition size, and the artist's name and biography. This discursive context designates the online image formally as an artwork. While images circulating on social media contribute promotional value to the artist, the images Mills circulates contribute an authentic value to her artworks sold in the gallery. In this way, the totality of the different ways in which artworks circulate in diverse economies contributes to the meaning of the artwork as a whole. The economies of scarcity and free circulation coexist, where there is also diversity in each practice, bringing different kinds of value to art.

Some artists prefer to harness scarcity online to encourage sales. For example, the studio Universal Everything released fifty unique iterations of the video animation *Walking City Citizens* (2014)[39] in which there was only one copy available of each iteration (see figure 3.3). Different textures were applied to the same image of a walking figure in each iteration, creating unique variations of the same piece. The works were sold for $150 each, and sold out nearly immediately, making Universal Everything one of the most successful artist profiles in terms of revenue and sales on Sedition. Universal Everything's works are popular, highly visual, and well suited for display on screens; however, the studio's recognition in the wider art market is limited, as it is a digital studio without gallery representation. Some artists on Sedition have large Instagram followings, but no gallery representation, circulating in other economies beyond the traditional art market. The online context enables the circulation of a certain kind of art to much broader audiences, with the result that artworks are not necessarily appreciated for the artists' reputation in the art world, but purely for the artworks' visual appeal and digital aesthetic.

Matt Pyke, founder and creative director of Universal Everything, explains that "it's because of the nature of digital, it's so malleable and easily distributable . . . how do you create something that is collectable, that is scarce, that is limited, and it still has this appeal [of being widely sharable]?"[40] Pyke is interested in finding a balance between having works viewed by large audiences and creating unique artworks that can be enjoyed by one person. The recognition of an artist grows as their works circulate as information online, contributing to their value in the art market on platforms like Sedition. In the age of social media, an image's circulation and reputation[41] become more important than its material value. Writer and scholar Mackenzie Wark states, "What establishes the value of the work is that people talk about it, write about it, circulate

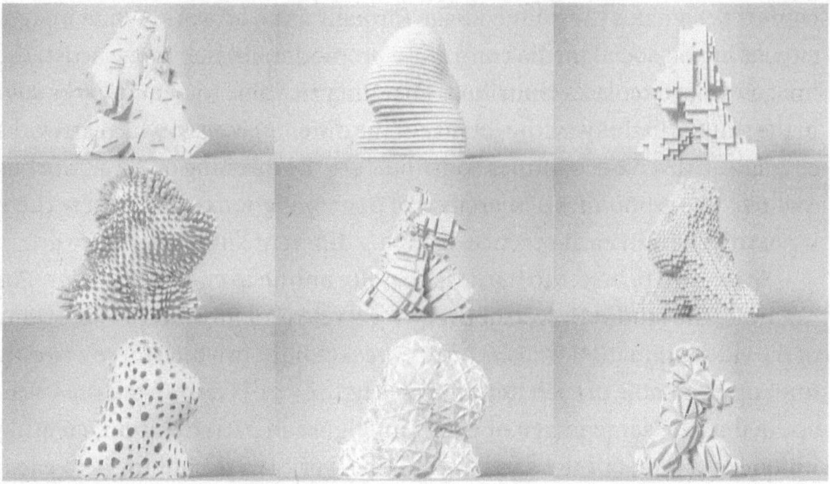

(unauthorized) pictures of it. The more it circulates, the more it has value. The actual work is a derivative of the value of its simulations."[42] The circulation of images becomes an indicator of value of a financial asset as we will find with NFTs, which clarifies and cements the relationship between digital art and finance, where the tension between the art market of scarcity and digital economies of free circulation is seemingly resolved.

NFTS AND THE FINANCIALIZATION OF ART

For decades, digital art lacked value in the art market, until, arguably, the NFT boom in 2021, which initiated a series of high-value sales.[43] Among the highest-grossing NFTs—such as Bored Ape Yacht Club and

3.3

Universal Everything, *Walking City Citizens*, composite image, fifty unique iterations, sold on Seditionart.com, 2014. Courtesy of Universal Everything.

Cryptopunks—are computer-generated images using variable algorithmic parameters designed as collectibles akin to sports trading cards or Beanie Babies. The serialization of generative artworks makes it easy to generate many different variations of the same artwork, where each unique iteration is valued for its scarcity and uniqueness among other iterations. The aesthetics of the artworks are based on internet memes, reflecting the populist digital cultures from which NFTs emerged. NFTs enable the sales of internet memes despite their existence online as part of free culture. For example, the well-known meme Nyan Cat sold on Foundation, a NFT marketplace, for 300ETH (Ethereum being a popular cryptocurrency), approximately $561,000. NFTs demonstrates how it becomes possible to monetize and sell internet memes as a form of "free culture" without limiting their circulation, as capitalism adapts to capture new forms of commodities. Prior to this, there was a tendency for artists to revert to traditional media and practices of enforcing the material value of art, as is the case with many post-internet artists.

NFTs essentially create an economy based upon scarcity using blockchain technology as a unique cryptographic hash that is associated with an artwork or digital file. The ability of NFTs to create unique digital assets has aided in the financialization of digital art, where it has existed in the art market for some time as assets managed through art investment funds.[44] However, NFTs have integrated new digital mechanisms and systems using digital currencies as a decentralized method for trading digital objects. Start-ups in the art world have been using blockchain in a variety of ways. Monegraph, for example, founded by Kevin McCoy, enables artists and creators to have greater control over how their works are distributed. Another start-up, Maecenas aims to create fractional ownership of blue-chip artworks, like owning shares of an artwork. Even within the practices of NFTs, these start-ups reflect the different cultures of circulation bringing together their varying conceptions of art, systems of valuing art, and techniques for selling art. It is not so much about *what* the technology is, but *how* it's being used and the implications it has for art as it is constituted in these economies.

As discussed in the previous section, artworks increase in value the more they circulate online on social media and as the recognition of the artist grows. When the market value of an artwork is determined partly by its provenance and the profile of the artist, it is important to note that its value is not quantitative. The more an artwork is viewed doesn't make it a better work, in the same way that a cat video viewed millions of times does not make it a better work (or art, for that matter). The numbers of views and followers on social media have become key performance indicators (KPIs), meaning they are often taken as signifiers of face value without further consideration. KPIs become powerful yet superficial (and even misleading) indicators of success. Not many artworks manage to circulate on social media and gain recognition, creating another sense of scarcity. Similarly, the valuation of art in the art market is often generated through systems of power and legitimacy within the art world.

For example, different exhibitions might be qualified differently; a solo exhibition at the MoMA might be valued greater than a group exhibition in a small gallery. The qualifiers of value in the art world are often dictated by the symbolic power of institutions, but also insiders as critics, curators, gallerists, and auction houses.[45] What gives an artwork its provenance is the information around the work, such as its exhibition history, press coverage, and reviews, alongside the comments and likes it receives online. These indexes are used to measure the value and success of an artist in the art market. The art market opening to the digital economies of social media and online distribution of blockchain technologies suggests that art's "free circulation is no longer antithetical to profit."[46] This is clearly evident with NFTs as the coexisting conceptions of art as scarce, ownable objects and freely circulated objects are resolved through blockchain-enhanced financial (smart) contracts. When taken as a financial asset, the physical ownership of the artwork is less important, while the proof of ownership and potential resale for profit take precedence.[47] Interest in a work lies in that work's perceived ability to circulate and gain cultural significance, which in effect raises its financial value. Blockchain technologies become a means to financialize artworks by tracking provenance that is connected to their value with less emphasis on the objects.

While there are attempts to connect the NFT to a unique object by storing it in the cloud, the issue of the unique files being lost when the links are broken was seemingly resolved with the development of the InterPlanetary File System (IPFS) protocol, which stores and shares data in a distributed file system. What has underpinned the hype in the market is less the ownership of the object and more the financial speculation on its growth in value. In this way, financialization creates an abstraction and separation from the art object: NFTs allow for anything to be owned and traded, even those works that are intangible, copied, and even destroyed. The destruction of the artwork does not mean it fails to exist; rather, it continues to circulate in the press and media as a publicity stunt and in the public consciousness, as in the case of Banksy burning his artwork after selling the NFT. With NFTs, the tensions between scarcity and free circulation are resolved. NFTs reduce artworks to financial assets, which are abstractions of value and ownership that refer to an art object that continues to exist in variable materialities.

For a short time, NFTs changed the economic landscape and potential for artists working in digital media to sell their work. However, the opportunities for artists were not evenly distributed. Some artists including software artists like LIA found some moderate success[48] and Mills found a means to develop a self-sustaining artistic practice without having to do other kinds of commercial work. Mills's work is aptly suited for the aesthetics of memes and internet culture and NFTs (see figure 3.4). However, Mills sees her engagement with NFTs as adjacent to her work with galleries. The NFTs Mills creates are derivatives of her pieces sold in galleries, where she does not need to invest time and energy creating new works for sale online. These NFTs exist as separate artworks circulating in different economies rather than viewed as part of the same artwork.

For LoVid, NFTs have brought new interest from collectors, giving value and validation in the art market for forms of digital art. Hinkis explains: "Definitely since the NFT thing blew up, my career has taken off in new ways. I've had more interest from people of all walks of life than ever before. It has normalized digital art."[49] Besides releasing digital editions on Sedition, LoVid has also released a series of works on Art Blocks, a platform supporting generative NFT artworks with initiatives to offset carbon emissions and donations to charitable organizations.[50] However, artists dedicating their practice to internet art or digital art does not mean their work will gain value and recognition in the NFT market. It requires significant investment of time and energy to self-promote on X (formerly Twitter) and Discord communities as platforms most commonly used by

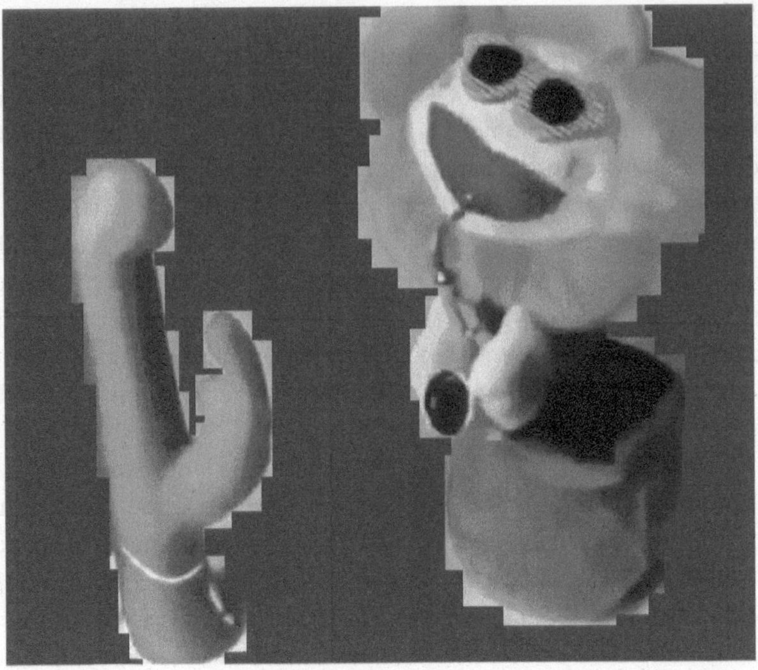

crypto collectors, a group of collectors often with little knowledge of the art market, and who are more interested in memes and self-referential artworks related to blockchain. In light of this generalization, there is diversity in the field, where many of those in the art world have also adopted collecting NFTs. Through her engagements in the community, Mills has also become an NFT collector herself, participating in the economy by supporting other artists and also discovering new younger artists.[51] The NFT market has created new communities of artists for sharing and supporting each other's work.

3.4

Lorna Mills, *Whorey Potter and the Sorcerer's Dick*, image still, 2021, NFT, part of *Honey, I Blew Up My Tits* presented in the exhibition *piecesofme.online* from TRANSFER and Left Gallery. Courtesy of the artist and TRANSFER.

In 2023, after ten years in business as a gallery, TRANSFER decided to take a break to pursue new ventures with TRANSFER Data Trust, a decentralized artist-owned archive and cooperative trust using blockchain technologies. While TRANSFER continues to present works in art fairs and exhibitions, it is now also a sponsored nonprofit organization with fiscal sponsorship from Gray Area, a cultural hub in San Francisco for arts, science, technology, and humanities, who made it possible for them to receive funds from Knight Art+Tech Expansion Fund in Miami, and the Filecoin Foundation for the Decentralized Web (FFDW). The project aims to open up to a peer-to-peer network for conservation, equitable distribution of value, and long-term sustainability and maintenance of artworks.[52] In addition to the speculative advances, blockchain technologies have opened a space for diverse practices and possibilities for artistic communities to converge.

Since the meteoric rise of NFTs in 2021, the market has entered a phase of decline. In 2023, two years after the boom, a group of collectors sue Sotheby's for overselling Bored Ape Yacht Club NFTs.[53] Auction houses like Sotheby's and Christie's have built a reputation for evaluating art to ensure its authenticity as secure investments. The authoritative power of the art market was seen to have been instrumentalized to promote and validate the use of cryptocurrencies. The *irrational exuberance* around NFTs and its fallout has only revealed the collusion between the technological elite and the art market, which has led to a small number of winners and a large number of losers. The cryptocurrency and NFT market continue to be largely dominated by speculators looking to "get rich quick." The lack of regulation means there are issues where it's not clear what a collector is actually buying, while platforms allow for the illegal upload of images without verification of authorship. There have also been numerous failed transactions,[54] where the hype around NFTs and blockchain is more a means to garner attention than any meaningful engagement with art. The NFT market turns digital objects into financial assets to be speculated upon. It equally relies on marketing and promotion to create positive feedback loops in which "everyone could be a winner" in the libertarian myth of the market. In the NFT winter, little can be said about the long-term sustainability of these communities, whose interests remain as short-term investments. Without a deeper engagement with art beyond speculation, the NFT economy will not be sustainable as collectors and artists lose interest or have already cashed out, leaving a glut of valueless detritus in the forgotten corners of the web. However, how can we ride out the hype cycles and shift the logic toward shared values, mutually supportive communities, and renewed visions for what art could be?

BEYOND SCARCITY, TOWARD ABUNDANCE

Digital art traditionally has not sat comfortably within an art market centered on the sales of material objects. The potentially infinite reproducibility of digital art hinders its value based upon scarcity and uniqueness. Efforts to promote online artwork on social media create contradictions regarding the value of the unique creations. At times these contradictions are resolved; for example, when Mills rationalizes online circulation as a means to allow the images to exist authentically as poor images from which they originated. For Sedition, the challenge of promoting a new way to collect artworks as digital limited editions prompted efforts to ensure that only low-resolution excerpts of the original artwork were shared on social media. However, there were still efforts and a desire to use the language of limited editions to ensure value through scarcity, when what people were actually buying was limited access to view the artworks.

For Sedition, the value of art's circulation online could not be ignored, which in turn contributes market value through its widespread recognition. A work's circulation online contributes to its symbolic value and the image of the artwork as a brand, subsequently influencing its market value. The circulation of art has been mobilized in promotional economies, wherein rapid and proliferating circulation is an indicator of success. It is used as a measure of the reputation and popularity of an artist as it contributes to the perceived value of the artist's work in the art market (despite the fact that not all artists choose to have a social media presence).

NFTs seemingly resolve the tension between scarcity and free circulation, where artworks become financial assets emphasizing the relation of speculative and exchange value, disconnected from a labor process. Many

NFT artworks are algorithmically generated with little artistic input following the initial programing and design of the NFT. The value lies in the prediction that the value of the asset will grow in the future, partly a result of its ability to circulate as viral media online. While NFTs attempt to identify with a unique object with links to files stored in the cloud, images such as memes are allowed to circulate freely and exist in permutation on the internet. As the image circulates it accrues value. However, as technologies and our conceptions of art evolve, so should the economies and methods for its presentation and distribution. This suggests expanding what may be understood as "art" and the "market." While NFTs created a new mechanism for the ownership of digital art, the market continues to follow a logic of speculation, scarcity, private ownership, and exclusivity. Instead, we might consider experimenting with diverse practices and perspectives that diverge from the use of blockchain for pure speculation and exchange. Blockchain technologies have also initiated a proliferation of practices for designing protocols for forms of collective organization with Decentralized Autonomous Organizations (DAOs) (as discussed in the conclusion).[55] In the following chapter, I look more closely at the role of corporations in the economies of artists to connect back to the practices and processes of creation and collaboration.

4

MECHANISMS OF CORPORATE PATRONAGE

While the rapid advancement of the technology sector has transformed the tools and mechanisms for the sale of digital artworks, the corporate sector has also developed collaborations with artists. Beyond government-funded grants and partnerships with public institutions, the private sector is playing a larger role in the creative economies of artistic production. I look at the different ways that artists working in media and technologies collaborate with corporations to create and circulate artworks, including through licensing for media facades, brand commissions, and corporate artist residencies. These various mechanisms of corporate patronage present different constraints and affordances on artistic practices, thereby shaping the kind of work produced. In this way, these economies condition the meaning and form of the artwork even as they serve particular corporate agendas.

This chapter explores how the technological environment and infrastructure available to corporations play a role in how artworks are circulated. With the proliferation of screens in public spaces, media facades have become potential platforms for presenting artwork beyond the confines of a gallery space. These spaces can include public squares and subway stations, as well as private venues such as hotels, corporate office lobbies, and events spaces. I consider how Mills and Sedition have employed licensing (in the form of rental contracts) to control and facilitate the circulation of existing works, rather than commissioning of new work, which often comes at a much higher cost. Licensing provides a means for corporations to gain access to artworks for temporary display. The format of videos as digital files can be more easily sent over a network, thus saving on logistical costs. The widespread accessibility of players and screens also makes these kinds of media easier to distribute.

For artists, licensing artworks for public display can provide another revenue stream beyond sales, while also increasing the visibility of an artist's work. Artworks in public space often take the place normally dedicated to advertisements, such as in the case of Art on the Underground, an initiative that brings art into the subway stations of the London Underground. Often, public screens feature spectacular artworks that will appeal to wide audiences as entertainment, however these artworks also have the potential to inspire and influence civic life.[1] At times, the perception of the artwork as art or advertisement blurs, such as when art is employed in the branding of cities. In contrast to commissions, however, licensing does not enable the means to make new work, but instead facilitates the circulation of existing works. Licensing is perhaps less valuable for artists' practices than commissions due to the lower cost to rent an existing artwork without production fees. In this sense, commissions allow artists to continue a practice through the creation of new work. Licensing for complex installations (as discussed in chapter 2) at times requires more creative input from the artist. Whereas chapter 2 looked at how licensing facilitates the sale of material installations, and chapter 3 examines how digital platforms have cultivated digital scarcity, this chapter examines how corporate patronage in the form of media licenses, commissions, and artist residencies provides a different avenue for securing the means to make.

For artists working between art and technology, corporations are playing a larger role in patronage, providing artists access to tools and support to realize new work through commissioning. However, brand commissions and sponsorship are not new. In 1970 the New York–based nonprofit organization known as Experiments in Art and Technology (E.A.T.) was sponsored by Pepsi to design a pavilion for Expo '70 in Osaka, Japan.[2] The project led to disagreements between the interests of the corporation and the avant-garde art group, and the collaboration was short-lived. It did, however, pave a way for innovative collaborations between corporations and artists. Today, these corporate collaborations are common. Companies like HTC VIVE Arts regularly commissions artists like Laurie Anderson, Marina Abramović, and Anish Kapoor to create new works across VR, XR, and blockchain technologies.[3] Companies like BMW have commissioned artists like Cao Fei to create an immersive digital art installation for the BMW Art Car.[4] In many of these initiatives, artworks serves to promote the brand either through the use of their technology, as in the case of HTC VIVE Arts, or to act as a form of advertisement, as for the BMW Art Car. Looking at the practices of Desmond Leung and onformative, this chapter examines the ways in which brands have adapted practices to work more closely with artists, where the art becomes integrated into the creative economies of branding. While the project with E.A.T. was highly experimental and did not make direct aesthetic connections to Pepsi, it also created friction with the corporation, which eventually tried to restrict the project. The projects with BMW and HTC VIVE Arts are more explicitly advertisements involving their cars and technology, presented in commercial showcases at art fairs like Art Basel. Not many corporations provide significant funding for artists in this way. More often art is treated as an investment whereby corporations from Microsoft (technology) to UBS (finance) to LVHM (fashion) to Progressive (insurance) have built up significant art collections by purchasing artworks as investments.

When receiving corporate funding to create work, artists are given a certain amount of freedom. However, artists are also chosen for a particular aesthetic or approach. Corporate agendas shape the kinds of artists and artworks that are produced. The ways the artworks are presented in lobbies and storefronts and written about in press releases contextualize the work as added value for the brand. Likewise, corporate commissions provide artists with the financial resources to create new work in ways that perhaps grants and other forms of public funding may not.

Artist residencies provide artists access to space and corporate resources to create work, operating as another mechanism that engages artists in a process of creation in collaboration with corporations. In particular, technology companies often fund artist residencies that contribute to innovation, knowledge exchange, and social impact agendas. While artist-in-residence (AIR) programs within technology corporations are not a new phenomenon—early AIR initiatives include those of Bell Labs in the 1960s and Xerox PARC's Artists-in-Residence program (PAIR) in the 1990s[5]—in recent years, there has been a proliferation of AIR programs in major technology corporations such as Google Creative Lab, Autodesk's Pier 9 Residency, and Microsoft's Artist in Residence program. Residencies provide valuable support for artists working with technology, but it is important to also consider how these initiatives enable or inhibit certain kinds of work. While business studies often focus on the benefits artists may provide to the corporation, the effects such relationships have on artists, the artistic community, and their practices typically are not deeply considered.

Building on my discussion of Mills's and Sedition's work with corporate media licenses and Leung's and onformative's corporate commissions, I conclude this chapter with a discussion of corporate artist residencies. To do so, I explore the case of Thoughtworks Arts as a unique example of a corporate collaboration with artists to create socially engaged projects with technology.[6] The program was founded in 2016 in New York by artist and engineer Andrew McWilliams and artist and scholar Ellen Pearlman. The program was an initiative by Thoughtworks, a multinational IT consultancy company founded in 1993. Through the Thoughtworks Arts Residency initiative, artists gained access to technology, knowledge, and resources to create new work and access to support from Thoughtworks' skilled employees who engaged in these projects as part of their professional development, feeding inspiration for their consulting work with clients. Thoughtworks employees were highly engaged and enthusiastic about the program at a time when the corporation was also keen to retain talent. While the corporation gave a lot of artistic freedom to the Thoughtworks team supporting the program, ultimately it remained rather low in the overall corporate priorities, resulting in the initiative eventually being cut following the COVID-19 pandemic. The success of collaborations with corporations is often dependent on individuals who can protect a space and access to resources for artists, playing a role in mediating between the interests of artists and the corporation. This example raises questions about how these initiatives could be designed to ensure the long-term sustainability of their collaborations with artists. As this example would indicate, there is a need to develop different approaches so that the private sector might better support the arts. Artists should play a role in the design of such initiatives. Artist residencies expand the understanding of the art market focusing more on the process of creation over an end product. Moving beyond the sale of finite material objects, these economies of art and technology center around research, development, and collaboration in innovative ways.

LICENSING FOR MEDIA FACADES

For artists working with video and media, licensing provides an economy beyond the sales of material objects for their works to circulate on public screens and media facades. Beyond the confines of a gallery space, artworks can engage wide audiences in the public life of cities. With the growing proliferation of screens in urban space, these become new exhibition platforms for video and media artworks.

Lorna Mills has presented a number of public displays on large outdoor screens, particularly New York's Midnight Moment program organized by Times Square Arts (see figure 4.1),[7] Everson Museum of Art in Syracuse, and the Sony screen in Potsdamer Platz in Berlin. However, Mills found a limitation in displaying her work on public screens; they do not allow for the often crude content of her works, drawn as they frequently are from porn sites and the dark net. She explains, "My only issue with those is that of course, it's public work so I can't be filthy; I can't be as free with my questionable taste as I normally would be on online. I have to mind my manners—I recognize that when I'm doing public work."[8] Public displays will almost always present a need to ensure the content is appropriate for all audiences. Politically sensitive works or works involving nudity or violence are not likely to be permitted, whereas within galleries or in an enclosed space, audiences can be warned of potentially offensive content.

The Times Square Arts' Midnight Moment[9] program presents the work of a new artist every month on an enormous media facade for three minutes (from 11:57 p.m. to12:00 a.m.) every night in the middle of this tourist magnet and heavily trafficked part of Manhattan. The publicly funded platform aims to enrich the life around Times Square with art. Often with media facades the works are presented alongside advertising

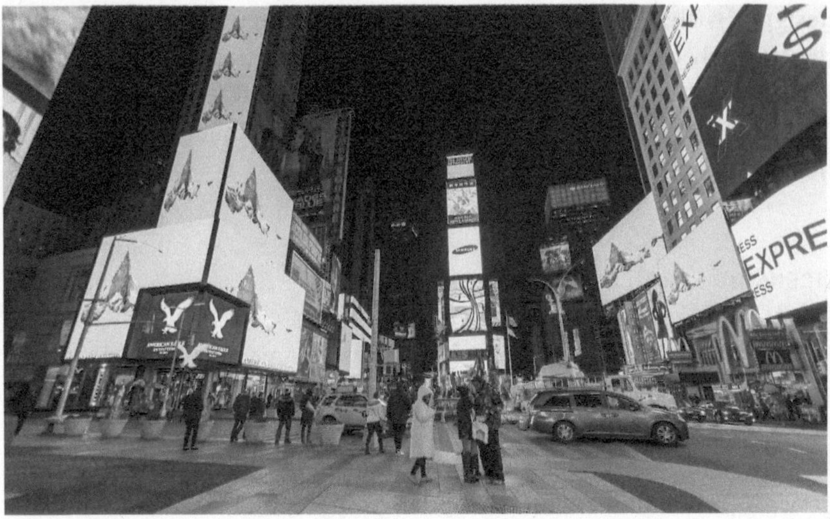

sequentially or next to other displays. The challenge is to stand out aesthetically within the backdrop of the city and lights. Mills considered her engagement there a success: "My piece for Times Square works so well because it was so graphic and so bright and so like monolithically yellow so that when it played, it just flooded suddenly amongst [the] cacophony of all the advertising."[10] To make a visual impact in Time Square, it becomes necessary to create something that looks and behaves differently to ensure that it is not mistaken for an advertisement. The context and space of the city partially dictates the form of the work. The visibility and presentation of the work is most important for Mills in these displays.

Beyond the extra income and publicity, Mills does not pay much attention to the displays, as they do not enable her to create new work; her commissions on average offer larger potential income streams, thereby

4.1

Lorna Mills, *Mountain Light/Time*, media facade display, Midnight Moment, Times Square, New York, 2016. Photo by Ka-Man Tse. Presented by Times Square Arts.

creating an opportunity to produce new work. Displays like Midnight Moment are noncommercial but use commercial screens funded by the city. Due to the commercial potential of such highly visible displays, it is difficult to keep them solely noncommercial due to the high running and maintenance costs. Another example, M+ Facade,[11] a display in Hong Kong on the M+ museum, overlooking the Victoria Harbor, aims to feature artistic content as well as messaging about the museum's programs, but refrains from any explicit advertisement beyond logo credits for sponsorship of exhibitions and commissions. However, it becomes difficult to separate art from commerce when art and museums are treated as spectacles to attract tourism and promote the city as a brand, where the screen simultaneously participates in citywide celebrations such as during New Year's Eve. In general, however, the screen is highly curated, presenting the videos as artworks in context of the museum.

Beyond the public-facing sales of digital editions on the platform, Sedition also has a business-to-business (B2B) side. Sedition has developed a method for distributing video works for media facades through public display licenses with corporate partners, providing them with long-term revenue streams. The sale of an edition on Sedition is essentially a license to stream a work on personal screens and devices. Works purchased from Sedition, however, can only be displayed for private use in a home or office space. A separate public display license is required to show the work in any public venue, exhibition, or screen. Sedition treats art as media but retains the qualities of an artwork (its copyright, accreditation of the artist, and display of the work), which ensure the work is recognized and valued appropriately, rather than as a piece of content.

Clients pay for a license to use the work in a specific venue or screen for a fixed period of time. Licenses are negotiated on a case-by-case basis, depending on the number of works, profile of the artists, and the duration and location of the display. For licensing, a digital download link is sent to the client upon their signing the contract, with the stipulation that the work must not be shared, distributed, copied, or used in any other capacity. The contract may also stipulate that the artwork must be deleted following the end of the display, while artists receive a share of the revenue for the display (usually 20–50 percent). Contracts ensure appropriate use and display of the artwork and accreditation of the artist.

Sedition has made licensing deals with clients like EDITION Hotels, which has boutique hotels in London, New York, Miami, Sanya, Bodrum, Barcelona, Shanghai, and other places. The hotel pays a fee per room and per year for a collection of artworks that are displayed on the TV in each guest room, with a catalogue about the curated art placed in every room. This arrangement provides a regular annual income for artists licensing works without the need for client to own and care for them. Sedition provides access to works by high-profile artists without paying large fees or requiring expensive shipping of physical works.

Other licensing deals have been arranged for nonprofit displays put on by arts organizations such as Public Art Screens in Norway and for museum exhibitions and festivals worldwide. Commercial displays include screens in showrooms, corporate offices, and lobbies (e.g., at Oxford Group Properties in Toronto) and displays for branding events hosted by fashion houses like Jimmy Choo in Korea. There is often an expectation from clients that works displayed in such contexts should be provided for free in exchange for publicity. After all, advertisers pay large sums in order to feature their advertising on a billboard.

The dual use of screens as art and advertising creates an ambiguity in how art is perceived when it is placed in contexts and on screens normally used for other purposes. It takes a trained eye to identify an artwork, particularly when advertisers employ artists and designers in the creation of ads that resemble artworks. For example, Will Benedict's Summer 2020 campaign for Balenciaga with music by experimental music group Wolf Eyes appears as a cyber-dystopian newscast that unsettles more than it sells.[12] The image exists both as branding and as an artwork. Art participates in perpetuating the market of commodities, where it has become fully entwined within our contemporary cultural economies. An artwork is valued and appreciated as art rather than advertisement when it is placed in context of a gallery, devoid of brand associations. At the same time, we also see how brands and corporate sponsorship are entering museum spaces, such as CHANEL's sponsorship of M+'s moving image programs for three years starting in 2023.[13] To create boundaries between an artwork and advertisements requires the attention and care of curators, to understand how artworks are perceived and appreciated in context and to safeguard their identity as art.

BRAND COMMISSIONS

Licensing as rental contracts provides a means for artists to distribute video and media-based artworks as temporary displays on media facades, providing a revenue stream for existing artworks. For some artists, commissions are more valuable than licensing for media facades or the potential sale of artworks that are difficult to sell on the art market, as it provides opportunities to continue a practice. When licensing a complex installation for restaging in an exhibition, more creative input is often required from artists and institutions to reinterpret the work for the space and context. However, when considering rentals of video artworks, the display and the artwork are often already fixed. Artists simply need to send the artwork file in the appropriate format. In this way, Mills does not find these collaborations interesting, but rather they provide another modest revenue stream. Licensing of video artworks for temporary displays is mostly transactional, requiring the artist to simply provide a file for display.

In terms of sales, artists may "cash out" where money is the end goal as "exchange value" (Money-Commodity-Money or "M-C-M")[14] serving for private accumulation. To shift our attention away from thinking of profit as a means to an end, is to understand how money circulates and contributes to enabling and sustaining artistic practices. Commissioning remains connected to a labor process; money retains its "use value" (Commodity-Money-Commodity or "C-M-C")[15] where artists are "put to work," rather than for the private accumulation of wealth. Money is not an end goal in and of itself, but something that enables the continuation of a process. While a client may own the completed artwork, the affordance of a commission is in the process it initiates, beyond the mere act of exchange. Commissions provide more resources to artists to create new artworks, where brands are playing a larger role in the economies of artists, such as for Leung and onformative.

The industries of fashion and art have formed a close relationship, where art has become aligned with luxury commodities. Fashion brands like CHANEL have a long history of collaborating with artists such as Jenny Holzer and Andy Warhol.[16] Desmond Leung worked with CHANEL on a year-long commission and found it to be a valuable experience for the development of his practice (figure 4.2). Having a history of working

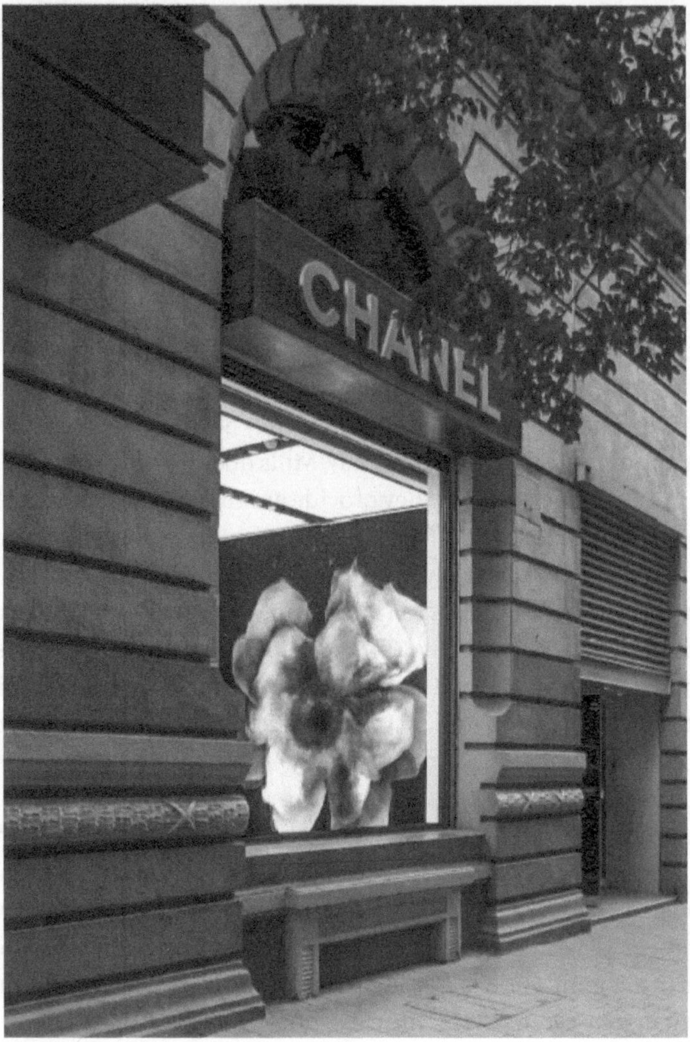

4.2

Desmond Leung, *Camellia*, in-store display at The Peninsula, Hong Kong, CHANEL Digital Art Program, 2011. Photo: Desmond Leung. Courtesy of the artist.

with artists and pioneering avant-garde strategies in fashion,[17] it can be said that CHANEL has a deeper understanding of the art world than most other brands. Leung was commissioned to create four artworks, which were displayed inside CHANEL stores and on building facades internationally. The collaboration enabled him to create work freely for the project and develop his practice over a long period of time as a rare long-term engagement with a brand.

At CHANEL, once an artist is selected from a shortlist, they are given significant freedom to produce the work. Leung remarks, "Maybe they treat themselves as art collectors rather than a brand. If they like the work, they just give you the space to work on it. So, they trust the artists a lot."[18] As part of the arrangement, CHANEL has exclusive rights to display the work internationally in their stores. Leung feels CHANEL is at the forefront of how brands can work with artists, given CHANEL's willingness to integrate commissioned art with their brand, and the fact that the opportunity gave him and his work international visibility. But again, the perception of art and advertising becomes blurred.

According to a 2018 survey on art and brand collaborations published by the trend forecasting agency Culture Projects, brands highly value a contracted artist's satisfaction with the project, as well as the art world's approval, and as a means of giving back to the community, alongside more business-minded values of brand perception.[19] Still, brands are becoming more attuned to the needs of artists through the development of meaningful collaborations. Brands employ artists to express values in association with luxury and sophistication. These economies produce kinds of art that are typically highly visual, decorative in function, and beautiful in contrast to works that are more conceptual or aesthetically challenging.

Commissions like Leung's provide important financial support for artists to further develop their artistic practices. In these arrangements, art becomes a service and a form of project-based work. Artists receive a fee for their vision and labor in the production of new work as a service, rather than for the sale of an artwork as a commodity. Artists participate in marketing and branding; according to Celia Lury, brands are assemblages of culture.[20] Art becomes part of the branded experience, contributing forms of symbolic and surplus value to the sponsoring corporation.

Surplus value (or *mehrwert*, in Marx's terms) is the value added to products sold at a premium due only to their association with art.[21]

Leung makes a distinction between a "design brief" and an "art commission." A design brief entails hiring a designer to produce work according to a client's request, and the client owns the result. For an art commission, the artist should be given the freedom to create the work according to their own vision, as the artist retains the copyrights to the work and control over its use and display. In chapter 1, onformative distinguishes between "self-initiated" artistic projects and their "commercial work" with clients. However, there is a blurring between the two when clients ask onformative to create works similar to the artworks they created on their own time and with their own resources. Leung asserts that the client should respect the artist's integrity: if a client selects an artist, they are giving the artist freedom to create the work and should not be able to ask for specific aesthetic changes. Artists value this freedom, and yet they may harbor hidden or unconscious desires to meet the client's expectations, which may influence the artistic process.

Leung now supports his work primarily through private and commercial art commissions, after self-funding his practice for several years. Leung estimates that one or two commissions can support his artistic practice for six to twelve months. He explains, "Art commissions have a very big impact on my practice because [they] brings more public awareness and connection with the city, but also financially, [they] has a much stronger impact than private sales."[22] Selling work in a gallery may also lead to private commissions, with collectors potentially building a relationship with the artist through the process of engaging them to create a new work.

While Leung continues to develop commissions with brands and corporations like Samsung and Hang Seng Bank, his practice has also evolved to become a more spiritual practice, incorporating abstract expression and animism through digital technologies. In 2021, he founded a multi-disciplinary studio named AHO to create holistic artistic experiences through immersive installations, performances, exhibitions, and workshops.[23] The work of the studio seeks to foster unity and connection within communities and global audiences. An example of such a work includes "The Evolution(s) by Visible Music" (2023), a collaboration with composer and musician Tsui Chin Hung, where Leung created live generated visuals that respond to pitch and rhythms of the musical performance, presented at Freespace in Hong Kong's West Kowloon Cultural District.[24] Alongside commercial commissions, Leung is able to explore more deeply his spiritual approaches to art making.

onformative also works closely with companies that commission them to create new work for their brands. In 2012, onformative produced a "self-initiated" project called *Unnamed Soundsculpture*.[25] The work involved using motion-capture technology to capture a dancer's movements, which were then used to create an abstract 3D audiovisual artwork. onformative was then approached by Dolby Laboratories team members, who had seen *Unnamed Soundsculpture*, and invited onformative to produce a work for their office lobby in San Francisco. Through this collaboration, onformative produced the work *Collide* (2016),[26] a site-specific audiovisual installation displayed on a sixty-two-foot-long digital ribbon screen using a fifty-four-channel speaker system (figure 4.3). With *Collide*, onformative created a synesthetic experience wherein they transformed motion data from the dancer into abstract visuals. These visuals were then displayed in VR headsets worn by three cellists, who played a composition responding to the work. The abstract visuals acted as a conductor for the musicians to play a composition in close relation to the image. This reflects onformative's collaborative and processed-based approach, in that *Collide* features a collaboration with the audio composers kling klang klong.

Collide showcased the technology of Dolby Laboratories, using their sound system and visual display. Working with clients often does not allow the time and budget to experiment with technology, but in the case of *Collide*, onformative artists were allowed the freedom to develop new techniques for their practice. As *Unnamed Soundsculpture* explored movement's interplay with visuals and sound, onformative challenged themselves to try a new method using VR. onformative tries to treat negotiations with brands as commercial opportunities to develop new ideas, bringing their client work closer to their artistic practice. Their commercial work allows them the larger budgets required to pursue collaborative projects with other musicians and designers. Working with Dolby also gave them access to advanced screen and audio technologies, as well as a highly visible platform to showcase their work. In this way, onformative's work in design becomes closer to art for which they are remunerated with

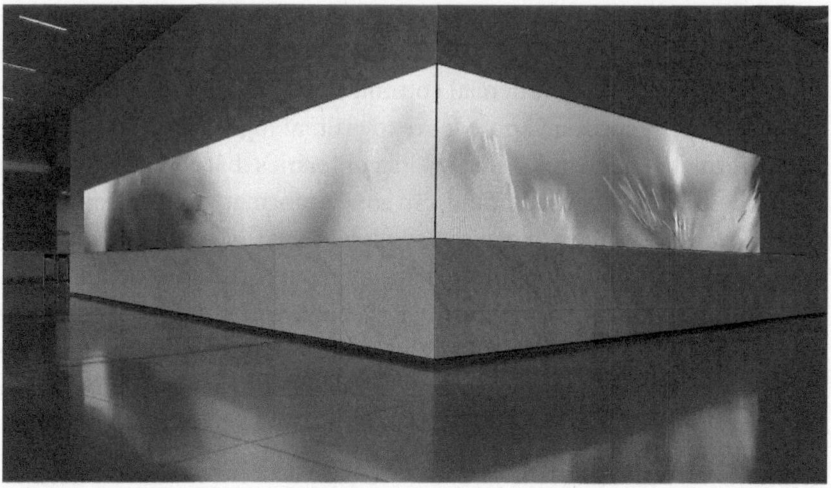

commercial budgets, allowing them to create more ambitious collaborative work with new technologies at a scale of funding that grants have not met. The relationship allows for the artists to have more agency, working between art, technology, and design to sustain their practice beyond the art market.

Thus, there are affordances of working with corporations, as they enable larger budgets for production and access to technology and public platforms to showcase art. While not every corporation will understand the different ways artists work, there are some clients who allow for experimentation, as seen in the case of Dolby Laboratories. Art contributes to the Dolby brand a sense of creativity and innovation, employing its aesthetics as marketing. While onformative artists are able to experiment in their collaborations with Dolby, they create a unique project that has

4.3

onformative, *Collide*, audiovisual installation, Dolby Laboratories, San Francisco, 2016. Courtesy of onformative.com.

both audio and visual output that allows the brand to also showcase their products. The authenticity of the work in allowing artists creative freedom brings symbolic value to the brand.

At the same time, the resources provided to artists also begin to shape the form of the work. For instance, Gork has received sponsorship from Meyer Sounds for speakers and sound equipment for her exhibitions in the United States. The notion of sponsorship suggests corporations provide monetary support, but more often these sponsorships provide in-kind support such as the loan of equipment for an exhibition. In exchange, sponsors receive credit within the exhibition with a logo and mention in press releases, wall text, and other promotional materials associated with the exhibition. Prior to getting sponsorship, Gork would make her own speakers. This DIY approach to technologies began to influence the design and aesthetic of her work, since the speakers became part of the installation visually, and also determined the quality of the sound. Meyer Sounds' interest in sponsoring the arts serves as promotion for their brand and creative applications of their technology. They provide valuable support, offering access to technologies most artists could not otherwise afford. An artist's practice may begin to shift according to what kinds of technology they have access to. These collaborations begin to influence the materiality of the work, with artists' access to professional equipment enabling certain kinds of technology-specific work.

Art has been appropriated in commercial economies, where brands are playing a larger role in patronage. There is a fine line between art and marketing, where there is still space for negotiating the terms of corporate collaborations to better serve the needs and interests of artists. Clarity in the definition of the relationship between the artist and corporation and the context in which the artwork is presented can help preserve the interest of artists and the recognition of the artwork as art. Artists should be allowed to present the artwork in other art contexts beyond their use as advertisements. However, as we see branding enter museum spaces, we can also see that designated spaces for art are also not neutral. Rather than trying to escape the grasp of commercialization, the economies of artistic production considered in this chapter reflect how resources may be channeled toward shared interests with the potential to transform ways of thinking and doing that have been taken for granted.

CORPORATE ARTIST RESIDENCIES

Like commissions, artist residencies engage artists in the process of creating new work by providing access to technology and space, and other kinds of in-kind support. At times production fees are provided in addition to support from staff to create the artwork. Residencies imply artists are working on site, where the corporation may be more closely involved in the production process. At times, the expectations for a residency are open ended; artists may be allowed to experiment and test out ideas without needing to complete the project by the end of the residency, whereas commissions are designed to yield a specific artwork as an output.

Some residencies are relatively well paid in comparison to nonprofit artist residencies. The Facebook Artists in Residence Program for instance, engages artists to create installations and murals in the Facebook corporate offices. The residency was started in 2007 by artist Drew Bennett, who proposed to expand the program to other artists in the San Francisco Bay Area after completing his own work there. In this sense, Facebook's residency could be considered "artist led." Bennett says, "We're not building an art collection. We're supporting the growth and development of local artists."[27] Facebook pays artists a fee for the commission and a space to produce the work, the latter of which is a scarce commodity in the Bay Area. Artists spend four to sixteen weeks in the workplace, where employees can also interact with the artist as a form of knowledge exchange. In this case, the Facebook Artist in Residence means artists are on site and contribute to the work ecology on the Facebook campus, where engagements with artists may inspire workers to think more creatively.

At the same time, artists are expected to create a new work as a final output of the Facebook's and other AIR programs, so they also function as commissions. At Facebook, commissions typically range anywhere from $10,000 to $40,000, a significant amount for many artists.[28] The artworks serve primarily decorative purposes for their offices, where Facebook owns the rights to the commissioned work.[29] The artists' work is embedded in the office building infrastructure and cannot be easily sold. Rather than collecting art as objects, Facebook turns the production of art into a service, where the artist's presence is imperative. Through associations with the arts and artists, companies gain credibility as socially engaged supporters of the arts.

Corporations like Facebook consider their role in the local art ecology as a philanthropic endeavor, seeking to offset the technology sector's role in the rising cost of living in the Bay Area. However, funding opportunities for artists are few and far between, given that corporate philanthropy normally serves more urgent concerns, such as the climate crisis. The emphasis on social justice follows the cultural logic of Silicon Valley, with its interest in bringing together progressive ideals and economic goals. Part of the Californian Ideology[30] celebrates a culture joining art (as an emblem of the progressive ideals of counterculture) and free market libertarianism of innovation. These seemingly contradictory logics continue to haunt the technology sector in the global context. Just as in art philanthropy, Silicon Valley's "philanthro-capitalism"[31] only reinforces preexisting social inequalities where the rich get richer. It becomes possible to see how seemingly ethical practices promoting the environment and social justice are employed as forms of virtue signaling that contribute to sustaining corporate interests.[32] Dichotomies of nonprofit versus commercial become less relevant, where the two are already entwined in today's cultural economies, where efforts to promote social good become a form of "art washing" as a means to distract consumers from other negative corporate impact. Virtue signaling may not always be explicitly directed at consumers, however, given that a positive image also helps attract and retain talent and also contributes to demonstrating knowledge to clients that today's consumers are attracted to ethical companies.

Often arts programs sit under the marketing department in corporate structures as part of their "corporate social responsibility" initiatives. This was the case for Thoughtworks Arts,[33] which sought to create mutually beneficial relationships between artists and corporations. As of this writing, the company has forty-eight offices in nineteen countries, with over ten thousand employees. At the time when the initiative started, they prided themselves on three pillars: sustainable business, software excellence, and social justice, a concept promoted by their chief scientist Martin Fowler.[34] Thoughtworks supports software development from the ground up, employing adaptive methods of project management such as

Agile, open source, and peer learning. As part of their mission to support social justice, in 2016 the company started the first Thoughtworks Arts program. Based in their New York offices on Madison Avenue, the program acted as a corporate interface for artists to work with the company. Thoughtworks Arts would host open calls each year, under a particular theme, and invited artists to create new works with the support of staff and resources at the company. The Thoughtworks Arts program had several strands, including the Thoughtworks Arts Residency, Art-A-Hack™,[35] an event that encouraged art and technology team collaborations, and the weekly Hardware Hack Lab,[36] which was open to anyone interested in exploring new technology over an evening at Thoughtworks' New York base. Reflecting this interest in public outreach and engagement, the New York office was also used to host regular public events, talks, and workshops.

The artist-corporation relationship was carefully mediated at Thoughtworks to ensure the residency maintained its artistic and curatorial autonomy. As practicing artists, the cofounders of Thoughtworks Arts, McWilliams and Pearlman, understood the need to create meaningful work. For Pearlman, the residency was a way to explore pressing social issues of our time, and the impacts of new technologies on society. The residency fed into her own practice as an artist by allowing her to witness how other artists developed their work and practice with new technologies. Pearlman thinks art should not simply be an appendix of corporate policy, explaining, "I do think corporate residencies should invite the artist in, show them what they have, and let the artist decide what to do, or what not to do. Art is a passion-driven experience. If you put art to work solely for the corporate interest, it usually does not sparkle."[37] A need arose to consider both the interests of the artist and the interest of Thoughtworks. As is the case when an artist negotiates any mutually beneficial corporate relationship, McWilliams explains, "It is highly important that the relationship between artist and corporate supporter be carefully designed and considered. The program must support the artist, be respectful of their practice, the subjects they investigate and the people they interact with. Equally the program must be valuable to the corporation."[38]

Supporting the arts was central to Thoughtworks' company culture, allowing them to engage with progressive individuals and organizations. The funding for the residency came from different departments within the company. Their running costs were relatively low, with most resources taking the form of in-kind support, including staff time and access to space and equipment. The residency participated in research into the social impact of technological innovation, which aided employees in their thinking on projects for clients. According to McWilliams, the projects were viewed as collaborative research ventures between artists and employees of Thoughtworks, where both discover and learn from each other along the way.[39] This approach allowed Thoughtworks to gain knowledge from artists of the emerging technological landscapes and encouraged dialogue among its employees. It introduced artistic and academic thinking to their work in the company as forms of knowledge exchange as acknowledged by McWilliams. Employees contributed their skills as forms of professional development, exploring new technologies and supporting artists in developing their work. Artists had the chance to be based in Midtown Manhattan in New York's central business district, to work with professional developers, and received access to the resources of a large corporation, all while retaining full creative control over their work.

Over the lifetime of the program, the residency supported artists such as Nouf Aljowaysir; Rashin Fahandej; Andy Slater; Olivia Ting; Miller Puckette; Neil Harbisson and Moon Ribas, cofounders of the Cyborg Foundation; Heather Dewey-Haborg; Karen Palmer; Hannes Bend; Adrianne Wortzel; and Catie Cuan. They had incubated an open-source AI system for emotion expression detection, cyborg "sensory organs," a comic illustration about genetic data privacy featuring the former political prisoner Chelsea Manning, and a biometric system for virtual reality. Projects they incubated won prizes and awards including the Lumen Prize and Ars Electronica Award of Distinction. In this arrangement, artists interacted with a corporation, its employees, and its resources to facilitate a project over a period of time. Themes for the residency were selected by McWilliams and Pearlman and were also generated through conversation with external partner organizations including AI Now, the Consortium for Research and Robotics, and Baltan Labs. After the first three years, the residency moved online in 2020 and had projects in their San Francisco office and globally.[40]

Artists were selected through thematic open calls, often involving projects engaging with technology and society. For participation in the residency, artists typically received $11,000 for approximately sixteen weeks, with an option to stay longer without monetary support. The fees provided were intended to cover accommodation and living expenses in New York for the duration of the residency. Artists were given a workspace at the Thoughtworks office and access to mentorship from Thoughtworks programmers and designers, who were free to contribute to projects as part of their jobs. Thoughtworks also provided some funds to purchase equipment and materials for projects.

The residency at Thoughtworks was led by individuals who were dedicated to supporting the arts. This can present a challenge if these individuals leave the company, as an employee's departure can result in the loss of a particular connection with the arts for the entire company. Thoughtworks required staff members who are able to negotiate within corporate structures, believed in a role for the arts within a corporation, and had the requisite skills to maintain these engagements. To get buy-in from the Thoughtworks management, McWilliams would submit an annual proposal highlighting their achievements, which was generally accepted without modification. The residency operated semi-autonomously within the organization, with the freedom to determine the direction and curatorial aspects of the program. Thoughtworks provided artists with an agreement stating that no intellectual property or client-related work will be sought from the artist.

Since Thoughtworks recognized the value of the arts, they allowed for critical and artistic experimentation and generally supported projects exploring social and political issues surrounding advanced technologies, such as surveillance and AI bias. The works produced at Thoughtworks did not serve as decoration for their office or branding as value added for a corporation, but as research in innovation, and as part of their mission toward social justice. The residency served as a means to support complex and socially engaged projects with technology, enabling art as an experiment and encouraging a process-driven approach. Given the size of the company, the residency remained a nonprofit and small-scale initiative, and its stakes remained low. Benefits of knowledge exchange and reputation building were enough to justify the investment in the arts. The residency brought together artists and corporations to work deeply with advanced technologies, where corporations play a role in advancing the artistic process. It required a negotiation of space and priorities to ensure a mutually beneficial relationship.

Artist residencies often provide access to space and equipment in ways that are beneficial to an artist's practice, where residencies tend to emphasize the process of developing and exploring new artistic tools or techniques over a specific output. In the case of Thoughtworks, artists gained access to the company's skilled staff as a form of knowledge exchange, while the company gained critical insight into the field of advanced tech. Artists working with Thoughtworks needed to find their own space and context for showcasing the work they produced in the residency, where the work was valued and recognized as art. In this way, perhaps the AIR in this case, as a space for R&D and collaboration is more conducive to preserving the needs and interests of artists.

THE ARTIST AND THE CORPORATION

The private sector is playing a larger role in patronage, particularly for those artists working with media and technology. Mechanisms such as licensing for media facades, brand commissions, and corporate artist residencies provide new opportunities for artists to collaborate with corporations. Licensing for media facades allows artists working with video to circulate their works while retaining the rights and ownership to their work, thereby moving away from the sale of art as a finite material object. However, unlike complex installations (as discussed in chapter 2) licensing with media facades does not initiate a creative process when regarded as a rental contract. By understanding how economic relationships may be appreciated beyond mere exchange, we can properly value the process and relations that these projects initiate. In this way, commissions are considered more valuable by artists like Mills and Leung because a commission engages them in a process of creation, with corporations providing substantial funding and resources that other kinds of nonprofit funding may not.

Corporations are becoming more attuned to the interests of artists by giving them freedom to experiment in a commission beyond the restrictions of a design brief, as described by Leung. While clients such as Dolby Laboratories have allowed onformative's artists to develop experimental collaborative works that are used to showcase Dolby technology, corporate interests in commissioning artists are often centered on employing the arts within marketing campaigns. In this way, art has become deeply entangled with the economies of marketing and branding and it often becomes difficult to differentiate between them. Care is needed in defining the terms of the relationship with artists and corporations and in the ways that artworks are presented. Media facade displays can be perceived as art for the informed viewer, while also serving the branding of cities for government clients. By preserving spaces for art to exist as art, we can emphasize the possibility of art shifting our normative habits. High-profile public displays and platforms provided by corporations may reach wider audiences with art.

In the case of Jacqueline Kiyomi Gork, the sponsorship from Meyer Sound provided access to high-end equipment for her sound installations, which began to shape the form of her work. In this way, corporate sponsorships have a material impact on the work itself. Rather than provide production budgets to commission an artwork, corporations are also able to provide in-kind support in exchange for a logo on marketing materials of an exhibition. In contrast to commissions, artist residencies center on the process of creation with access to space and equipment that often take place on site. While artist residencies may overlap with commissions (as with the Facebook AIR program), residencies do not have to result in an output. For the Thoughtworks Arts Residency, the process of knowledge exchange with artists was valued over the creation of an ownable or presentable artwork. Instead, as a technology consultancy Thoughtworks was interested in the arts to achieve their social impact mission. The socially engaged projects they have supported have become a means of dialoging with artists and experimenting with technology. By examining these diverse examples, this chapter has demonstrated how art and technology supports an economy that prioritizes the process of creation over the final output. The process of negotiating relationship between artists and corporations requires dedicated individuals who are able to communicate the needs of both parties in a mutually beneficial relationship. However, the long-term sustainability of such initiatives is difficult to maintain due to the low priority given to the arts in the overall corporate agenda.

To imagine economies centered on the process of creation shifts away from an understanding of art as finite material objects that can be bought and sold. This calls for reenvisioning the art market and creative economies based on a dynamic creative process. Within these processes, there is a need to tend to the quality of our interaction and engagement with art and artists. In chapter 5, I look at artists *as* corporations and at how the corporate entity may be mobilized to initiate larger-scale artistic collaborations.

5

COLLABORATIVE PRODUCTION

In this chapter, I look at how artists experiment with organizational forms to facilitate collaborative production at different scales. By examining how artists have taken advantage of the legal entity of the corporation, I consider the aesthetics and politics of entrepreneurship as a practice. In these instances, registering a company or business can be a creative means to find new ways of working collaboratively. For instance, Xu Zhen has employed the corporate entity as artwork in itself with the XU ZHEN® brand, while simultaneously mobilizing the company form to support artistic production with and by others through MadeIn Company. In another example, teamLab, an interdisciplinary collective of artists founded in Tokyo, formed a flexible and experimental internal structure that enables large-scale artistic collaborations with technology. Finally, my own company, MetaObjects, facilitates digital production with artists and cultural institutions to support deeper engagement with advanced technologies. In each of these cases, artists and practitioners have experimented with different aspects of organizational structure to allow for new possibilities of engaging within contemporary cultural economies.

The case studies examined in this chapter occur alongside of what has been described as contemporary art's "organizational turn."[1] They are engaged in the functional economy of creating work, rather than overtly critiquing it. The artist-led organizations examined here are all developing a means to support art—either their own practices, those of others, or those of a collective. As the practices under discussion here demonstrate, there are multiple ways of moving, operating, and acting that are part of the process of "making do."[2] Organizational practice and entrepreneurship do not need to follow the logic of growth and accumulation. For organization studies scholars Daniel Hjorth, Robin Holt and Chris Steyaert, the firm is always changing and can only be studied in motion in a flow of transaction and change.[3] Rather than thinking of organizations as fixed entities, I view them as relational and emerging in time. I argue that by looking closely at *how* different economic practices are enacted on a case-by-case basis we can better understand the possibilities in a complex field. Entrepreneurship is here understood as a creative process of creating an organization that is temporally open to the future with the potential for becoming. To think about entrepreneurship ecologically is to consider the organization as a platform for relational engagements, in connection with others and responding to changes in the environment.

Artists have long experimented with organizational forms as part of their artistic practices, including as a form of conceptual art and as an appropriation of corporate aesthetics. Early interventions with corporate aesthetics include the work of the Artist Placement Group and Andy Warhol[4] in the 1960s and 1970s, Superflex in the 1990s, whose work blurred art and business as a political strategy, and, more recently, the work of post-internet artists including Shanzhai Biennial, K-Hole, GCC, and Jennifer Lyn Morone whose practices reflect on our digital post-Fordist economies.[5] As parodies of the real world, these practices are treated as artistic interventions and as experiments that are not required to succeed and function well in the economy (though it is a bonus if they do succeed). For example, N.E. Thing Co. formed by Iain and Ingrid Baxter in Vancouver, Canada, between 1966 and 1979, registered as a commercial enterprise in order to parody commercial culture but also to experiment with increasing their financial sustainability through commercial artistic projects. The group's intention was also to dissolve their respective identities into a collaborative entity, an act that had the effect of obscuring their genders and challenging notions of authorship prevalent in the art world.[6] Dissolving identities into a collective also acknowledges and enables large-scale collaborations, such as in the case of teamLab. Artist, critic, curator, and entrepreneur Xu Zhen, introduced in the introduction, also treats the companies he creates as a way to also obscure his identity as an artist behind the brand, where art is produced under a common name beyond the individual artist.

Artists, through their practices, raise questions about the normative practices of the industry, whether it's the art market or the technology industry. For example, Jeremy Bailey employs the practices and language of the technology sector to create the LEAN Artist Incubator,[7] a project designed as a Silicon Valley-style seed accelerator for artists, where a group of artists are brought together in short three-day "boot camps." The work subverts the practices of start-ups to empower artists to engage with entrepreneurship and design thinking methodologies as both art and a pitch for a sustainable business. As a means to earn a living wage, Bailey works within the tech start-up industry, where he gains inspiration for his work. His work makes it possible to conceive of start-ups and organizational forms as a material for experimentation, providing a means for artists, particularly those from disadvantaged communities, to participate within contemporary systems of production and also to challenge and raise unique business concepts that the industry would not normally consider. For instance, one of the Lean Artist participants, Mashaun Ali Hendricks, created Trap House Chicago, an apparel shop and community hub, as a social enterprise to support employment and education in Chicago's South Side communities. Through the project, Bailey seeks to raise questions about the fact that, on average, artists make less than $10,000 per year (including himself). Like Xu Zhen, Bailey employs the aesthetics of design and branding as a tactic to intervene in contemporary modes of production. While Bailey engages in the start-up economies of rapid innovation, Xu Zhen engages with economies of mass manufacturing and branding as mode of production prevalent in China. Both employ these modern economic techniques as a means to produce and circulate art as products.

In other ways, artists may also treat their studio practices as an experimental project. For instance, Olafur Eliasson's studio in Berlin ran an experimental art education program as Institut für Raumexperimente from 2009 to 2014 linking with the activities of Berlin University of the Arts, where he was a professor. The practice of his studio does much more than produce art and architectural projects: it has also developed the institute as a platform for spatial research. The studio houses a communal kitchen and in-house chef for their staff and guests, to encourage discussion and creativity as a form of "relational aesthetics," a term coined by curator Nicolas Bourriaud to describe the aesthetics of social interactions.[8] Institut für Raumexperimente's website states: "This model is not something to be imitated—not a model for mimicry and imitation, but rather is an activator, a cultural catalyst for the right here right now, a now that resonates in the rest of the world. The Institute's model allowed the unique micro ecologies and needs of the place or institution to shape their own direction. The purpose of this education model has been to help think and work critically at the same time, and at the same time be organically grown into a particular place—for us Berlin—without excluding the rest of the world."[9] As an art and architecture studio, Eliasson considers its role and function in the community as participating in education and providing a discursive platform through social events and gatherings around food and cooking. The model is not intended to be copied or followed, but rather seeks to understand how organizations could evolve in conversation and connection with the people involved and the local communities it is connected to. The work of MetaObjects resonates with Eliasson's vision of how organizations respond to and evolve with the communities in which they are embedded, though at our own scale and capacities as individuals situated in the context of Hong Kong. We take an ecological approach to building and developing an organization, designed in response to the people and social, political, economic, and technological environments that surrounds us. The environment in this sense is not only the natural environment but also the social and cultural contexts in which we operate.

Embedded in the daily realities of our contemporary cultural economies, the organizational practice of Xu Zhen is taken as part of his art, in which the XU ZHEN® brand and the MadeIn Gallery are mobilized to help strengthen the art ecology in Shanghai. For teamLab, forms of collaboration and R&D are integrated into the internal practices of the organization, supporting transdisciplinary and experimental projects with technology at a large scale. For MetaObjects, collaboration and knowledge sharing are built into the way we work with artists and cultural institutions, where process is emphasized over the end product. As a studio our role is not predefined. We act as mediators to support deeper engagements with advanced technologies. Each example presents a different approach and role affecting the wider art community, the internal processes of collaboration, and knowledge across sectors. These practices demonstrate how notions of "work" and "organizations" may be considered not simply as employment or a means to gain profit. For Bernard Stiegler, "work" (*travaille* in French) or *oeuvre* (artwork), refers to meaningful participation and knowledge creation. This is differentiated from "employment," which is characterized as mindless, uncritical labor.[10] In the latter, we lose our capacity to create and imagine the future. Rather than treating work as employment purely for profit, artists can mobilize organizational forms to create new ways of working collaboratively.

XU ZHEN: THE ART OF INCORPORATING

Well known in the Shanghai art scene, in 1997, Xu Zhen cofounded the nonprofit Biz Art Centre, which has played a key role in fostering an emerging local art scene at a time when there was little infrastructure for supporting artists. The Biz Art Centre was an organization and alternative art space that supported experimental exhibitions by young artists through advertising, design, and commercial services.[11] At a time when China's economy was growing rapidly, Xu Zhen became one of the early promoters of contemporary art in the city. In 2006, Xu Zhen cofounded Art-Ba-Ba, an online community and art platform for the discussion and criticism of contemporary art.[12] In 2009, he combined his art practice into MadeIn Company, which he described as a "contemporary art creation company." This company worked to dissolve his individual identity as an artist and to facilitate his practice, as well as to present exhibitions and promote the work of other artists in Shanghai. The project is treated both as an art project and as an art production company, created as a rejection of the notions of individual authorship and artist personalities that dominate the art world.[13] In an interview Xu Zhen explains:

> We found out that a "company" cannot operate solely for one artist; it also has to be a platform, a corporate, a structure. The "company" with its rational business

system, represents a breakthrough in the traditional relationship between art and culture: now the creativity of artists can evolve at different levels, it can change the surviving value of art by experiencing new models. In a way that makes it all the more innovative. . . . In fact, MadeIn Company is progressively modifying the famous relationship between artist and creativity. The company is the artist of today; in this sense, art possesses an even more "sharing" spirit.[14]

Still largely directed by Xu Zhen, the company plays a role in blurring the boundaries between commodity and art in order for art to exist and circulate in contemporary cultural economies in new forms. Works produced by MadeIn Company include unusual cartoon plush toys as sculptures, such as *Sphynxxxxxxxxx* (2014) and *The Sausage Voice* (2015). *Physique of Consciousness* (2011), a performance and installation that features cultural fitness exercises combining religious rituals and new age spiritualism presented as videos on a CD-ROM, and museological displays of objects exploring different cultures and histories based on the exercises (see figure 5.1). Blurring the lines between product and art, MadeIn Company's works engage traditional and contemporary aesthetics and modes of production. While in other instances artworks may become commodities to promote a brand, the products that Xu Zhen creates are artworks that can be circulated as commodities.

Spinning off from his growing enterprise, the artist launched the XU ZHEN® brand in 2013. Following that, he launched MadeIn Gallery[15] in 2014, a commercial gallery focused on emerging artists in China. Xu Zhen playfully reinforces the artist-as-brand in his XU ZHEN® brand, while also removing the distinction between the artist and collective practices. Works by the brand include *MadeIn Curved Vase* (2014), a series of porcelain vases with traditional Chinese motifs, the vase necks curved ninety degrees, rendering them useless (figure 5.2). The brand creates artworks as a means to intervene in and reflect on the contemporary conditions of production as institutional critique: the works satirize and mock the practices and contexts in which art is presented. While Xu Zhen does not necessarily engage with advanced technologies like some of the other cases I have discussed, his practice crosses design and branding, all while interrogating contemporary systems of production. As described by art writer, Chris Moore, MadeIn Company "'inhabits' the idea and legal personality

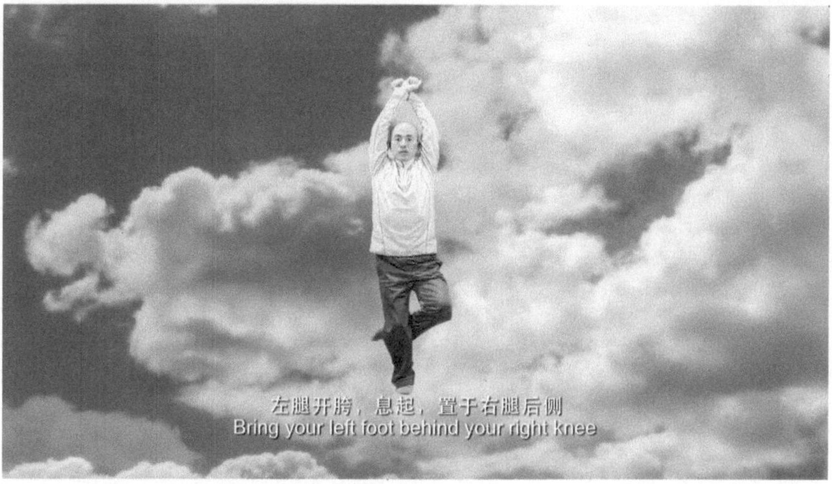

of a corporate structure. It is simultaneously a 'real' company—a company of people—but also a conceptual virus, a cell of subversives tunnelling into the hierarchy."[16]

For Xu Zhen, branding becomes part of an aesthetics of practice in his play on the corporate entity. There is some ambiguity in his work's intention and meaning, the result of working in an environment in China where creating certain kinds of art can be risky. Some works exhibited by MadeIn Company feature provocatively sexual or offensive material including plush toys like an Energizer bunny with the head of Osama bin Laden or collages of political and children's cartoons. Other works involving taking photographs of sculptural works and then destroying the original object.[17] He plays with nationalist, consumerist, and art historical symbols and aesthetics, and takes them to the extreme through

5.1

XU ZHEN®, *Physique of Consciousness, Exercise 8 #22*, video still, 2011. Courtesy of the artist Xu Zhen and performer Wu Jianxin.

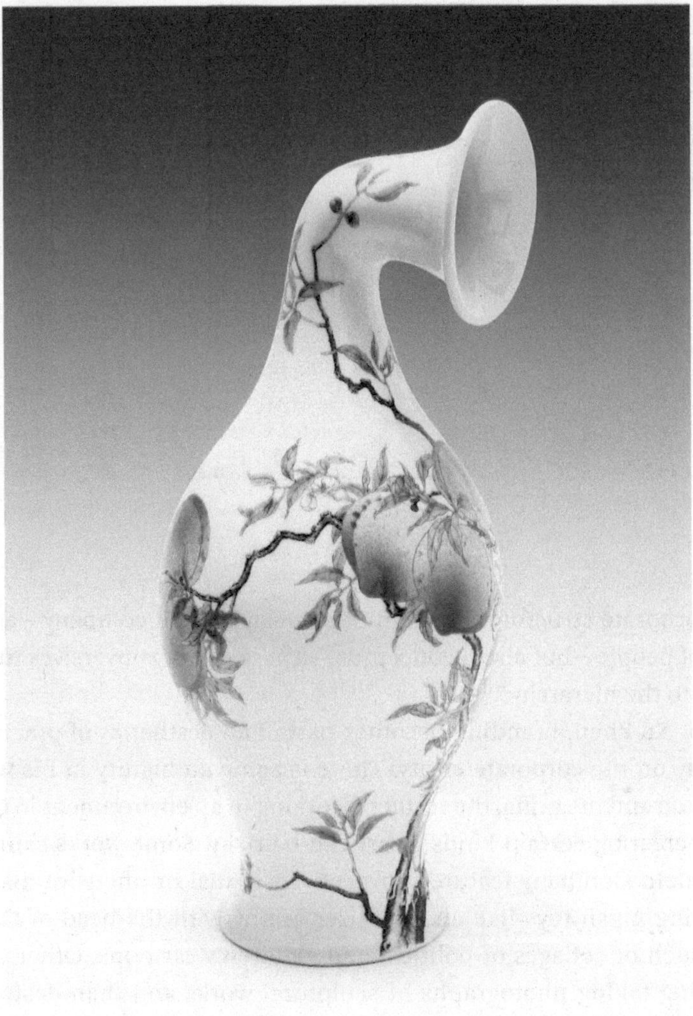

5.2

MadeIn Curved Vase—Famille-rose Olive Vase with Bat and Peach Design, Yongzheng Period, Qing Dynasty, 2013. Porcelain, 17 x 17 x 40 cm. Produced by MadeIn Company. Courtesy of the artist Xu Zhen.

satire and the creation of absurd juxtapositions. A company may also be a means to distract and gain legitimacy in a political environment that does not value critical or morally challenging artistic practices. While Xu Zhen is not immune to censorship in China, he has developed various approaches to obscure the meaning of his works.

In China, the development of the contemporary art industry is connected to its economic advancement and role in global markets. As discussed in chapter 4, the private sector is playing a larger role in the economies of art, particularly in China where there is a blurring of the roles of public and private institutions:[18] for example, K11 Art Foundation and K11 Art Malls, billionaire Adrian Cheng's cultural-retail empire.[19] Cheng's model uses contemporary art to promote his malls as lifestyle venues to engage digitally savvy millennials as Cheng's target audience. The commercial businesses directly support the programs of the nonprofit K11 Art Foundation including residencies and commissions intended to incubate a new generation of artists and cultivate audiences in China.[20] Both public and private initiatives are intertwined and feed into each other. While contemporary artists become complicit in these consumerist economies, K11 at the same time has the resources to appropriately remunerate artists and hire professional curators who can develop successful collaborations with artists.[21] The extreme commercialization of the cultural sector in China means artists are oriented toward markets, where artists like Xu Zhen have found a means to embrace commerce, while subverting it and creating new opportunities for artists, through the MadeIn Gallery, for example.

For artists, registering as a business offers specific affordances, particularly in Hong Kong where organizations have more rights than individuals do. Registering as a company or organization provides certain legal rights and visibility within the economic and political sphere, while also protecting individuals from personal financial responsibility.[22] In Hong Kong, the "artist"[23] often falls under the category of the self-employed, who have fewer rights than salaried full-time employees and registered businesses or organizations—a disparity reflected in the imbalance between subsidies provided to big businesses and those for individuals during the COVID-19 pandemic. Commercial entities can find other sources of funding beyond government grants, which largely serve political agendas in

China. In this way, the private sector in China provides more resources and possibilities for experimentation beyond nationalist narratives. Corporate entities can simultaneously provide a platform for forms of art that may not otherwise have opportunities to show in public institutions.

As an artist, Xu Zhen simultaneously creates conceptual artworks and installations that reflect on consumerism in China. He received success early on as the youngest Chinese artist to exhibit in the 49th Venice Biennale in 2001 with a video artwork called *Rainbow* (1998).[24] The work features a bare back being slapped where the hand has been edited out leaving the sound, as the viewers sees the skin on the back slowly changing color from the violent gesture, a reflection on the desensitization to violence in mass media. Xu Zhen's work often plays on and subverts stereotypical Chinese and Western iconography, while also challenging the social and cultural norms and practices of art and galleries. For example, the work *Action of Consciousness* (2011) challenges the viewer's expectations by presenting various sculptures on top of a white cube. The sculptures feature clichéd cultural symbols juxtaposed to each other, such as a Chinese lantern on top of an Ionic Greek column or a swastika made of cacti, which are seen briefly before dropping out of view. This artwork mocks gallery audiences pandering to the spectacle of art.[25]

When discussing his work, Xu Zhen explains, "It isn't critique; in fact, we hope to use these kind of 'market characteristics' to produce new aesthetics and possibilities. . . . I believe that the culture of the future will be centered on different methods of production and diffusion."[26] In this sense, Xu Zhen shifts to what Jacques Rancière calls a "distribution of the sensible," where "artistic practices are 'ways of doing and making' that intervene in the general distribution of ways of doing and making as well as in the relationships they maintain to modes of being and forms of visibility."[27] Artistic practice begins to open up ways to think about our institutions and economic forms that are up for constant renegotiation. Through experimentation with market characteristics, this work presents new aesthetic possibilities by making visible different ways of doing and making that unfold their own logic.[28] Xu Zhen's approach does not aim to critique, but rather leads to different ways of thinking and doing in the process of creating a company that affirms new ways of being in contemporary society.

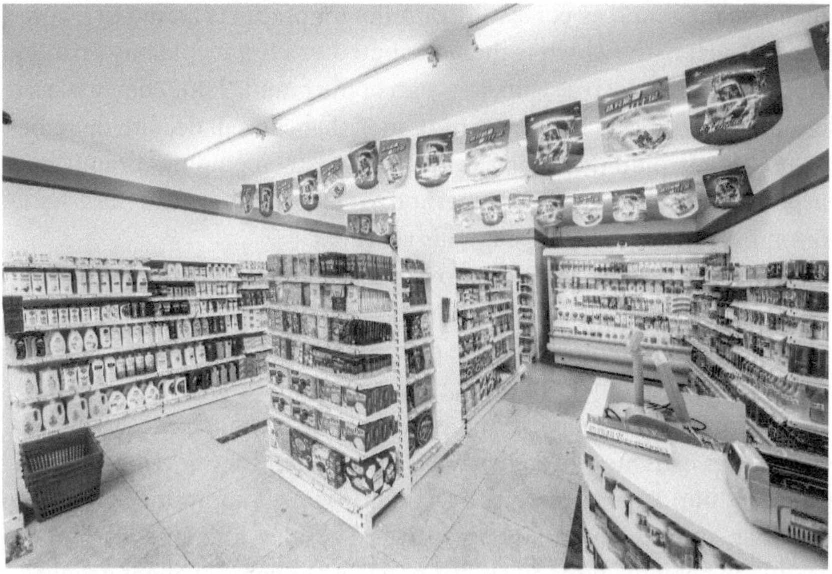

His artwork self-consciously interrogates the aesthetics of advertising, such as in *XU ZHEN SUPERMARKET* (2007/2017), a work created under his brand name (figure 5.3). It features a replica of a supermarket stocked with empty packages of everyday products with the storefront rebranded by the artist. The first version of the work was presented at Art Basel Miami in 2007 as *ShangART SUPERMARKET*, which was subsequently sold at auction by Sotheby's Hong Kong for $2 million HKD as the first concept ever sold at auction in Asia.[29] Acknowledging the capitalist society we live in, Xu Zhen appropriates the brand as an image devoid of substance that is also a commentary on the art market itself. According to sociologist Adam Arvidsson, brands are a "context of consumption"[30] that pertains to the marketing of a corporate identity, while Celia Lury

5.3

XU ZHEN®, *XU ZHEN SUPERMARKET* Yuyuan Road, Shanghai, 2007/2016. Photo: Mao Xingyu. Courtesy of the artist.

considers the brand as consisting of different products linked by a common characteristic, which is then attributed to a brand, placing primary importance on a "logo as icon, as a sign of the brand."[31] Xu Zhen makes a statement to indicate the power of brands that can sell despite there being nothing behind the image as an icon. Xu Zhen employs brands and corporations as a language and method to support his art and the artistic community in Shanghai through his ventures.

Xu Zhen's work enables him to support emerging artists, suggesting a way that these organizational forms can be mobilized as part of an aesthetic practice. His companies are considered a part of his art, a shifting of tactics and techniques in the contemporary conditions of production. His practice simultaneously conforms to the market and actively engages with it to its extremes through what UCCA Center for Contemporary Art director Philip Tinari describes as "a gently violent appropriation in service of an ambivalent and irreverently universalist humanism."[32] When considering organizing as an artistic practice, the concept opens a renegotiation of normative ways of thinking and doing. Here practices of branding, organizational roles, and products are considered as aesthetic forms for reflection and intervention. Whereas institutional critique raises awareness of the inequalities of museums and art institutions, artist-led organizations offer a set of practices that may be mobilized creatively to intervene in society, blurring the boundaries of art and life.

Even in the mundane aspects of everyday life, there is a need for everyone to be creative. Joseph Beuys would proclaim that "everyone is an artist." Xu Zhen demonstrates the desire to be creative even as he enables and encourages other artists in the local art community. In a conversation with leading economists in the book *What Is Money?*, Beuys claims, "Money has to undergo a metamorphosis again; it has to relinquish its role in the market economy and engage in an economy of capacities."[33] In this Beuys refers to human capacities as co-creators of the future as *social sculpture*. The economy is viewed as a social organism in which we are required to participate beyond the notion of private property. Profit should not be an end in itself, but rather a means of serving the needs of others, and forms of paid labor (or "employment" in Stiegler's term) should not restrict creative capacities.[34] Through his various businesses, galleries, and platforms,

Xu Zhen seeks to encourage the creative capacities of others by building platforms for art and discourse as part of a shared social responsibility.

While not every artist can build enterprises like Xu Zhen has with MadeIn Company and his various brands and platforms, his work opens ways in which incorporating could enable new forms of collaborative production. While corporate entities can also be viewed as exploiting the market to sell products, Xu Zhen's work also serves to enable other artists by presenting them at MadeIn Gallery and creating an art production business that engages in collaborative work. Through his success, Xu Zhen has supported the artistic community in Shanghai, which could be seen as a form of philanthropy or wealth redistribution, unique but similar to Eliasson's studio practice in Berlin. Successful artists can play a role in fostering emerging artists as a social responsibility, suggesting that commercial entities can be employed strategically to mobilize resources to build discursive platforms or support artistic production in the community. Organizations become a conduit to enable the flow of money, where profit is not the end goal, to support the development of the local art ecology.[35] The term "organizing" also refers to political activism. Commercial entities and corporations, despite seemingly apolitical, foster tangible effects and meaningful exchanges in the artistic community. An organization can also enable practices beyond the individual artist. The next section considers teamLab as a collective that employs a unique organizational approach that enables large-scale collaborations with technology.

TEAMLAB: LARGE-SCALE ARTISTIC COLLABORATIONS

Like onformative (discussed in chapter 1), but at a much larger scale, teamLab operates as a commercial company providing service for clients, while also creating their own collaborative artworks with technology. teamLab tests and builds new concepts and ideas that become immersive installations and artistic experiences. Working with technology necessitates collaboration with others with diverse skillsets. As such, incorporating as an organizational entity shifts the focus from the artist as an individual genius, and challenges notions of authorship in the art market.

Founded in 2001 in Tokyo by Toshiyuki Inoko with four friends, teamLab comprises artists, programmers, engineers, CG animators, mathematicians, and architects. Since the beginning, the collective has always created art, but also provides digital solutions for a wide range of clients. Their artistic practice is collaborative, requiring teams of people with different skills producing works through an organic process. Inoko explains, "Inspiration doesn't suddenly happen. We have a lot of specialists and when they work in teams, they are co-thinking. They're not only thinking of their own territories, but over their boundaries, thinking together with other people."[36] teamLab has expanded their artistic practice to stage large-scale immersive art installations that have garnered worldwide attention. Collaboration is core to teamLab's philosophy and practice. Says founder Toshiyuki Inoko, "The kind of people whom I want to come here are those who believe in the importance of a repeated process of collective experimentation for the purpose of creation."[37]

Internally, teamLab works in smaller teams on specific projects and approach their work through their diverse perspectives as engineers, artists, or architects to see if something interesting emerges.[38] For Takashi Kudo, the communication director of teamLab, the difference between art and design is that design provides answers, while art asks questions.[39] At times, questions cannot be easily answered; the resulting artwork cannot be expressed through words and operates beyond language and the rational mind, which for Kudo, is a form of art. The creative process is one of experimentation and unknowingness, which does not rely on simply providing answers, but also on asking questions.

teamLab's artistic processes are also reflected in how they are organized as a company. They do not strive to define what they do or even put it into words, nor are they centered on individual authorship. Through a holistic approach that does not create separations between individuals or disciplines, teamLab's artwork simultaneously seeks to transcend boundaries between the self and the world.[40] The notion of overcoming boundaries and categories through a process of self-discovery is also found within Buddhist philosophy.[41] Inoko describes teamLab's practice as a "co-intelligence" in the way they work in teams, starting with a concept to collectively address a problem to approach new questions and keep investigating until they discover a new form of art.[42] They may start with no more than intuition, an inkling of an idea, then assemble teams to create prototypes and engage in a problem-solving process to realize an abstract vision where there is no preconceived end goal. Kudo explains, "So we'll talk in teams and ask questions and start to make some kind of image. We try to make a prototype. It's trial and error, again and again and again."[43] Their process is iterative, experimental, and collaborative so that they may come to a shared understanding of whether a project is moving in the right direction. These unarticulated ways of collective thinking and doing move teamLab away from the rational and mechanistic modes typical to most businesses. At teamLab there is a process of identifying problems and solving them, but also discovering new questions.

Harvard Business School's Japan Research Center published a case study on teamLab that describes the organization's success in having grown without borrowing external capital: "teamLab had evolved into a unique company with few corporate practices and organization structures typical of firms in Japan or elsewhere. . . . They are a collective, although at a scale that is unusual, to say the least. This process also means, of course, that no single person has to develop on their own an expertise in all of the technologies necessary to realize their vision."[44] teamLab is organized horizontally, inspired by other technology companies using nonhierarchical and decentralized forms of management. There is no company figurehead; rather, they are self-organized into teams around projects.[45] In the technology industry, horizontal corporate management structures and processes such Holacracy, a method of decentralized organizational management allows for the self-management of teams.[46] Such practices give a sense of autonomy to individual workers to define their work to facilitate collaboration within teams and a workflow between other teams. Adaptive and learning protocols integrate creativity into their processes to allow room for iteration and innovation. These management methods are flexible and agile to respond dynamically to changes to ensure successful outcomes. Methods of horizontal management make working cultures more appealing for employees who have more control over their work, ensuring greater productivity for the company. Ultimately, such practices remain under the legal and financial control of the corporation with directives from the top, which end up serving interests in growth and profit. Perhaps teamLab's horizontal approach is viewed less as a method for productivity, but rather a spiritual and creative practice that is shared with their team members to encourage artistic concepts to emerge organically.

As a studio, teamLab did not gain recognition in the art world until later in its founders' careers, ten years after starting the company. In the beginning, they struggled to find support for their artistic projects, says a member of teamLab. "We were creating art installations from the beginning, but we had neither the opportunities to present them, nor could we imagine how to economically sustain our teams producing art."[47] Employees felt a strong desire to create artistic work, despite not having much support for their work in the art world. It wasn't until 2011, when they were invited by artist Takashi Murakami to present an exhibition titled *We Are the Future*, featuring a 360-degree screen at his gallery Kaikai Kiki[48] in Taipei, that teamLab started to gain recognition in the art world. They were supported by Singapore-based gallerist Ikkan Sanada as their art advisor for the Murakami show, which eventually led them to be represented by Pace Gallery in 2014. Sanada explains, "I knew working with them was what I wanted to do. I had two main goals as teamLab's official art adviser. First was convincing Inoko that this was fine art. The second was getting recognition from museums and collectors and establishing real value to the work."[49] Their connection to key individuals in the art world helped position their work in the art market context. There was also an element of luck where the unexpected invitation to show with Murakami opened up new possibilities for their work. However, Kudo has remarked on the challenges of selling their works on the art market due to the scale of their work, as well as the technical complexity and cost for making and maintaining them.[50] In addition to the art market, teamLab has also developed a format of presenting their works through ticketed immersive experiences.

teamLab's work attracts large audiences beyond the art market, who pay entry fees to experience their installations. Time-based experiences with ticketed entry follow the model of film, theater, and performing arts, and can be considered part of the experience economy.[51] While there have been immersive installations in the past, such as the *Dreamspace V* (1996)[52] inflatable project of Maurice Agis, they have not engaged advanced technologies as teamLab has. teamLab expanded this model of large-scale interactive immersive experiences to a scale that allows them to be presented around the globe. Among their largest installations is the digital art museum *teamLab Borderless* in Tokyo, which spans 7,000 square meters with more than seventy exhibits spread over numerous rooms, featuring both large-scale experiences and interactive installations (figure 5.4). Other permanent exhibition locations include Macau and Singapore. The notion of *teamLab Borderless* is to allow audiences to move seamlessly through different spatial experiences, ideas, and concepts. Their work typically features a flatness evocative of Japanese landscape paintings, which lacks modern Western perspective, an aesthetic technique teamLab calls "ultrasubjective space." This technique gives the viewer the sense of being inside the space, rather than observing it from an individual point of view. These highly popular works create an economy that can and does support teamLab's large-scale collaborative productions with technology. Their revenues are primarily based upon ticket sales, where they depend on a high number of audiences in order to sustain the scale of their work. Their practice emerged through their interest in digital art experiences, as well as a chance opportunity to present their works in the art world. teamLab has retained their collaborative practice between art and technology, which has formed its own unique position between spectacle and art market as they gain recognition for their work. Their approach enables them to create works at unprecedented scales, developing their own definition of art and practices for sustaining their work.

This can also be said of organizing when it is considered as the process of engaging in the world. For teamLab, their practice wasn't planned; instead, their intuitive approach to their art also influences how they are organized collectively. The economies for teamLab's work evolved over time, from primarily supporting their work through commercial software development, to developing their own model for their art through immersive events. They hold a number of patents, including the teamLabBall, which is an interactive interface that emits color and sound.[53] teamLab's practice straddles different economies of the art market and mass culture, reaching diverse audiences as a shifting of techniques in the conditions of production. Some may disregard their engagements with art as entertainment, populist, and superficial; however, teamLab has carved out a unique practice and a means for creating large-scale work with art and technology—both within and beyond the art market. Initially supporting

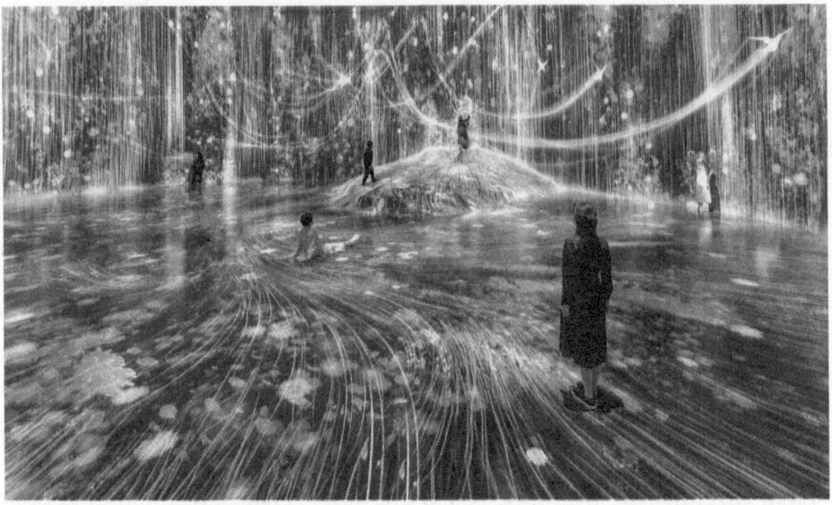

their work through commercial software development, they continued developing their work without defining it as fine art until they received the help of art advisors to contextualize their work in the art world. Their success in the art world also challenges and redefines notions of artistic practice, as well as which economies are able to support complex works that require large audiences to sustain them.

While teamLab presents uniquely collaborative internal structures and modes of practices, we can see that many start-ups have adopted flexible practices, recognizing that creativity is required for productivity. However, the nature of teamLabs work continues to explore and define its own mode of practice that challenges the art market, which also has adapted to accommodate their unique form of practice that embodies a philosophy toward collaboration and artistic creation. With my own work

5.4

teamLab, exhibition view of *teamLab Borderless: MORI Building DIGITAL ART MUSEUM*, 2024, Azabudai Hills, Tokyo. © teamLab, Courtesy of Pace Gallery.

at MetaObjects, while we do not call ourselves artists, artistic processes are involved in how we organize and consider our practice as a studio.

METAOBJECTS: ART FABRICATORS AS MEDIATORS

Working across VR, 3D printing, motion capture, audiovisual production, and web development, MetaObjects encourages the sharing of knowledge of new digital tools and processes through a collective and collaborative process of learning through doing. Founded with technical director Andrew Crowe, the studio is more interested in supporting and enabling artistic practice than in finite and formally resolved artworks that can easily be bought and sold. MetaObjects chooses to emphasize process over product, where we do not create artworks ourselves, but rather extend the possibilities for artists to engage more closely with advanced technologies. Through our work, we have developed long-term collaborations with artists and cultural institutions by leveraging resources across sectors and disciplines of art, technology, and academia.

Founded in 2017 in Hong Kong, we chose to register as a limited company to support the business by providing technical and curatorial services, while providing subsidized rates for artists. Each project is considered an opportunity to learn new techniques and skills, but also a means to understand the possibilities emerging in the moment. By leaving our roles open, we did not start with a preconception of what we would do and chose not to follow typical paths of a start-up industry or gallery. Rather than being predetermined, our identity and practice is not fixed, but is co-constituted in relation and subject to constant reconfiguration in a shifting environment. The name "MetaObjects" is conceived as a fluid *thing*, a self-reflexive entity that continually defines and redefines itself in practice as it exists in and through various relations with artists, technologies, and institutions.[54] We are a commercial studio that caters to working with artists and cultural institutions. We are not motivated by profit and our focus is projects that are not technically but rather artistically and conceptually challenging.

As discussed in the introduction of this book, one of our early collaborations was with artist Samson Young on a 3D printed sculpture. As a sound artist and composer, Young felt 3D printing was a way to explore sculpture in his practice. From this one project our work with Young has evolved into a long-term collaboration in which we support one another by sharing knowledge and resources. Rather than assuming a predefined role in collaboration with Young, we allowed the relationship to develop organically.

In 2017, Young was selected to represent Hong Kong at the 57th Venice Biennale. With an ambitious vision of creating large-scale installations with sculpture, performance, video, and sound, he took this opportunity to extend his practice using technologies such as 3D printing. For his exhibition *Songs for Disaster Relief*, he wanted to develop a large-scale 3D printed sculpture[55] as part of his installation *Palazzo Gundane (homage to the mythmaker who fell to earth* (figure 5.5). While Young is technically skilled at producing his own animations and compositions, he sought help to work with a new medium. MetaObjects consulted with Young on different materials, printing processes, and modeling of the piece to ensure it was printable and structurally sound, while Young assembled the basic design of the sculpture in 3D rendering software. The sculpture combines the ancient Greek sculpture of the *Winged Victory of Samothrace* with digital sculpts of the philosopher Pythagoras, a bust of Ronald Reagan, a space station, and a bugle as symbols of the rise of neoliberalism and technological hubris. Our engagement with this project was a collaborative process of showing the artist the possibilities of 3D printing, describing the different methods available, and making practical suggestions, all of which feeds into the artistic process and shapes the form of the work itself. Young worked with 3D specialist Cosmo Wegman in California to apply a coating to make the piece look like rusted bronze. The model was printed, assembled, and finished in California before being shipped to Venice.

Young then purchased large-format 3D printers, which we agreed to help manage and maintain and also make available for other artists' use (figure 5.6). MetaObjects has helped Young produce numerous large-scale 3D printed sculptures, including musical instrument pieces exhibited at the Guggenheim Museum in New York, a bumper-car shoe presented at Edouard Malingue Gallery in Shanghai and Art Basel Hong Kong, and a large-scale mini-golf course for K11 Musea, a new cultural-retail venue in Hong Kong. We also produced a series of frames for the artist's sound

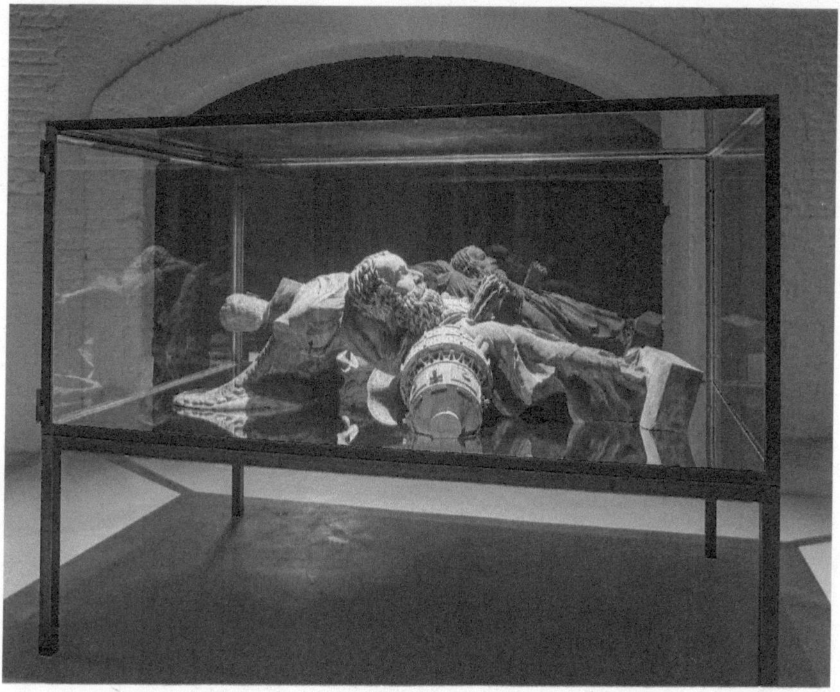

5.5

Samson Young, *Palazzo Gundane (homage to the myth-maker who fell to earth)*, 3D printed sculpture, Hong Kong Pavilion, 57th Venice Biennale, 2017. 3D printing technical support by Cosmo Wenmen and MetaObjects. Photo: Simon Vogel. Commissioned by M+, Hong Kong.

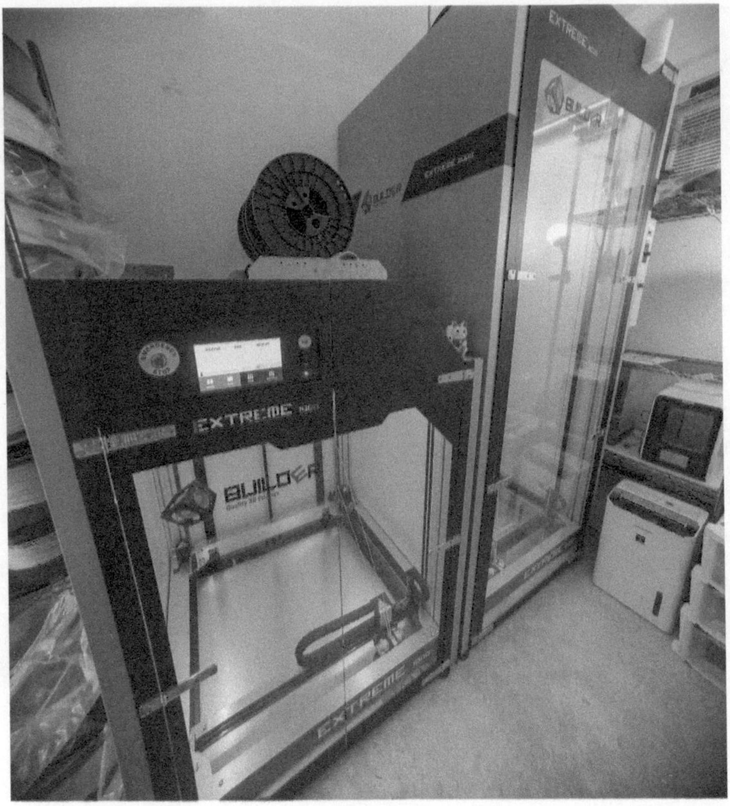

5.6

3D printers at Samson Young's studio, Hong Kong.

drawings. In addition, we helped develop a technique with 3D printing by feeding two different-color filaments into the dual nozzle of the printer to create a gradient effect. We created an algorithm to mix the two colors at different rates to resemble marble. Owning the printer allowed for quick trial and error experiments in a collaborative process of exploring the creative possibilities and applications of the tool. As a sociotechnical ensemble, the 3D printer, artist, technician, and studio space are bounded in relations of art making.[56] Young, in a sense, owns the means of production, just as artisans working with ceramics would own their kilns. MetaObjects becomes studio technicians, not only by helping maintain the printers and ensure effective functioning by adding sensors to detect and stop errors and cameras for monitoring the prints, but also by modifying the printing process to produce new results.

In her book *Working Aesthetics*,[57] Danielle Child discusses art fabrication companies that emerged with conceptual art, where artists are no longer masters of their craft, and rather focus on the conceptual development while seeking collaborators to create their artworks. Artists in the post-media condition are effectively deskilled, and their collaborators may be studio assistants, or outsourced labor from external companies. In this way, art fabricators become part of the invisible labor that sustains the art market. While MetaObjects acknowledges that we are contributing to the artistic system, we care less about authorship and ownership of artworks, and value the process of collaboration. Child emphasizes the deskilling of artists who are cut off from the production process; MetaObjects understands our work as a sharing of skills and knowledge.

While Young is very technically capable, there are also limits to learning new tools and software. MetaObjects helps bridge the gaps in knowledge, in a collective process of learning and discovery of what these technologies can do. Through this approach, Young has also gained new knowledge and skills in 3D printing. With Young, we are able to achieve things beyond our individual capacities, while also enabling other artists to engage with technology.

For Bernard Stiegler, the problem of "proletarianization" (also described in chapter 1) is where the transfer of knowledge becomes "short-circuited" and people no longer have the informational means to modify or adapt technologies, such as our mobile phones. Stiegler's "economy of contribution"[58] supports an ethics of care and long-term engagement with technology to create "long circuits" and communities based on the collective sharing of knowledge, contributing to a way of life with technology that is not only structured around moneymaking. MetaObjects likewise seeks to create long circuits of engagement with technology with artists. Young could easily send his models to be printed in China, but then he would be cut off from the production process, unable to learn and experiment with the machine firsthand. Our arrangement enables a long-term engagement with technology and allows for a two-way feedback process, through which unexpected results may emerge through mutual experimentation, expanding the possibilities of the technology.

In addition to Young, MetaObjects has worked with artists Lu Yang, Helen Knowles, Wong Kit Yi, Clon & NWRMNTC, Rachel Monosov, Gordon Cheung, Carla Chan, and others. We are an artist-led studio, meaning we do not start with a technology, but rather try to understand which tools and techniques are most appropriate for the artwork and available resources. We have also developed long-term collaborations to provide technical and curatorial services for exhibitions and artist commissions with cultural institutions that include M+, Museum of Visual Culture, Tai Kwun Centre for Heritage and Arts, Hong Kong Design Centre, and Asia Society Hong Kong. We are regular suppliers for several institutions and work on a contract and project basis on diverse projects. We also are approached to work on specific projects with an artist, or to consult on an institution's digital and online projects. This flexibility allows us to play a role in facilitating production for the cultural sector, bridging knowledge gaps in the applications of advanced technologies, while providing a steady stream of work to support the artist-led projects. MetaObjects becomes more than a production company or services provider, but a collaborator and mediator between sectors and disciplines.

Our role as an external entity and registered company allows us to navigate in between sectors to help mediate relations between art, industry, and academia. Working both inside and outside the academic institution also has affordances. MetaObjects has worked with a number of academic institutions to run workshops and to bring knowledge from the field into the institution, as well as to support production on research projects.

We have conducted workshops with motion capture, VR, and 360-degree video and animation workshops with institutions that include Toronto Metropolitan University; the School of Creative Media, City University of Hong Kong; Pratt Institute, New York; the University of Melbourne; Freespace, West Kowloon Cultural District; and the Hong Kong Academy for Performing Arts. The workshops are a nonprofit endeavor; we value bringing knowledge back to support education for students and emerging artists. We have also worked on R&D projects for university professors including artist Scott Hessels at City University of Hong Kong, and music professor Christopher Keyes at Hong Kong Baptist University.

Through our work in academia, we quickly discovered a challenge faced by many universities that are acquiring expensive equipment to remain competitive and attract students, but without the appropriate systems in place to allow student use. Equipment is often left sitting underused after completion of a particular research project without appropriate technical support or available training for students. Conducting workshops tests possibilities within the university setting to gain access to high-end equipment, while exploring the potential to become trusted technicians and extend access to labs and equipment for artists and students to create work. In this way, MetaObjects negotiates a role within the community based on how we can best contribute our knowledge and skills. As an organizational entity, MetaObjects becomes a vehicle for experimentation, whereby we test and explore the possibilities for artistic collaboration with technology within local cultural contexts.

Adopting a pragmatic approach to organizational practice, MetaObjects seeks to operate immanently within the field to encourage collective learning and knowledge-sharing with our artists and institutional collaborators. In Braidotti's terms, a "nomadic subjectivity" is "generated affirmatively and creatively by efforts geared to creating possible futures, by mobilizing resources and visions that have been left untapped and by actualizing them in daily practices of interconnection with others."[59] In this way, MetaObjects operates nomadically, playing different roles in local art ecologies by enabling artistic practices and supporting others to create work through our skills, knowledge, and experiences. In practice, we differentiate ourselves from a creative agency[60] in how we undertake work for commercial and institutional clients. Rather than serve as a design studio, we seek to develop long-term collaborations by aiding the technical process. As an embodied approach, we do not follow models set by the industry, but rather respond in our work to the possibilities available to us in a particular environment, with and alongside others in an open-ended and evolving practice.

THE COMPANY AS COLLECTIVE

As legal entities, companies or enterprises offer specific opportunities for artists in today's cultural economies. Incorporation can enable new forms of collaborative production. For artists like Xu Zhen, incorporation enabled the artist to experiment with brand identities and art production practices in ways that also reflect on the normative behaviors and practices of the art and cultural industries that are taken for granted. Xu Zhen also critiques the centrality of individual authorship and spectatorship in our cultural economies by using the corporate entity to facilitate forms of collaborative production. By producing products as artworks, he embraces the corporate form to allow art to circulate in the contemporary modes of production, while simultaneously raising questions about the hyper-commercialization of the arts. As philosopher Brian Massumi explains, "Complicity is an ontological condition under neoliberalism. It cannot be avoided, but it is not all-defining. It should not just be critiqued. It should be practiced strategically, in ways aimed at always upping the ratio of escape over capture."[61] By acknowledging this complicity, Xu Zhen's practice creates new platforms and contexts for art. In this way, he opens a space for experimentation and opportunities for critical discourse through Art-Ba-Ba and exhibitions for artists through the MadeIn Gallery. The impact and influence of his companies in the Shanghai art community are undeniable. He has built a place where he can uniquely tread the line between artist and entrepreneur in a way that appropriates the corporate form to create new possibilities for artists. By doing so, Xu Zhen raises awareness of the economic structures in which we operate. As described by Tinari, "Xu Zhen is interested in the company less as a strategy and more as a form; not so much as a vehicle for enterprise or an agent of branding, but as a social construct, an educational institution, an extended clan."[62] His practice therefore exemplifies how economies shape the meaning, form, and reception of artworks, as well as a model for how experiments with economic practices can become part of the artistic process itself and produce new social relations. Xu Zhen's artistic practice is not just about branding. His works also demonstrate and enact the possibilities for art as a social experiment to exist within accelerated economies.

To think of the company as a collective is to subsume individual identities into a unified brand. Collaborative processes are integral in the work of teamLab, which in fact calls itself an international art collective. For teamLab, the internal structure and processes of collaboration of the large-scale organization is fluid rather than fixed. Arranged in self-organized interdisciplinary teams with a horizontal structure, teamLab allows its members to engage in an open-ended process of discovery. Embracing an experimental process, teamLab has developed new concepts for installations collectively and tested out new ideas with immersive technologies. They have innovated a unique model of presenting large-scale immersive installations as ticketed events with interactive environments that engage wide audiences, including young people. While their work has not gained the attention of the art market, their popularity has attracted interest from commercial galleries like Pace Gallery. They now transform their practice into media displays and objects that can be sold on the art market.

While flexible and creative work environments have become the norm in the creative industries, teamLab brings a deeper philosophical approach that values the process of creation and experimentation. Normally, horizontal practices within corporations ultimately serve the interests of internal stakeholders of the corporation; teamLab's horizontal approach is connected to a spiritual and philosophical purpose. The internal organization of their teams is a practice that connects with each other's creative capacities beyond the individual. Without predefined roles, team members can freely explore creative possibilities and contribute in any way they can. In this sense, the organization exemplifies how individuals embody diverse knowledge that can contribute to projects beyond their designated roles or fields of study. Rather than a model that ensures efficiency and productivity, teamLab's open-ended process allows for creative concepts and practices to emerge organically. This approach has the potential to open up new practices that allow for the emergence of new forms of cultural experiences that can be sustained at scale.

In our work with MetaObjects, we choose to work with a wide range of external collaborators rather than working at a large scale with internal teams. These collaborators include artists and cultural institutions in Hong Kong and internationally. Without a predefined concept of what we would be or do as a studio, we discovered a role for ourselves in the artistic community through the projects and collaborations we have developed over time. This open-ended approach allows us to navigate the possibilities within the field across disciplines and sectors of art, technology, and academia. By operating immanently in the field, we can identify obstacles and challenges that emerge in the present moment and seek to bridge the gaps in knowledge through our role as a registered business. In this way, the commercial entity can be mobilized as a vehicle to support artistic practices in Hong Kong, where companies have more rights than individuals. There are affordances to registering a company that gives a certain legitimacy to one's work, while remaining financially independent.

Artists based in Hong Kong are encountering increasing influence from China and top-down policies from the Chinese government, such that grants programs in the current political climate are recognized as not neutral. A government-funded system means only certain kinds of artists and artworks get funding, with implicit biases against work that may present an unfavorable image of the government. It requires fitting a project into particular granting streams to fulfill certain social and political agendas, because these programs are more likely to support work that does not challenge official narratives. In contrast, by registering as a commercial enterprise, Xu Zhen has afforded himself the possibility of presenting challenging and subversive narratives in the name of art.

While the Hong Kong government is currently funding new Art Tech initiatives, their interests lie in employing the arts and advanced technologies for their own branding initiatives as Asia's World City to present an image of modernity. While MetaObjects is not closed to receiving government grants, we feel the bureaucratic granting system in Hong Kong hinders rather than encourages creativity. By operating commercially, MetaObjects can be self-sustainable without being motivated by profit, so that we are able to continue to explore artistic projects with artists. While our role is hidden in the economies of art centered on artists, we value the process of collaboration and enabling the circulation of knowledge as we constantly renegotiate our role in the community, decentering the product and process of exchange within art markets.

Together, these cases present a set of examples of the ways in which commercial enterprises can be deployed in service to artistic practice. Such modes of thinking and practice are not defined by fixed roles, institutional practices, or disciplines, but rather these modes respond to and explore the possibilities that emerge in the present moment. Beyond the end goal of profit, commercial entities may allow the flow of resources to enable and support artists and others in the community in the process.

6

CONCLUSION: ARTISTIC PRACTICES IN PROCESS

This book was written as an effort to think through methods for sustaining artistic practices within a capitalist economy. The intention is not to present a complete picture of the field as it is, but rather to examine a range of possibilities for thinking and doing in the contemporary condition. The economy is not singular and monolithic, but rather consists of multiple and diverse situated practices that evolve over time. Throughout the book, I argue that creative economies are constituted via the dynamic relationships between the artists, galleries, corporations, and platforms that help bring artworks into existence. Artworks circulate in diverse contexts, such as in galleries, on media facades, on online platforms, or as NFTs. Through each of these different modes of circulation, the artwork accrues different meanings and values. This way of understanding artistic practice—as a dynamic, nonlinear process—suggests an ecological understanding of economies, focused on examining how practices change over time and in relationship to broader social, technological, economic, and cultural shifts. To better understand the notion of value in our contemporary cultural economies, there is a need to understand *for whom* and *in what ways* practices matter. By paying attention to artists and the economic realities that shape their work (a perspective often ignored by economists), we can gain a deeper understanding of the contemporary environment and ways to navigate it.

By considering art not as objects that can be owned, but as the result of dynamic sets of practices and relationships, we can begin to reimagine cultural economies around shared processes. To some extent, the hegemony of an art market focused on the buying and selling of material objects has blinded practitioners and scholars from taking seriously the different kinds of cultural economies for art that are already in existence. For instance, practitioners who prop up the market by reinforcing notions of authorship and uniqueness of art objects, as well as scholars who focus on a critique of the art market rather than identifying the diverse practices as artists negotiate a means to make, obscure the possibilities within a dominant market. As the market continues to adapt to capture new forms of art, new models and paradigms emerge. However, within an all-encompassing neoliberal environment, this book has followed a different set of possibilities. Rather than imposing values from without, I ask, how can we generate our own values and practices? Operating within the field dominated by corporate and financial interests may seem on the surface complicit with these larger systems. However, the practices discussed in each chapter offer possibilities for different conceptions and values of art: for example, understanding art as a variable object, valuing experimental and open-ended processes of creation, sharing knowledge and resources, and participating as part of a community.

Through the book, I have described contemporary artworks as distributed and variable objects, rather than simply scarce and unique objects. This demands that we, as scholars and practitioners, focus on the processes of making and circulating in order to expand our perspective of the art market. The practices I have covered in this book offer an iterative conception of art that exists as shared experiences and events, rather than as a unit of exchange. By examining circulation beyond the sale of an artwork, we can see how artworks manifest in different forms and contexts through various restagings. Artworks in this sense are temporal processes sustained in time, rather than discrete objects that can be owned or acquired. In order to foreground this conception of art, I use the term artistic *practices* rather than art *objects*. Artistic practices are open-ended and experimental; the process of creation is valued over the finished product. This focus on making turns our attention toward labor processes (that need to be properly remunerated) and the need to safeguard the time and space to experiment with technology. In the post-media condition, contemporary art is inherently collaborative and shifts away from notions of individual authorship. Organizations such as galleries, corporations, and institutional partners also contribute to the artistic process, as well as curators, technicians, fabricators, and studio assistants. Scholarship must acknowledge these shared processes as these social, technical, and economic environments shape the emergence of an artwork through the constraints and affordances inherent to the process of making.

Artworks are not produced in isolation, but through interconnectedness. There is a flow of knowledge between different sectors and disciplines to sustain the arts. Money initiates or enables the continuation of an artistic process, shifting away from profit as an end goal. Money can be channeled to sustain artistic practices or serve an artistic community. Correspondingly, there is value in long-term and sustained engagements with art and technology, beyond short-term gratification and spectacle. Furthermore, we should consider how to sustain long-term engagements with art and technology, rather than treating them as commodities or as added value for brands, such as when artworks are employed as corporate advertisements or in the branding of cities. These provisional conclusions aim to broaden inquiry into a diversity of practices that do not follow the chronology of the book, but rather draw together threads from each of the chapters to illuminate new perspectives.

PROCESSES OVER PRODUCTS

The artistic practices surveyed in this book are open-ended and experimental, valuing the process of creation over the finished product. Working with technology requires the time to hone new skills and experiment. Valuing the process of creation turns our attention to artists residencies, universities, and collaborative production spaces that also extend to organizational entities, makerspaces, and media labs[1] that can enable shared knowledge and resources, and open-ended processes of experimentation. Likewise, corporations are playing a larger role in the ecosystems of artists working with technology, where there are possibilities to design corporate collaborations that can better support artistic practices. However, as the case studies examined in this book indicate, we must consider how these collaborations can be designed to better support artistic practices by meeting the needs and interests of artists with mutual benefit to corporations.[2]

In chapter 1, I looked at the ways in which artists negotiate a means to make art by balancing between different forms of paid labor and often unpaid artistic labor. Within the artistic process, working with technology requires time to experiment and develop new skills. In the case of onformative, this process is integrated into the practice of the studio as "self-initiated projects." While they have found a unique model balancing commercial work and unpaid artistic work, it raises questions about how we can safeguard the time and space for knowledge sharing, and open-ended experimentation with technology. Through their artistic works, onformative has found clients who value their practice and allow them to experiment as part of their commercial work, carving out a practice between art, generative design, and technology.

The necessity to develop and maintain skills is viewed as a challenge by the artist Lorna Mills who has struggled to keep up with skills and changing software in her day job. Working in the technology or media sectors requires time spent on reskilling and upskilling that may not be remunerated. Yet this work remains vital for artists like Lorna Mills who sustained their artistic practice via work in other industries. In this sense, knowledge flows from other sectors to sustain the arts forming a larger conception of the cultural economy. For Tali Hinkis and Kyle Lapidus of LoVid, the university setting becomes important to sustain R&D. Through their work in psychology, LoVid's founders have established support for developing collaborations with scientific institutions and universities. While universities are also mobilizing to promote knowledge transfer, build digital literacy, and produce social impact, there are also initiatives that bring artists into academic institutions to conduct research.[3] Research is often open-ended and exploratory, providing spaces for artists to develop and test out ideas.

LoVid's practice has evolved over the years, their work evolving alongside the diverse opportunities they have made the most of, spanning grant applications, performing and touring, selling limited-edition scarves, presenting video installations and NFTs in commercial galleries. The means for sustaining their practice evolved alongside social, technological, and economic changes, where different income sources have shaped their workflow and artistic practice. They shifted to working more commercially as the market for digital works developed, and as they have exhausted the possibilities for grants. Working with commercial galleries and the art market reinforces value in unique objects. Practices in this sense are not static but evolve over an artist's career and acquire different meanings and forms as they engage with different economies.

In chapter 4, I discussed the role of the corporate sector in supporting artists through commissions and artist residencies that provide access to space and resources to produce work. At times, the latter may be open-ended, other times, artists may be expected to produce a work by the end of the residency, as is the case of the Facebook Artist in Residence Program, which functions more like a commission. The Thoughtworks Arts program, which ended in 2023, supported socially engaged projects with technology, providing space, resources, and staff to realize artists' projects. Thoughtworks Art-A-Hack™ and Hardware Hack Lab events facilitated open-ended experimentation with the community. While residency ceased after eight years, it raised important questions about how to sustain such collaborations and design them in the interests of artists.

Corporate patronage (or patronage in general) should not be viewed simply as a transaction but should be considered in ways that recognize how money initiates or enables the continuation of an artistic process. Desmond Leung, discussed in chapter 4, finds commissions highly valuable because they enable him to continue his practice for some time. His year-long collaboration with CHANEL shows how brands are becoming more attuned to the interests of artists, which include providing him public platforms to share his work and stability in funding. Additionally, Leung has developed long-term relationships with collectors who have commissioned him to create works. Beyond simply purchasing an artwork, commissions allow collectors to build closer relationships with artists by consulting with them during the production of new work. The opportunity the commission provides for furthering the artist's practice, and the interpersonal connections generated via these economic relationships, go beyond mere exchange. Profit is not thought of as an end goal, but rather a means to continue a creative process.

Money may also be channeled to contribute to building the artistic community, as the case of Xu Zhen demonstrates in chapter 5. Xu Zhen employs the brand and corporate entity both as art and intervention with contemporary systems of production. Through his various businesses and platforms like Art-Ba-Ba, MadeIn Company, and XU ZHEN®, he also creates discourse around art and hosts exhibitions by other artists, playing a key role in fostering the art community in Shanghai. As a successful artist and entrepreneur, Xu Zhen plays multiple roles, which at times blurs his intentions, but shows how the corporate entity may be mobilized to channel resources that also contribute to supporting other artists. Xu Zhen's practice is self-interested, but also performs as institutional critique revealing how money may be channeled for artistic purposes and ends, in the guise of a corporate enterprise.

ARTWORKS IN PERMUTATION

Contemporary artworks are distributed and variable objects rather than simply scarce and unique objects. In this way, they exist in permutation and iteration as shared experiences and events. Beyond ownership, licensing as rental contracts allows for artists to retain control over their artworks, so that they continue to earn from their artworks and participate in their circulation in future restagings. Licensing agreements could be approached creatively such as in practices of legal design, where the terms and conditions can be experimented with and where these contracts play a key role in constituting the artwork and ensuring appropriate remuneration of the artist.

As discussed in chapter 2, since the emergence of conceptual art, contemporary artworks often lack a fixed materiality. Conceptual artworks exist as installations and performances that can be restaged in future exhibitions, while with digital art, files need to be executed on a device in order to be experienced. The variable materiality of conceptual and digital artworks poses challenges for their sale on the art market. Working with Empty Gallery, Gork sells her sound installations as documentation, sets of materials, digital files, and a license agreement that stipulates how the work is to be displayed. In this way, licensing plays a larger role in the sale of conceptual and digital artworks, because the documentation and contract define what the artwork is, its use, and method of display. When considering licensing as rental contracts, as a method of circulation of artworks beyond ownership and sales of artwork, artists retain the rights and control over their work. Rather than treating artworks as finite objects that can be bought and sold, legal instruments such as licensing allow artworks to exist in a plurality of forms. Licensing is an under-regarded practice in the arts market, where the focus on selling obscures the potential to reorient around a rental economy. For conceptual artworks and media installations, the possibilities for restaging a work opens a labor process in which the artist installs artwork as a "service provision." Gork's sound installations manifest in different forms as site-specific installations that need to be "tuned" to their space, requiring her to be on site to install the work. By recentering the economies of art on circulation, rather than the abstract value of an object, artworks become shared processes rather than objects of ownership.

Artworks also circulate as images online, where for digital artworks, the images are not simply reproductions as photographs of original works, but the digital object is the artwork itself, where any copies of the file are virtually the same as the original. Regardless of whether the image is a reproduction or an original digital artwork, the circulation of art online contributes to our understanding and experience of art and its value as André Malraux's *musée imaginaire* (museum without walls) might suggest.[4] Malraux, whose book was published in 1949, could not comment on the internet, where these experiences of art within networked mass media extend far beyond the walls of a museum and contribute to our understanding of the work in the social imaginaries. The variable materialities of contemporary art and infinite reproducibility of digital art raise questions on whether the model of ownership of unique objects is still relevant for these art forms.

While Sedition (as discussed in chapter 3) attempts to enforce a value of scarcity of digital art through digital limited editions, the value of its visibility and circulation on social media is also undeniable. The desire to go viral becomes part of the attention economies creating another kind of value through mass recognition. While at times a work's free circulation online poses tensions with the economies of the art market, NFTs reinforce scarcity and ownership of digital objects as financial assets, allowing images to circulate freely and contributing financial value to the artwork as it goes viral. Participating in internet culture, the images exist in permutation as viral memes. The NFT market represents the extremes of the art market, reinforcing the logic of speculation, scarcity, and ownership. However, technologies can be put to different uses, where some practices are more supportive and others more exploitative of art and artists.

There is a value in long-term and sustained engagements with art and technology. However, with the advancement of technologies like blockchain and NFTs, our attentions have become short-circuited in the interest of short-term gains. At the same time, there is an intertwining with commercial interests, where art becomes blurred with commodities/advertisements, where licensing artworks for public displays often needs to appeal to wide audiences, often valuing spectacular displays. In corporate commissions such as Desmond Leung's collaboration with CHANEL, the arts are used to promote a product as added value to the brand. This creates a confusion between art and advertising, highlighting a need to preserve the spaces in which art can circulate and be appreciated as art. As video artworks are licensed for media facades normally used for advertising, there is ambiguity in the meaning and interpretation of the works. Curated displays like the M+ Facade experiment with different kinds of temporalities for art on public screens, where the displays are presented and treated as works of art. Allowing artworks to circulate in contexts in which they can be appreciated and valued as art can be a challenge as we also see commerce entering the museums through gift shops and corporate sponsorships. In other ways, a sustained engagement with technology suggests working closely with artists through knowledge sharing, which is intrinsic to the practice of MetaObjects. To take care of our collective psychology is to create not only sustained engagements with art beyond commodity, spectacles, and short-term profits, but also engaged processes of learning with and through technology.

COLLABORATIVE CULTURES

Contemporary art is inherently collaborative. Contemporary artists are no longer masters of their trade, but work across diverse media, such as conceptual art for which the ideas become more central to the work.

Working with technology also requires collaborating with others who have diverse skillsets, thereby extending artistic practice beyond notions of individual authorship. Organizations such as galleries, corporations, and institutional partners also contribute to the creative process. To acknowledge this condition in which artworks are created is to understand how contemporary art requires contribution from a wide range of partners including curators, other artists, producers, and fabricators.

As discussed in chapter 2, gallerists and curators also play a role in the artistic process when they stage a work in an exhibition space, or invent methods for selling conceptual, digital, or ephemeral art forms in the case of TRANSFER and Empty Gallery. To allow artworks to exist in permutation is to acknowledge the creative work of curators involved in restaging an artwork, where it undergoes a modification as it is translated into a new space (for instance, TRANSFER's interpretation of VR artworks into immersive three-channel installations with the TRANSFER Download format). Considering variations in art allows culture and creativity to thrive through the multiple forms and approaches of artworks, beyond notions of individual authorship. It becomes possible to consider exhibitions as versions or instances of an artwork that build upon the past in future iterations.[5] This type of versioning has been discussed in the field of conservation, where the conservator's role in restoring the artwork also contributes to the creation of a new version of it.[6] Conceptual and digital artworks have a "temporal materiality" that changes and evolves in future instantiations and variations.[7] The focus is less on a fixed material object frozen in time, but rather on artworks as concepts that can be transposed into different forms. These concepts belong less to individual creators but rather are sustained through our shared practices and engagements with the artworks (as artists, audiences, conservators, curators, researchers, or others). Mechanisms for versioning could be developed that are more representative of how culture actually circulates and exists in the world. Different versions or iterations of artworks could potentially be recorded on the blockchain as a technology that enables a public ledger of changes. Artworks in this sense are living, active processes through shared experiences.

Chapter 5 brings the discussion of how artists employ commercial entities to facilitate collaborative production. Working as a collective, studio, or commercial entity obscures individual identity under a common name, as we see in the examples of LoVid, onformative, MadeIn Company, and teamLab. As a large-scale collective who have also worked in commercial production to sustain their artistic interests, team Lab values a fluid and intuitive process in their work. Working in interdisciplinary teams, without hierarchies of roles and tasks, allows for ideas to emerge organically as conversations between members. The value of open-ended experimentation contrasts with the need to produce output and generate revenue, with economic constraints shaping the work. By studying the conditions that bring artworks into existence, we gain a broader understanding of cultural economies and the complex processes behind the creation of artworks. To register a company also has affordances in enabling collaborative forms of work, beyond the capacities of an individual author, where there are possibilities to work at larger scales. At the same time, experiences become commodities beyond objects of individual authorship as the economy evolves alongside artistic practices.

As discussed in chapter 5, MetaObjects seeks to support engagements with technology by helping bridge gaps in knowledge. We co-learn with artists and partners to develop a deeper and sustained engagement with advanced technologies, while developing mutually beneficial trust-based collaborations through the sharing of knowledge and resources, such as with artist Samson Young and 3D printing. This suggests ways studios and organizations could support artistic practices with technology in open circuits of knowledge production to wider audiences to form collaborative culture.

To elaborate on a speculative project that proposes to rethink cultural economies around collaboration, I briefly discussed *Ensembl*,[8] a conceptual prototype designed as a decentralized autonomous organization (DAO) (see figure 6.1). Conceived by Samson Young with anthropologist Massimiliano Mollona and MetaObjects, the project fosters the self-organization and management of artistic collaborations. Young developed this concept based on his own practice as a composer and also a contemporary artist working across diverse media, collaborating with many others to produce works. Inspired by the concept of the open musical score—one that can be freely interpreted and improvised by performers, with each performance a unique iteration of the work, *Ensembl*

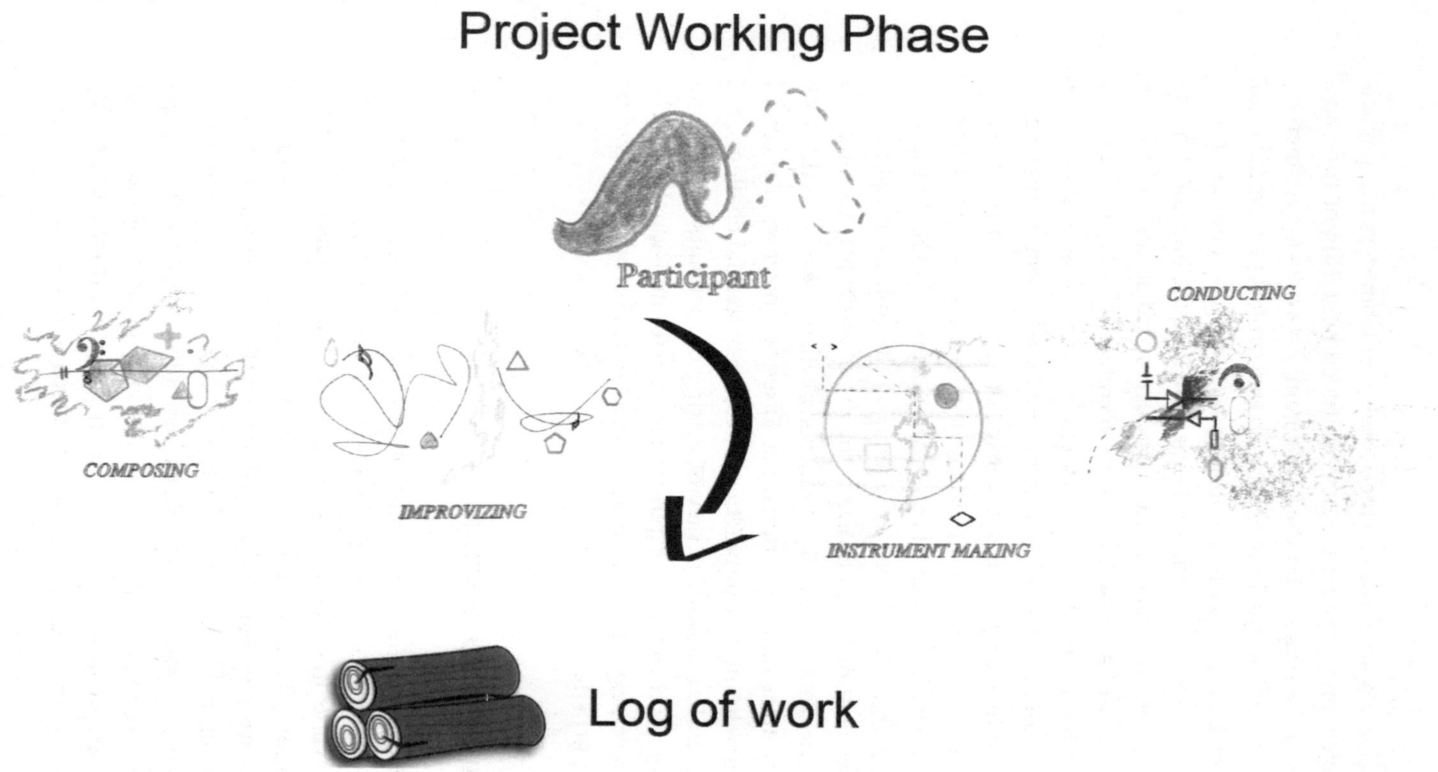

6.1

Ensembl, decentralized autonomous organization, concept diagram with drawings by Samson Young and MetaObjects, 2021.

intended to create a platform in which diverse collaborators can participate in a project and create a log of work (documentation of time and contribution to the project) on the blockchain. Artworks are defined by the project (rather than the individuals), so that project participants can also change over time as members join or leave the project and can "fork"[9] collaborations with other members. Participants can include not only artists and performers, but also curators, producers, and designers involved in staging the work. A platform is used to collectively vote on who can join; the distribution of shares to participants according to their stake in the project; and the use of resources, facilitating decentralized governance. Individual participants can leave the project and return their shares, for which they receive funds from the group. *Ensembl* imagines a cultural economy in which artists and participants are brought together for a project decentering the artist to focus on the collaborative process, with artworks continuing to evolve through subsequent iterations and participants. Artworks are not finite objects but instead evolve as the work is restaged in subsequent iterations. The *Ensembl* project was conceived only speculatively and not in practice. There are potential challenges of self-governance in the bureaucracy of getting participants to vote and possibilities for individuals to exploit the system for individual gain. The project, however, explores possibilities for a cultural economy based on collaborative artistic production.

SHIFTING ROLES, FLUID IDENTITIES

While this book has focused on the practices of artist practitioners, it presents an insider's view of what takes place behind the scenes when bringing artworks into the world. It calls for a wider perspective on cultural economies, beyond consumer-driven supply and demand. One thinks about art in process in terms of not only the processes of creation and circulation, but also how audiences engage with art. While this is not discussed at length in this book, with socially engaged and participatory art practices today,[10] audiences also become creators of the artwork beyond the authority of artist, which is an area for further research. We also see the emerging role of AI and other technologies that will impact how artworks are created in the future. Artists (e.g., onformative) are developing new workflows to experiment with generative AI in their creative process.[11] Discussions dominated by antagonistic views of technology replacing humans miss the point: we are already immersed in technologies, and emerging forms can enhance the creative possibilities as prosthetics to the human imagination.[12] Ideas around *digital rewilding* connect the development of technology to the natural evolutions of the biosphere rather than to a monoculture of an extractive industry.[13]

As avenues for further inquiry, my work with Yuk Hui and the Research Network of Philosophy and Technology engages in philosophical discussions about how we might diverge from notions of technological progress. Hui's concept of *cosmotechnics* as "the unification of the cosmos and the moral through technical activities, whether craft-making or art-making considers the importance of local and indigenous knowledges that may inform the development of technology."[14] He explores concepts from Chinese philosophy that inform the development of art and technology with applications across wider society.[15] His work points toward other possible technological futures.

As I complete this book, I am entering a new phase in my professional practice as an academic. My work in the field has informed my view of industry, which, correspondingly, has informed my approach to research from within the sectors described in these chapters. This research was a means to come to terms with my own practice and role in cultural economies, and to articulate the nature of my relationships with the artists I have encountered along the way. While most research about art analyzes artworks, my focus has been on the ecosystems enable artworks to exist—a process in which I am also implicated as a cultural worker through my work at Sedition and then with MetaObjects. While I do not consider myself an artist, I have studied art and have worked closely with artists and thus view every aspect of life through an artistic lens, even the mundane daily practices of administration, contracts, marketing, and management. This includes academic research, since research strives to introduce new ways of thinking and seeing the world. At the same time, I also treat research and learning as an ongoing process, where ideas and concepts are continually rethought and reiterated in every paper, book, or presentation. Repetition is always iterative and never truly the same;

it yields small differences each time, which can initiate a new thought or findings in the process. There is a need to embrace art and research as part of the eternal change and flow of life in connection with nature. By continually challenging our roles and boundaries we can create a fluid connection with our work and deepen our engagement in society through repetition and practice.

The role of the cultural researcher is to apply professional skills to articulate concrete issues and problems in the complexity and situatedness of social conditions.[16] It is through this book and through direct experiences with artists and organizations that I view my work in cultural research as an opportunity to play a role both inside and outside academia. There is an observable need for cultural researchers to engage within the contemporary cultural economies and conditions of labor. To bridge these domains is to develop a practice wherein research can have impact in the world, but also provides me with a more intimate understanding of the field as a researcher, where real-world problems are brought into the academic realm. This exchange serves the purpose of destabilizing assumptions within canons of critique and policy while also developing and actualizing new, emerging possibilities within contemporary cultural economies. Whether my role constitutes a curator, scholar, researcher, writer, or other, identities are also fluid and open to exceed their roles in practice, where practice is viewed not as it is, but as what it could become.

NOTES

INTRODUCTION

1. Homo economicus is the notion of the ideal man who was the subject of the Enlightenment in the emergence of humanism premised on scientific innovation and the progress of knowledge. Originating in the nineteenth and twentieth centuries the term was used by economists like John Stuart Mill. See John Stuart Mill, *Principles of Political Economy*, ed. J. Laurence Laughlin (New York: D. Appleton, 1884).
2. Matthew Fuller and Olga Goriunova, *Bleak Joys: Aesthetics of Ecology and Impossibility*, vol. 53, Posthumanities (Minneapolis: University of Minnesota Press, 2019), 148.
3. Ecology has been addressed in a number of disciplines across biology, media studies and communications, business, anthropology, and sociology. It has also been applied to museum studies; on thinking of museums as ecosystems, see Amalia Sabiescu and Katerina Charatzopoulou, "The Museum as Ecosystem and Museums in Learning Ecosystems," in *Museum Experience Design: Crowds, Ecosystems, and Novel Technologies*, ed. Arnold Vermeeren, Licia Calvi, and Amalia Sabiescu. (Switzerland: Springer International Publishing AG, 2018), 325–345.
4. Anthropologist Julian Steward uses the term *cultural ecology* to refer to how humans and specific cultural communities adapt to the natural environment. See Julian Steward, "The Concept and Method of Cultural Ecology," in *The Environment in Anthropology: A Reader in Ecology, Culture, and Sustainable Living*, ed. Nora Haenn and Richard Wils (New York: New York University Press, 2020), 12–17. However, in this book I consider the environment to be both natural and artificial, where ecology is used more as an analytic to look not at people but at practices and processes that enable artwork to exist.
5. Systems theory and cybernetics are interdisciplinary fields connecting biological and technological systems into interconnected wholes: rather than thinking of the distinctions between humans (living) and machines (nonliving), the focus is on understanding how they evolve together in constant communication with each other. For further reading, see Francisco Miranda, *Systems Theory: Perspectives, Applications and Developments*, Systems Science series (New York: Nova Publishers, 2014).
6. Scholars such as Guy Standing, Angela McRobbie, Mark Banks, Rosalind Gill and Stephanie Taylor, Maurizio Lazzarato, Isabell Lorey, and Andrew Ross have written extensively on labor conditions in the creative economy and technology industry in post-industrial society.

7. Michael Siciliano describes how creative labor presents a double-edged sword where there is a sense of ambivalence in the form of finding excitement in one's work while also experiencing precarity and alienation from one's work. Workers engage in a form of self-exploitation in the pursuit of doing work that is creative and enjoyable. See Michael L. Siciliano, *Creative Control: The Ambivalence of Work in the Culture Industries* (New York: Columbia University Press, 2021); Miya Tokumitsu, *Do What You Love: And Other Lies About Success and Happiness* (New York: Regan Arts, 2015).
8. Silvio Lorusso, *Entreprecariat: Everyone Is an Entrepreneur. Nobody Is Safe* (Eindhoven, NL: Onomatopee, 2019).
9. Zygmunt Bauman, *Liquid Modernity* (Cambridge, UK: Polity Press, 2000), viii.
10. Platform cooperativism employs digital tools to enable cooperative forms of organizations. It supports models of shared ownership through decentralized forms of management and development of platforms to challenge monopolies on digital platforms by large corporations, such as Google and Facebook. While many of these platforms may function on a small scale, they become difficult to scale and maintain, making it hard to compete with the dominance of multinationals that have the resources to develop sophisticated systems. See Trebor Scholz and Nathan Schneider, *Ours to Hack and to Own: The Rise of Platform Cooperativism, A New Vision for the Future of Work and a Fairer Internet*, ed. Trebor Scholz and Nathan Schneider (New York: OR Books, 2016), https://doi.org/10.2307/j.ctv62hfq7. Social enterprises justify commercial gain for social good as an alternative to pure market economies. See Grace McQuilten and Anthony White, *Art as Enterprise: Social and Economic Engagement in Contemporary Art* (London; New York: I. B. Tauris & Co. Ltd., 2016). On the peer-to-peer model, Michel Bauwens, founder of the P2P Foundation, supports and promotes open source and commons-based approaches to considering the development of technology and society. See Michel Bauwens, Vasilis Kostakis, and Alex Pazaitis, *Peer to Peer: The Commons Manifesto* (London: University of Westminster Press, 2019).
11. Gregory Sholette, *Dark Matter: Art and Politics in the Age of Enterprise Culture* (London: Pluto Press, 2011); emphasis added.
12. For further reading on the co-optation of critique by the market, see Ashley L. Wong, "Artists in the Creative Economy: Inoperative Modes of Resistance," *A Peer-Reviewed Journal About* 7, no. 1 (2018): Research Values, https://doi.org/10.7146/aprja.v7i1.116059.
13. Andrew Barry and Don Slater, "Introduction: The Technological Economy," *Economy and Society* 31, no. 2 (2002): 175–193, https://doi.org/10.1080/03085140220123117.
14. Neil De Marchi and Hans J. Van Miegroet, "The History of Art Markets," in *Handbook of the Economics of Art and Culture*, ed. Victor A. Ginsburgh and David Throsby (Amsterdam: Elsevier B.V., 2006), 71.
15. In May 2021, I presented a paper titled "Temporalization in Art, Digital Cultures and Institutions" in the Collecting Art and Exhibiting Cultures in Asia

Conference at Lingnan University, Hong Kong. The papers touch upon a temporal understanding of art and artistic practices in contrast to modern conceptions of art.

16. According to philosophers Yuk Hui, François Jullien, and Byung-Chul Han, Chinese conceptions of art are founded in the changing variables of life, rather than fixed entities and stable objects. See Yuk Hui, *Art and Cosmotechnics* (Minneapolis: University of Minnesota Press, 2020); François Jullien, *From Being to Living: A Euro-Chinese Lexicon of Thought*, trans. Michael Richardson and Krzysztof Fijalkowski (London: SAGE Publications Ltd, 2020); Byung-Chul Han, *Shanzhai: Deconstruction in Chinese*, trans. Philippa Hurd (Cambridge, MA: MIT Press, 2017).

17. Han, *Shanzhai*, 4.

18. See https://www.loudspkr.org, an independent sound and experimental music platform that was active from around 2005 to 2012.

19. Through my work with DOXA (www.doxacollective.org), a collective I cofounded with Yuk Hui from around 2010 to 2014, we sought to bring together artists, activists, and professionals to address issues including art's role in gentrification, funding cuts to the arts and education sectors, precarity and flexibilization of the labor market, and efforts to find collaborative ways of organizing culture. DOXA published, participated in conferences, and organized events in London and Hong Kong, but as a form of independent organization without a formal structure, it became difficult to sustain when there was a need to develop new strategies in relation to the current political and economic environment.

20. See *Sound in Context* (2009), https://vimeo.com/6033559, an early documentary I produced with Sound and Music in the UK, exploring the practice of sound in the contemporary art world.

21. Notable Canadian philosopher Marshall McLuhan coined the phrase "the medium is the message": the medium (or technology) contains signifiers and serves as content in how it transforms how we receive and process information as a society, thereby having an effect on how the message or content is delivered. See Marshall McLuhan, *Understanding Media: The Extensions of Man* (Cambridge, MA: MIT Press, 1994).

22. Christiane Paul, *New Media in the White Cube and Beyond: Curatorial Models for Digital Art* (Berkeley: University of California Press, 2008), 2.

23. See https://www.seditionart.com.

24. In his essay "Why Has Critique Run Out of Steam?" Bruno Latour sees critique as the act of subverting power structures, and revealing dark truths about our social reality as a habit of academic culture. A mode of critique loses its meaning and value when practiced in a culture of critique for the sake of critique. Latour attempts to reframe the role of the critic in the conclusion of his paper: "The critic is not the one who debunks, but the one who assembles. The critic is not the one who lifts the rugs from under the feet of the naïve believers, but the one who offers the participants arenas in which to gather. The critic is not the

one who alternates haphazardly between antifetishism and positivism like the drunk iconoclast drawn by Goya, but the one for whom, if something is constructed, then it means it is fragile and thus in great need of care and caution." By continually employing critique against critique itself, Latour seeks to find a mode of practice that doesn't create polarizing and dichotomous positions, but rather constructively brings people together to generate real change. It does not involve defining the moment in the negative but rather seeks to build platforms to enable the emergence of new collective imaginaries. See Bruno Latour, "Why Has Critique Run out of Steam? From Matters of Fact to Matters of Concern," *Critical Inquiry* 30, no. 2 (2004): 225–248.

25. Rosi Braidotti, "Nomadic Ethics," *Deleuze Studies* 7, no. 3 (2013): 343.

26. Xavier Greffe, *The Artist–Enterprise in the Digital Age* (Tokyo: Springer Japan, 2017); David Throsby, *Economics and Culture* (Cambridge, UK: Cambridge University Press, 2001); David Throsby, "The Production and Consumption of the Arts: A View of Cultural Economics," *Journal of Economic Literature* 32, no. 1 (1994), http://www.jstor.org/stable/2728421.

27. Dave Beech, *Art and Value: Art's Economic Exceptionalism in Classical, Neoclassical and Marxist Economics* (Boston: BRILL, 2015).

28. The notion of "what works" is drawn from Pragmatism, a philosophical movement that emerged in the late 1800s, led by Charles Sanders Peirce, William James, and John Dewey. The method of "what works" intends to employ concepts as a means of problem-solving and usefulness. Pragmatists sought to bring together the divide between subject/object and mind/body, proposing that human experience is a combination of both thoughts and sense perceptions of events as temporal processes. It favors knowledge drawn from experience as an a posteriori (as opposed to an a priori) understanding of the world. Plato and Aristotle first created a distinction between a theory of the mind as a deductive a priori thinking, which is in opposition to inductive, practical, a posteriori "thinking of the body" favored by the pragmatists and empiricists. Kant's transcendental idealism sees experience and sensation as playing a key role in the cognitive faculty of reason. While placing emphasis on ways of knowing a priori, Kant claims that our knowing must be confirmed a posteriori as a ground to knowledge. While pragmatism emphasizes a posteriori way of knowing through experience and sensation, it allows that both faculties operate together in a process of thinking-feeling. Pragmatism, in contrast to Kant, privileges knowledge not drawn from pre-existing concepts, but rather through experiences of a phenomenon.

29. Michel de Certeau, *The Practice of Everyday Life*, trans. Steven Rendall (Berkeley: University of California Press, 1984).

30. De Certeau, *The Practice of Everyday Life*, 19–30.

31. American economist Alan Greenspan used the term "irrational exuberance" during a speech in 1996 regarding the dot-com boom when he was the chair of the Federal Reserve Board in the United States. The term was later used for the title of Nobel Laureate Robert J. Shiller's book *Irrational Exuberance* (2000), referring

to different financial speculative bubbles. See Robert J. Shiller, *Irrational Exuberance* (Princeton, NJ: Princeton University Press, 2000).

32. *No Logo* has been a seminal book in outlining the globalization process in the late 1990s, the rise of multinational companies, and the exploitation of labor in the global south. See Naomi Klein, *No Logo: Taking Aim at the Brand Bullies* (New York: Picador, 2000).

33. This article describes the ongoing arts funding budget cuts in the UK and the impact on organizations and institutions across the sector. See Charlotte Higgins, "Arts Funding in England Is a Thin Gruel That Organizations Are Forced to Beg For," *The Guardian*, September 2, 2022, https://www.theguardian.com/commentisfree/2022/sep/02/arts-funding-england-government-levelling-up.

34. See DesignSingapore Council, "Singapore, UNESCO Creative City of Design," accessed September 27, 2024, https://www.designsingapore.org/about-us/unesco-creative-city-of-design.html.

35. See UNSECO, "Changsha," Creative Cities Network, accessed September 27, 2024, https://www.unesco.org/en/creative-cities/changsha.

36. See The Government of the Hong Kong Special Administrative Region, "LCQ6: Art Tech," Press Releases, February 24, 2021, https://www.info.gov.hk/gia/general/202102/24/P2021022400540.htm.

37. These books discuss the relationship between art and commerce in neoliberal cultures. The books focus more on contemporary art rather than artists working with technology. Chin-tao Wu, *Privatising Culture: Corporate Art Intervention since the 1980s* (London: Verso, 2002); Isabelle Graw, *High Price: Art Between the Market and Celebrity Culture* (Berlin: Sternberg Press, 2009); Martha Buskirk, *Creative Enterprise: Contemporary Art between Museum and Marketplace*, ed. Francisco J. Ricardo (New York: Continuum International Publishing Group, 2012).

38. This book describes how the digital economy has transformed the ways in which artists make art and sustain their practices in an age when it seems everyone can be an artist by promoting their work online. William Deresiewicz, *The Death of the Artist: How Creators Are Struggling to Survive in the Age of Billionaires and Big Tech* (New York: Henry Holt and Co., 2020).

39. Edward A. Shanken, "Contemporary Art and New Media: Digital Divide or Hybrid Discourse," in *A Companion to Digital Art*, ed. Christiane Paul, Blackwell Companions to Art History (Chichester: John Wiley & Sons, 2016), 80.

40. Mark Tribe, Reena Jana, and Uta Grosenick, eds., *New Media Art* (Cologne: Taschen, 2006), 21.

41. Further details can be found in Ashley L. Wong, "Comment se confronter au marché: les nouveaux médias face au marché de l'art," *Marges*, no. 28 (2019), https://doi.org/https://doi.org/10.4000/marges.1760.

42. Marisa Olson, "Postinternet: Art after the Internet," *Foam Magazine*, no. 29 (2011): 59–63; Artie Vierkant, "The Image Object Post-Internet," 2010, http://jstchillin.org/artie/pdf/The_Image_Object_Post-Internet_a4.pdf.

43. Drawing from Julie Graham and Katherine Gibson's (aka J. K. Gibson-Graham) notion of "diverse economies," economies are performatively enacted in a process of doing thinking, where artists may seek to "cultivate themselves as ethical subjects of economic possibility." Diverse economies take a postcapitalist perspective to explore the economies of art and technology as experimental, performative, and open to possibilities. This provides a mapping of diverging and proliferating economic practices in a complex field. Gibson-Graham seeks to navigate opportunities, understand challenges, and find ways to support and elevate shared values. Grounded in everyday practices and experiences of artists and practitioners, this research aims to open up "opportunities for elaborating a radically heterogeneous economy and theorizing economic dynamics that foster and strengthen different economies." See J. K Gibson-Graham, "Diverse Economies: Performative Practices for 'Other Worlds,'" *Progress in Human Geography* 32, no. 5 (2008): 618, https://doi.org/10.1177/0309132508090821.

44. Benjamin Lee and Edward LiPuma, "Cultures of Circulation: The Imaginations of Modernity," *Public Culture* 14, no. 1 (2002): 192.

45. For anthropologist Arjun Appadurai, all objects, including artworks, are social *things* (rather than fixed and finite objects), where in a situation of transaction and exchange, such as selling an artwork in a gallery or art fair, the art objects become commodities as one phase of their existence. In another phase of their existence, they may become objects held in a museum collection and recognized for their social and cultural value. In their movement through different systems, art objects are constituted in their relations. See Arjun Appadurai, *The Social Life of Things: Commodities in Cultural Perspective* (Cambridge, UK: Cambridge University Press, 1986), 15.

46. Isabelle Stengers, "Introductory Notes on an Ecology of Practices," *Cultural Studies Review* 11, no. 1 (2005): 195.

47. The examples discussed do not include those artists who are privileged and independently wealthy and free to pursue art without the concerns of making a living. The cases derive from artists who are required to support themselves and their practices as part of the middle class.

48. See Jagmeet Singh, "Thoughtworks Lays Off around 500 Employees amid Ongoing Slowdown," *TechCrunch*, March 1, 2023, https://techcrunch.com/2023/03/01/Thoughtworks-layoffs-economic-slowdown/.

49. Dilip Parameshwar Gaonkar and Elizabeth A. Povinelli, "Technologies of Public Forms: Circulation, Transfiguration, Recognition," *Public Culture* 15, no. 3 (2003): 385–398.

CHAPTER 1

1. Niamh Crawford and Sabina Dewfield, *A Design Sprint for the Creative Industries Sector Vision: Maximising the Spillover Value of the Creative Industries to the Wider*

Economy (London: Design Council UK, 2022), https://assets.publishing.service.gov.uk/media/62e10b63e90e0766b251ab73/Creative_Industries_Sector_Vision_Report_FINAL.pdf.

2. James J. Gilson, *The Ecological Approach to Visual Perception* (New York: Psychology Press, 2015), 119.
3. Lorna Mills, interview by Ashley L. Wong, May 3, 2019.
4. Bernard Stiegler, *For a New Critique of Political Economy* (Cambridge, UK: Polity Press, 2010), 37.
5. Bernard Stiegler, *What Makes Life Worth Living: On Pharmacology*, trans. Daniel Ross (Cambridge, UK: Polity Press, 2013), 31.
6. Karen Barad's onto-epistemological perspective decenters the human within complex relationships that are conditioned by the environment. Barad explains: "Parts of the world are always intra-acting with other parts of the world, and it is through specific intra-actions that a differential sense of being—with boundaries, properties, cause, and effect—is enacted in the ongoing ebb and flow of agency. There are no preexisting, separately determinate entities called 'humans' that are either detached spectators or necessary components of all intra-actions. Rather, to the extent that 'humans' emerge as having a role to play in the constitution of specific phenomena, they do so as part of the larger material configuration, or rather the ongoing reconfiguring, of the world." The social and material are always entangled where and when meaning and knowledge emerge from intra-actions of humans and nonhumans. It is through this emergent practice of intra-acting entities that economies are understood, which acknowledges the world as constantly in flux. See Karen Barad, *Meeting the Universe Halfway: Quantum Physics and the Entanglement of Matter and Meaning* (Durham, NC: Duke University Press, 2007), 338.
7. Viviana A. Rotman Zelizer, *Economic Lives: How Culture Shapes the Economy* (Princeton, NJ: Princeton University Press, 2011), 5.
8. Alison Gerber, *The Work of Art: Value in Creative Careers* (Palo Alto, CA: Stanford University Press, 2017), 26.
9. Chalmers Arts Fellowships, provided by the Ontario Arts Council, provide grants from C$30,000–$50,000 for one year for artists with at least ten years of professional experience. See https://www.arts.on.ca/grants/chalmers-arts-fellowships.
10. Merja Heikkinen, *The Nordic Model for Supporting Artists* (Helsinki: Arts Council of Finland, 2003), 18. https://www.taike.fi/en/file-download/download/public/235.
11. Sissel M. Bergh, "Notes on Artists, Workers and Cooperation in Norway," *Art Production in Restriction: Possibilities of Transformative Art Production and Coalition-Building*, 2015, http://transformativeartproduction.net/notes-on-artists-workers-and-cooperation-in-norway/.
12. See https://www.hkadc.org.hk/?p=3184&lang=en.
13. See https://creative-capital.org.

14. Cedric Kiefer, interview by Ashley L. Wong, May 31, 2019.

15. We can relate these struggles to Silvia Federici's *Wages for Housework* campaign (1972), whose participants sought payment for forms of unpaid reproductive labor such as housework and childcare. Artistic labor and education are also often unpaid forms of labor or "free labor" in Marxist and autonomist worker's movements, but also in new forms of digital labor. See Trebor Scholz, *Uberworked and Underpaid* (Oxford: Polity Press, 2016); Trebor Scholz, ed., *Digital Labour: The Internet as Playground and Factory* (New York: Routledge, 2012).; Christian Fuchs, "The Digital Labour Theory of Value and Karl Marx in the Age of Facebook, YouTube, Twitter, and Weibo," in *Reconsidering Value and Labour in the Digital Age*, ed. Eran Fisher and Christian Fuchs, Dynamics of Virtual Work series (Berlin: Springer, 2015), 26–41; Tiziana Terranova, "Free Labor: Producing Culture for the Digital Economy," *Social Text* 18, no. 2 (2000), https://doi.org/10.1215/01642472-18-2_63-33.

16. Economist Gary S. Becker developed studies of *human capital* as the investments on the individual such as education and training. Humans are seen as a resource to be made productive in the economy, just as investing in machinery or pieces of equipment. See Gary S. Becker, *Human Capital: A Theoretical and Empirical Analysis, with Special Reference to Education*, 3rd ed. (Chicago: University of Chicago Press, 1993).

17. Kiefer, interview.

18. Kiefer, interview.

19. FIELD, a creative, design and innovation studio based in London, was founded in 2009 by Marcus Wendt and Vera-Maria Glahn. See https://www.field.io. fuse* is a studio based in Modena, Italy exploring the intersections of art and science founded in 2007. See https://www.fuseworks.it. Zeitguised is a digital art and design studio based in Berlin, founded by Jamie Raap and Henrik Mauler in 2001. See https://www.zeitguised.com.

20. See https://zeitguised.studio and https://fyihenriksson.com, and formerly foam Studio.

21. Kiefer, interview.

22. The Staatliches Bauhaus was an art school active from 1919–1933 founded by Walter Gropius in Weimar, Germany. The school sought to bring together craft and fine arts, merging art with design and functional mass consumer objects. It became a movement that introduced artistic sensibilities into practices of graphic design, printmaking, advertising, product design, interior design, and architecture inspired by modernism. Gropius's notion of the *gesamtkunstwerk* as the "total work of art" brought all the art forms together, where art and aesthetics were applied to considerations of all aspects of daily life. Ushering in the modern age of design, Bauhaus reconciled dichotomies between mass production and high art, fine arts and crafts, while navigating tensions between form and function and embracing new industrial materials and production techniques. Bauhaus embraced collaboration across disciplines from print and architecture

to product design creating an equality among disciplines. It was a response to technologies of the times that created a new aesthetic for the industrial age.

23. Aristotle's concept of *hylemorphism* creates a separation between form and matter as constituting the substance of a thing, whereas for Simondon, it is a dynamism of individuation or becoming: beyond a dualism of form and matter, it is inherent in the material processes. See Simon Mills, *Gilbert Simondon: Information, Technology and Media* (Lanham, MD: Rowman & Littlefield International, 2016), 11–12.

24. Kiefer, interview.

25. Tali Hinkis, *What It Really Means to Be A Mid-Career Artist: A Talk with LoViD's Tali Hinkis*, podcast audio, Explain Me, 2018, http://artfcity.com/2018/08/21/explain-me-what-it-really-means-to-be-a-mid-career-artist-a-talk-with-lovids-tali-hinkis/.

26. Lars Jan, an artist I met in Los Angeles, remarked on the challenges of being a mid-career artist. He feels he has reached a limit in his career where he is unable to grow or sustain the scale of his practice, particularly at a stage in his life where he also has to support his family and his collaborators. He teaches drama at CalArts as a stable form of income and works with large-scale performances and emerging technologies.

27. Hinkis, *What It Really Means.*

28. See LoVid, "Telephone Rewired," accessed September 27, 2024, https://www.lovid.org/works/telephone_rewired/.

29. See section toward the bottom of the page on "LoVid (Tali Hinkis & Kyle Lapidus) & Sean Montgomery" from Harvestworks, "Creativity+Technology=Enterprise Residency," accessed September 27, 2024, https://www.harvestworks.org/creativity-technology-enterprise-residency/.

30. Hinkis, *What It Really Means.*

31. Hinkis, *What It Really Means.*

32. Groups like W.A.G.E and the Precarious Workers Brigade fight against forms of "free labor" and exploitation of artistic labor in the arts. While there continues to be a need to fight exploitation by institutions and the industry, this book does not begin with a critique, but rather seeks to find a constructive and affirmative approach to developing sustainable economies for art and technology.

33. Tali Hinkis, interview by Ashley L. Wong, May 20, 2019.

34. Marcel Mauss, *The Gift: The Form and Reason for Exchange in Archaic Societies*, ed. Mary Douglas and W. D. Halls (London: Routledge, 2002).

35. Hinkis, interview, May 20, 2019.

36. Hans Abbing, *Why Are Artists Poor? The Exceptional Economy of the Arts* (Amsterdam: Amsterdam University Press, 2002), 81.

37. The work was presented in LoVid's first solo exhibition at Southfirst Gallery in Brooklyn, New York, in 2003. The work was presented as an audiovisual performance and as a video installation (without sound) in the gallery. See http://www.southfirst.org/PR%20LOVID%205-6%202003.htm.

38. I have previously written about the challenges of participating in independent and DIY cultures, both representing an ideology that was considered empowering in the 1980s and 1990s, but became increasingly subsumed by the neoliberal culture. See Ashley L. Wong, "Work in the Creative Economy: Living Contradictions Between the Market and Creative Collaboration," in *Collaborative Production in the Creative Industries*, ed. James Graham and Alessandro Gandini (London: University of Westminster Press, 2017).
39. Dale Dougherty, "The Maker Movement," *Innovations* 7, no. 3 (2012): 12.
40. See https://www.postmastersart.com/archive/lovid22/lovid22.html.
41. See https://whitney.org/collection/works/66845.
42. Gilles Deleuze, *Bergsonism*, trans. Hugh Tomlinson and Barbara Habberjam (New York: Zone Books, 1991), 31–32.

CHAPTER 2

1. Lucy R. Lippard, *Six Years: The Dematerialization of the Art Object from 1966 to 1972*, ed. Lucy R. Lippard (Los Angeles: University of California Press, [1973] 1997), 5.
2. Rosalind Krauss, *A Voyage on Art in the Age of the North Sea: Post-Medium Condition* (New York: Thames & Hudson, 1999), 7.
3. Peter Weibel, "The Post-Media Condition," Mute, March 19, 2012, http://www.metamute.org/editorial/lab/post-media-condition.
4. Lev Manovich, "Post-Media Aesthetics," 2001, http://manovich.net/index.php/projects/post-media-aesthetics.
5. Yoko Ono, *Instruction Paintings* (New York: Weatherhill, 1995).
6. Yuk Hui, "What Is a Digital Object?," *Metaphilosophy* 43, no. 4 (2012): 394, https://doi.org/10.1111/j.1467-9973.2012.01761.x.
7. William Mitchell draws on the writings of philosopher Nelson Goodman in *Languages of Art: An Approach to a Theory of Symbols* (1968), in which Mitchell describes the difference between a pencil sketch as a one-stage process, and music as a two-stage process with the score and performance. See William J. Mitchell, *The Reconfigured Eye: Visual Truth in the Post-Photographic Era* (Cambridge, MA: MIT Press, 1992), 50–51.
8. Yuk Hui, *On the Existence of Digital Objects*, (Minneapolis: University of Minnesota Press, 2016), 141.
9. Sections of this text are also discussed in my chapter: Ashley L. Wong, "Beyond Ownership: Sustaining Art as Practices and Processes," forthcoming in *Curating Superintelligences: A Reader on AI and Future Curating*, DATA browser 10, ed. Joasia Krysa and Magdalena Tyżlik-Carver (London: Open Humanities Press, 2024).
10. Edward A. Shanken, "Art in the Information Age: Technology and Conceptual Art," *Leonardo* 35, no. 4 (2002): 437.

11. Melissa Gronlund, *Contemporary Art and Digital Culture* (Abingdon, UK: Routledge, 2017), 61.

12. The term "new media art" was often used to describe artworks engaging with new technologies. However, the terminology of "new" became problematic as technologies were no longer considered new. Media artists wanted to resist their practices being defined by the medium and to be recognized and validated as contemporary artists in general. At the same time, there continues to be a digital divide where, at times, artists working with technology continue to operate on the margins of the contemporary art world. For further reading on the relationship of media art to the art market, see Wong, "Comment se confronter au marché."

13. Florian Cramer points out that the word "digital" is anything that is broken up into countable units, therefore, a guitar with frets is also digital despite being an analog instrument. "Digital" as pertains to electronic media, however, embodies both digital and physical. For the sake of clarity, I use *digital* to refer specifically to electronic media. See Florian Cramer, "What is 'Post-Digital'?," *A Peer-Reviewed Journal About* 3, no. 1 (2014): Post-digital Research, https://aprja.net/article/view/116068.

14. Erika Balsom, *Exhibiting Cinema in Contemporary Art* (Amsterdam: Amsterdam University Press, 2013), 39; Brian O'Doherty, *Inside the White Cube: The Ideology of the Gallery Space* (Santa Monica, CA: Lapis Press, 1976), 13.

15. This page features a detailed description, images, and a video documentation of Gork's artwork from the SFMOM Collection. See SFMOMA, "Jacqueline Kiyomi Gork: Inside You Is Me, 2016," December 2018, https://www.sfmoma.org/read/jacqueline-kiyomi-gordon.

16. This page features Gork's installation and events at The Lab in San Francisco and a detailed description of The Lab Box created for the artwork *Inside You Is Me*. See The Lab, "Jacqueline Kiyomi Gork," accessed September 27, 2024, https://www.thelab.org/2016/2016/10/1/jacqueline-gordon.

17. This shift in the preservation strategies of museums and the role of institutions (away from objects, toward their continual reinterpretation and restaging in different forms and formats) can be understood as different epistemologies coexisting in the contemporary condition, valuing both material permanence and forms of work as process and derivatives. Currently, preservation strategies as outlined by The Variable Media Initiative include storage (or documentation), emulation of works on new systems, migration of works to new platforms, and reinterpretation of the works in other forms. These methods are developed on a case-by-case basis in conversation with the artist, as every artwork has different considerations to preserve the original meaning or intention of the artist. See Guggenheim, "The Variable Media Initiative," n.d., accessed Mar 28, 2020, https://www.guggenheim.org/conservation/the-variable-media-initiative.

18. Eric Golo Stone, "Legal Implications: Cameron Rowland's Rental Contract," *October 164*, 2018, 112.

19. Jacqueline Kiyomi Gork, interview by Ashley L. Wong, November 13, 2019.

20. Hans Abbing, *Why Are Artists Poor? The Exceptional Economy of the Arts* (Amsterdam: Amsterdam University Press, 2002), 81.

21. Sarah Whatmore, *Hybrid Geographies* (London: Sage Publications, 2002), 61.

22. Celia Lury, "Brand as Assemblage: Assembling Culture," *Journal of Cultural Economy* 2, no. 1–2 (2009): 67, https://doi.org/10.1080/17530350903064022.

23. Licensing pertains to the use of intellectual property, often for a limited period of time. Intellectual property as a legal construct has been around since the Statute of Monopolies (1624) and British Statute of Anne (1710). It also relates to patents and trademarks, of which Mickey Mouse is an early iconic example of the control of use of images.

24. Balsom, *Exhibiting Cinema*, 13.

25. Daniel McClean, "The Artist's Contract / from the Contract of Aesthetics to the Aesthetics of the Contract," *Mousse Magazine*, 2010, http://moussemagazine.it/daniel-mcclean-the-artists-contract-2010/.

26. See Victoria Ivanova, Alana Kushnir, and Jasper Salomonsz, *Legal Lab Report 1: Art + Tech/Science Collaborations*, Serpentine Galleries (London, 2021), https://d37zoqglehb9o7.cloudfront.net/uploads/2021/07/Serpentine-Legal-Lab-Report-Final_V3.pdf.; https://futureartecosystems.org.

27. Sven Lütticken, "Legal Forms, Value-Forms, Forms of Resistance," *The Online Journal of Contour Biennale* (2017), http://hearings.contour8.be/2017/01/12/legal-forms-value-forms-forms-of-resistance/.

28. Alain Servais, "Video Art Market: The Right Time to Rethink the Structure," *Texte zur Welt*, no. 19 (2016).

29. "TRANSFER," 2019, accessed August 1, 2019, http://transfergallery.com/.

30. Documentation as art stems back to early experiments with conceptual and performance art in the 1960s. Documentation is considered in the process of creating an ephemeral artwork, such as a performance, which would serve as the only remaining object of art following the event. Such image objects—for example, a photograph—constitute the artwork itself and become part of the information about the artwork that continues to circulate. An example is the iconic image of Chris Burden's *Shoot* (1971), which represents an original and unique moment captured in time. The scarcity of the event and the image and its cultural significance as it is circulated by the press and media are what create the social and material value for the work. Additionally, Annet Dekker has written extensive on documentation and preservation of digital art and the implications it has for museums. See Annet Dekker and Gabriella Giannachi, eds., *Documentation as Art: Expanded Digital Practices* (Abingdon: Routledge, 2023).

31. Seth Siegelaub and Robert Projansky, *The Artist's Reserved Rights Transfer and Sale Agreement*, [1971] 2012, accessed October 19, 2019, http://www.primaryinformation.org/product/siegelaub-the-artists-reserved-rights-transfer-and-sale-agreement/.

32. See Kelani Nichole. "Experiments in Distribution of Time-Based Media Artworks," ed. MetaObjects (Medium, 2018), https://medium.com/@metaobjects/experiments-in-distribution-of-time-based-media-artworks-716c601d653c.

33. See Rosa Menkman, *Behind White Shadows* (2017) exhibition, https://beyondresolution.info/BEHIND-WHITE-SHADOWS-2.

34. See https://www.berlinerfestspiele.de/en/immersion/reihe/allgemein/allgemein.html.

CHAPTER 3

1. Peter Osborne, *The Postconceptual Condition: Critical Essays* (London: Verso, 2018), 18–19.

2. I have also discussed a need to move beyond scarcity and ownership in a paper presented at the 7th Annual Conference of The International Art Market Studies Association (TIAMSA), The University of Melbourne, in 2024 titled "Beyond Scarcity: Intangible Art Markets of Digital and Conceptual Art."

3. Douglas Davis, "The Work of Art in the Age of Digital Reproduction (An Evolving Thesis: 1991–1995)," *Leonardo* 28, no. 5 (1995): 381–386.

4. *Shanzhai* refers to imitations of branded products produced in China. Products take on multiple variations and forms at a rapid pace of innovation in places like Shenzhen. However, China is increasingly clamping down on trademark infringements in the professionalization of the technology and manufacturing sectors to follow international standards. In 2018, I presented the paper "Emergent Economies of Art and Technology in Shenzhen" at Crossroads in Cultural Studies Conference, Shanghai University, which explored some of these developments.

5. Han, *Shanzhai*, 11.

6. Founded by Casey Reas and Ben Fry in 2001, Processing is a free graphics library and development environment that has been widely used by digital artists and designers as tool to do visual programming. Used to create generative art, the tool has spawned a community whose members share code and build upon each other's work through an open-source ethics.

7. Jean Baudrillard, *The Consumer Society: Myths and Structures* (London: Sage Publications, [1970] 1998), 106–107.

8. Lawrence Lessig, *Free Culture: The Nature and Future of Creativity*, ed. Lawrence Lessig (New York: Penguin Books, 2005).

9. Lawrence Lessig developed Creative Commons as an alternative to restrictive copyrights, to allow creators to have more control over how their artworks may be used and distributed. Through customizable terms artists may allow for artworks to be modified, remixed, shared, and distributed, while protecting their interests from commercial use of their work. Copyleft presents various licensing models for software and artistic works with varying degrees of control over

the use of intellectual property. These include the rights to use, study, copy, share, modify, and distribute the works for commercial or noncommercial purposes. It created a middle ground between free distribution and protecting an artist's work, while allowing for remixing within its terms.

10. For more details on appropriation in art and art history, see Tate, "Appropriation," accessed September 27, 2024, https://www.tate.org.uk/art/art-terms/a/appropriation.

11. See India Bourke, "Hong Kong Protesters Transform Alt-Right Pepe the Frog into Pro-Democracy Symbol," Hong Kong Free Press, October 3, 2024, https://hongkongfp.com/2019/10/03/hong-kong-protesters-transform-alt-right-pepe-frog-pro-democracy-symbol/.

12. See Jacob Kastrenakes, "A Key Feature of NFTs Has Completely Broken," *The Verge*, August 18, 2023, https://www.theverge.com/2023/8/17/23836440/nft-creator-royalty-fees-are-dead-opensea-optional.

13. Blockchain technologies were first implemented in 2008 by a person (or group) under the name Satoshi Nakamoto who worked to develop Bitcoin using cryptographic functions to verify transactions computationally across a distributed network. Ethereum, developed by programmer Vitalik Buterin in 2013, created a layer on top of the blockchain to develop smart contracts to automate transaction protocols. The origins of blockchain date back to the cypherpunk movement in the early 1980s and 1990s, which sought to defend individual privacy through anonymity such as monetary transactions. The cypherpunk discussions on mailing lists seeded the technological foundations for bitcoin. However, there is often a conflation of social libertarianism and market libertarianism, where the ideological perspectives feed into each other at times in contradictory ways. More often than not, the market prevails as the dominating logic. Grounded in the countercultural ideologies of Silicon Valley, blockchain technologies were developed with a techno-utopian and libertarian ideal to empower individuals through peer-to-peer networks circumventing the middleman (similar to the development of the internet).

14. Clare McAndrew, *Fine Art and High Finance: Expert Advice on the Economics of Ownership* (New York: Bloomberg Press, 2010), 32.

15. Noah Horowitz, *Art of the Deal: Contemporary Art in a Global Financial Market* (Princeton, NJ: Princeton University Press, 2011).

16. See Cristina Criddle, "Banksy Art Burned, Destroyed and Sold as Token in 'Money-Making Stunt,'" BBC, March 9, 2021, https://www.bbc.com/news/technology-56335948. Radical gestures of destroying artworks stem back to conceptual art practices, including Gustav Metzger's auto-destructive art or John Latham's book burning, which has not stopped the market from its monetization.

17. Early developments of this section were presented in the short paper "Speculation and Acceleration: Financialization, Art & the Blockchain" in Art Machines: International Symposium on Computational Media Art, School of Creative Media, City University of Hong Kong, 2019.

18. Mills, interview, May 3, 2019.

19. See Artprice.com, "The Contemporary Art Rush," in *ARTPRICE REPORT: 20 Years of Contemporary Art Auction History 2000–2020*, accessed September 27, 2024, https://www.artprice.com/artprice-reports/the-contemporary-art-market-report-2020/the-contemporary-art-rush.

20. Graw, *High Price*, 136.

21. Jason Eppink, "A Brief History of the GIF (So Far)," *Journal of Visual Culture* 13, no. 3 (2014): 301, https://doi.org/10.1177/1470412914553365.

22. Olav Velthuis, "Symbolic Meanings of Prices: Constructing the Value of Contemporary Art in Amsterdam and New York Galleries," *Theory and Society* 32 (2003): 184.

23. Olav Velthuis, *Talking Prices: Symbolic Meanings of Prices on the Market for Contemporary Art* (Princeton, NJ: Princeton University Press, 2005), 117.

24. Velthuis, *Talking Prices*, 118.

25. Velthuis, 118.

26. Mills, interview, May 3, 2019.

27. Hito Steyerl, "In Defense of the Poor Image," *e-flux Journal* 10 (2009), https://www.e-flux.com/journal/10/61362/in-defense-of-the-poor-image/.

28. Steyerl, "In Defense of the Poor Image."

29. Marcel Duchamp's readymades are considered among the first conceptual art objects, which placed everyday found objects within the context of a gallery. The intention was to challenge bourgeois notions of high art in which any object could be art when placed in a gallery. Among the first readymades were *Bicycle Wheel* (1913) and *Fountain* (1917), a urinal signed "R.Mutt."

30. Artie Vierkant, "The Image Object Post-Internet," (2010), http://jstchillin.org/artie/pdf/The_Image_Object_Post-Internet_a4.pdf.

31. See Kelani Nichole, "Experiments in Distribution of Time-Based Media Artworks."

32. In the 1990s, Andrew Wernick coined the term "promotional cultures" to refer to the ways in which advertising has become an ideology of contemporary life. Leading on from Wernick, Aeron Davis relates promotional cultures to the rise of social media and digital marketing, where user-generated content produces value as organic forms of publicity, and notions of self-promotion and self-branding becomes a requirement in entrepreneurial cultural economies. See Andrew Wernick, *Promotional Culture: Advertising, Ideology and Symbolic Expression* (London: Sage Publications, 1991); Aeron Davis, *Promotional Cultures: The Rise and Spread of Advertising, Public Relations, Marketing and Branding* (Cambridge, UK: Polity, 2013).

33. Povinelli and Gaonkar use the term "transfiguration" to describe the shifting ontology of cultural form as it is circulated via material technologies. See Gaonkar and Povinelli, "Technologies of Public Forms."

34. John Law and Vicky Singleton, "Object Lessons" (July 2, 2004): 10, http://www.heterogeneities.net/publications/LawSingleton2004ObjectLessons.pdf.

35. Boris Groys, *In the Flow* (London: Verso, 2016).

36. These artist relationships stem from the gallery business of Sedition's founder Harry Blain and helped support the development of the platform. Harry Blain and Blain|Southern closed galleries in London, Berlin, and New York in 2020; however, Sedition continues to remain in operation remotely.

37. Clay Shirky, *Here Comes Everybody: The Power of Organizing Without Organizations* (London: Penguin Books, 2008).

38. Desmond Leung, interview by Ashley L. Wong, June 19, 2019.

39. This is the page on Sedition featuring the *Walking City Citizens* fifty unique iterations as a sold-out series. See https://www.seditionart.com/universal-everything/walking-city-citizens, accessed September 27, 2024.

40. Matt Pyke, "Universal Everything on Art Collecting in the Digital Age," ed. Sedition (Vimeo, 2014). https://vimeo.com/98913293.

41. Scholars have discussed the reputation economy in relation to creative and digital labor, where one's reputation and online presence contribute to one's value and career prospects in the real-world. See Alessandro Gandini, *The Reputation Economy: Understanding Knowledge Work in Digital Society* (London: Palgrave Macmillan, 2016).

42. Mckenzie Wark, "My Collectible Ass," *e-flux* 85 (2017), http://www.e-flux.com/journal/85/156418/my-collectible-ass/.

43. For further discussion of NFTs, see Ashley L. Wong, "NFTs and Digital Collectibles: Creating Systems of Ownership for Digital Objects," *Visual Culture Studies*, no. 3 (2022): 211–237.

44. Horowitz, *Art of the Deal*, 143.

45. Paolo Cirio's *Art Derivatives* (2020) is a tactical media artwork featuring a website selling images of high selling artworks at auction that are sold for a fraction of its original auction price. The work is a direct comment on the role played by auction houses in controlling and manipulating the art market. See https://art-derivatives.com/?/l/About/. See Ashley L. Wong, "Paolo Cirio, Political Aesthetics of the Art Market," *Clot Magazine*, August 4, 2020, https://www.clotmag.com/interviews/paolo-cirio-political-aesthetics-of-the-art-market.

46. Rachel O'Dwyer, "Limited Edition: Producing Artificial Scarcity for Digital Art on the Blockchain and Its Implications for the Cultural Industries," *Convergence: The International Journal of Research into New Media Technologies* (2018): 3, https://doi.org/10.1177/1354856518795097.

47. *Real Flow* (2015) by Diann Bauer, Victoria Ivanova, Christopher Kulendran-Thomas, and Suhail Malik presented at P! Gallery in New York, provides one example, creating a series of financial derivatives for investing in art where the collector does not need to care for the work, but earns the more the work is exhibited. It is pure financialization in which the value of art becomes entirely speculation. See Diann Bauer's description of the project on her website, http://diannbauer.net/real-flow.

48. In Sedition's "Ask Me Anything" conversation on Twitter on April 6, 2022, LIA discussed her difficulties during the pandemic and then success after some NFT drops that enabled her to buy a new house in Vienna. NFTs provided her an important market for her work that has been traditionally difficult to sell on the conventional art market.
49. Tali Hinkis, interview by Ashley L. Wong, March 22, 2022.
50. See https://www.artblocks.io/legacy/artist/lovid.
51. Lorna Mills, interview by Ashley L. Wong, April 13, 2022.
52. See https://transfergallery.com/data-trust/.
53. Vivienne Chow, "A Group of Collectors Is Suing Sotheby's over Its 'Misleading' Marketing of Bored Ape Yacht Club NFTs," *Art Net*, August 15, 2023, https://news.artnet.com/art-world/collectors-sue-sothebys-bored-ape-yacht-club-nfts-2349974.
54. Toronto-based artist Alex McLeod collaborated with Nissan Canada to create an NFT to be sold at auction to promote their new car model. The winning bid of $2.8 million failed to go through and instead the NFT was sold for $220,000, which is the actual price of the car. Winners of the auction also receive a car along with the NFT. The blunder around the NFT's price—likely an error of adding one extra zero to the bid—created hype around its sale in the media, followed by the embarrassing actual result. See Kathy Renwald, "US$2.3-Million Bid on Canadian Nissan NFT Fails, Art Sells for US$220,000," *Driving* 2021, https://driving.ca/auto-news/entertainment/us2-3-million-bid-on-canadian-nissan-nft-fails-art-sells-for-us220000.
55. For instance, Economic Space Agency is a digital economy organization and an international network of radical economists, developers, and artists that seeks to "design new systems of value creation and distributions" to imagine the economy in a post-capitalist, post-scarcity society; see https://economicspace.agency. Also see Ruth Catlow and Penny Rafferty, eds., *Radical Friends: Decentralised Autonomous Organisations and the Arts* (Lancaster: Torque Editions, 2022).

CHAPTER 4

1. Susa Pop et al., *What Urban Media Art Can Do: Why When Where & How* (Stuttgart: Avedition, 2016).
2. The project by E.A.T. brought together artists and engineers to create *Great Big Mirror Dome* (1970), an experimental immersive dome space with a complex feedback system enabling audience interaction with fog, mirrors, sound, and performances. See Jimmy Stamp, "When PepsiCola Allowed a Team of Artists to Wreak Creative Havoc," *Smithsonian Magazine*, September 26, 2013, https://www.smithsonianmag.com/arts-culture/when-pepsicola-allowed-a-team-of-artists-to-wreak-creative-havoc-109661/. Art historian, Michelle Kuo has also written extensively on E.A.T. in her PhD thesis, see Michelle Kuo, "To Avoid the Waste of

a Cultural Revolution: Experiments in Art and Technology," doctoral dissertation, Harvard University, 2018.

3. The HTC Vive Arts website features projects they have supported through the initiative. See https://www.vivearts.com/.

4. See https://www.artnews.com/art-news/sponsored-content/bmw-digital-art-cars-cao-fei-1234624856/.

5. Edward A. Shanken, "Artists in Industry and the Academy: Collaborative Research, Interdisciplinary Scholarship and the Creation and Interpretation of Hybrid Forms," *Leonardo* 38, no. 5 (2005): 415–418.

6. Also see an interview with McWilliams and Pearlman in Ashley L. Wong, "Thoughtworks Arts Residency: Leveraging Corporate Resources for Art & Social Change," *Clot Magazine*, September 27, 2018, https://www.clotmag.com/biomedia/thoughtworks-arts-residency-leveraging-corporate-resources-for-art-social-change-by-ashley-lee-wong.

7. View video of Lorna Mills's work in Times Square: https://www.youtube.com/watch?v=w1x5cJ-5gzI.

8. Mills, interview, April 13, 2022.

9. Sedition presented the work of Tracey Emin for the Times Square Midnight Moment in 2013. Presenting high-profile artists on such a display serves promotional purposes by generating media attention. The artist was present for the launch and a social media campaign was organized to encourage engagement with the work and also with Sedition, which sold Emin's work as limited editions. As a publicly funded, noncommercial display, the social media publicity stunt that Sedition staged sought to take advantage of the site's visibility and popularity to promote the platform through digital edition giveaways as a reward for sharing photos of the artwork and tagging Sedition on Instagram. This opportunist did not sit well with the nonprofit aims of Times Square Arts, the public arts program of the Times Square Alliance, revealing tensions in the diverse uses of media facades and their organizational intentions.

10. Mills, interview, April 13, 2022.

11. Our studio MetaObjects has been contracted by M+ to consult on their media facade including the development of art commissions and to support the development of interactive artworks such as Studio Moniker's commissioned work *Touch for Luck* (2022) and a commission by Pipilotti Rist. See Alison Fung, "Behind the Screen: The M+ Facade," *M+ Magazine*, accessed September 27, 2024, https://www.mplus.org.hk/en/magazine/mplus-building-hong-kong-showcases-art-on-led-facade/.

12. Some brands seek to be aesthetically challenging as an alternate means to draw attention, such as Balenciaga in its Summer 2020 campaign, which featured surreal dystopian newscasters and the music of Wolf Eyes. See https://www.youtube.com/watch?v=kHSeIK6tmfg. Also discussed in Wong, "Beyond Ownership."

13. See M+, "CHANEL becomes M+'s Major Partner and supports a lead curatorial position dedicated to M+'s moving image programmes," press release, July 13 2023,

https://www.mplus.org.hk/en/press/chanel-major-partner-and-supports-moving-image/.

14. Karl Marx, *Capital: A Critique of Political Economy*, vol. 1, trans. Ben Fowkes (London: Penguin Books, [1867] 1976), 247–248.
15. Marx, *Capital*.
16. Lars Svendsen, *Fashion: A Philosophy*, trans. John Irons (London: Reaktion Books, 2006), 96.
17. Svendsen, *Fashion*.
18. Leung, interview, June 19, 2019.
19. Culture Projects, *Second Cultural Citizenship Survey*, Report No. 2, 2018. https://www.pradagroup.com/pradagroupjournal/e4f74ca298b9eeaeb23436599fa34f63/wp-content/uploads/2019/02/Press-release_Culture-Projects-Cultural-Citizenship-Report-Issue-2.-pdf-1.pdf.
20. Lury, "Brand as Assemblage," 67.
21. Diedrich Diederichsen, *On (Surplus) Value in Art*, vol. 1, Reflections (Rotterdam: Sternberg Press, 2008), 21. Also see a paper presented by DOXA in Madrid in 2010: Yuk Hui and Ashley Wong, "Reclaiming Culture and Creativity from Industry and the UK Creative Economy: Towards New Configurations of the Artistic System," *Societies in Crisis, European Congress on Aesthetics* (2011): 472–477.
22. Leung, interview, June 19, 2019.
23. See https://www.aho.art.
24. See https://www.aho.art/the-evolutions-by-visible-music.
25. See *Unnamed Soundsculpture*, embodiment of sound (2012), https://onformative.com/work/unnamed-soundsculpture.
26. See *Collide*, synaesthetic art installation (2016), https://onformative.com/work/collide.
27. Drew Bennett, "Drew Bennett on Using Art to Build Community," *If So What*, April 11, 2018, https://www.ifsowhat.com/isw/2018/4/11/drew-bennett-on-using-art-to-build-community.
28. Gork, interview, November 13, 2019. In my interview with her, Gork mentioned the general amounts artists receive based on the experiences of her friends and artists she knows who have participated in the Facebook residency.
29. Cade Metz, "The Amazing Murals Created by Facebook's Artist-in-Residence," *Wired*, November 24, 2014, https://www.wired.com/2014/11/take-tour-facebooks-giant-corporate-art-lab/.
30. Richard Barbrook and Andy Cameron, "The Californian Ideology," *Mute* 1, no. 3 (September 1, 1995), http://www.metamute.org/editorial/articles/californian-ideology.
31. Linsey McGoey, *No Such Thing as a Free Gift: The Gates Foundation and the Price of Philanthropy* (London & New York: Verso, 2015).

32. McGoey, *No Such Thing as a Free Gift*.
33. Wong, "Thoughtworks Arts Residency."
34. Martin Fowler, "Three Pillars," May 11, 2011, https://martinfowler.com/bliki/ThreePillars.html.
35. See https://artahack.io.
36. See https://hardwarehacklab.io.
37. Wong, "Thoughtworks Arts Residency."
38. Wong, "Thoughtworks Arts Residency."
39. Wong, "Thoughtworks Arts Residency."
40. See https://ainowinstitute.org; http://consortiumrr.com; http://www.baltanlaboratories.org.

CHAPTER 5

1. Ditte Vilstrup Holm and Timon Beyes, "How Art Becomes Organization: Reimagining Aesthetics, Sites and Politics of Entrepreneurship," *Organization Studies* 43, no. 2 (2022): 228, https://doi.org/10.1177/0170840621998571.
2. See the introduction for a definition and elaboration on "making do." Also see de Certeau, *The Practice of Everyday Life*.
3. Daniel Hjorth, Robin Holt, and Chris Steyaert, "Entrepreneurship and Process Studies," *International Small Business Journal* 33, no. 6 (2015): 602, https://doi.org/10.1177/0266242615583566, https://journals.sagepub.com/doi/abs/10.1177/0266242615583566.
4. Andy Warhol can be considered an early example of the artist as brand through his approach to mass production in The Factory in the 1960s. The Factory churned out artworks such as silk-screened prints that were sold in the art market by employing the aesthetics of mass-produced products. It operated as a Fordist assembly line, where the artist also owned the means of production, which simultaneously served to sustain an artistic community and their hedonistic cultural activities. Warhol employed the language of advertising, blurring the distinction between the irony and sincerity of his work as high art. Through mass circulation of products and symbols, he created his own brand and celebrity image, which also functioned economically to support his practice and others in his community. The Factory became a space for underground culture in New York City, which would perhaps be less possible today, considering the high cost of rent in cities.
5. Nate Cohan, "Corporate Aesthetics: Shanzhai Biennial," *Art in America*, April 30, 2014, https://www.artnews.com/art-in-america/interviews/corporate-aesthetics-shanzhai-biennial-56395/; Huw Lemmey, "Mission Creep: K-Hole and Trend Forecasting as Creative Practice," *Rhizome*, March 26, 2013, https://rhizome.org/editorial/2013/mar/26/mission-creep/; Kira Josefsson, "Corporate Aesthetics: The

GCC at MoMA PS1," *Art in America*, April 24, 2014, https://www.artnews.com/art-in-america/interviews/corporate-aesthetics-the-gcc-at-moma-ps1-56393/; Alexia Mellor, "Professional Parody: An Examination of Artist Practices Parodying and Disrupting Business Models to New Ends," *Organizational Aesthetics* 4, no. 1 (January 19, 2015), https://oa.journals.publicknowledgeproject.org/index.php/oa/article/view/50.

6. See "Corporate Aesthetics: Ingrid Baxter of N.E. Thing Co.," *Art in America*, April 8, 2014, https://www.artnews.com/art-in-america/interviews/corporate-aesthetics-ingrid-baxter-of-ne-thing-co-56388/.
7. Bailey's LEAN Artist Incubator was first presented in Hamburg in 2016, and subsequently as part of the *I Was Raised on the Internet* exhibition at the Museum of Contemporary Art Chicago in 2018. See https://mcachicago.org/calendar/2018/06/talk-lean-artist-chicago-demo-day-with-jeremy-bailey.
8. Nicolas Bourriaud, *Relational Aesthetics* (Dijon: Les Presses du réel, 2002).
9. See "Five Years of Institut für Raumexperimente: We Have Only Just Begun," n.d., accessed September 27, 2024, http://raumexperimente.net/en/meta/about/.
10. Bernard Stiegler, "Too Late? The Final Warning," in *Work Marathon 2018*, ed. Serpentine Galleries (YouTube, 2018), accessed August 16, 2021, https://youtu.be/EsGVN7UEopw.
11. Barbara Pollack, "Risky Business," *ARTnews*, March 29, 2012, https://www.artnews.com/art-news/artists/risky-business-524/.
12. The name is a play on words with the name of Alibaba, as one of the largest e-commerce platforms in China.
13. *Xu Zhen: A MadeIn Company Production*, exhibition catalogue (Beijing: Ullens Center for Contemporary Art, 2014).
14. Xu Zhen, *Corporate*, produced by MadeIn Company, ed. Katrin Bucher Trantow and Peter Pakesch (Vienna: Verlag für Moderne Kunst, 2015), 67.
15. See http://www.madeingallery.com.
16. Chris Moore, ed., *Xu Zhen* (Berlin: Distanz, 2014), 9.
17. Moore, *Xu Zhen*. Also see chapter 3 in this book for discussion of artists like Banksy destroying NFTs as a statement on the extreme financialization of the art market.
18. The designation between public and private institutions is more clearly defined in a Western context, where the concept of "art mall" may be considered a strange concept to audiences who understand museums as public institutions. However, Tinari has remarked, the word for "company" in Chinese combines the characters for "public" and "private." See Zhen, *Corporate*, 78–79.
19. Adrian Cheng is the son of business tycoon Henry Cheng, who founded K11 with a series of art malls and hotels around China. The Cheng empire includes the K11 Art Foundation and an Art Village in Wuhan, which hosts artist residencies and collaborations with international institutions to develop exhibitions, programs, and exchanges. The K11 Art Foundation aims to groom young

contemporary artists in China and to facilitate exchange while educating audiences about art. The Cheng enterprise also caters to digitally savvy millennials and has invested in technology-driven brands through its C Ventures investment fund. At the same time, Adrian Cheng sits on the board of a number of international art institutions including The Metropolitan Museum of Art, New York, and the Royal Academy of Arts in London and is a member of the International Circle of Centre Pompidou.

20. Enid Tsui, "How New World Heir Adrian Cheng Combines His Passion for Art with Entrepreneurship," *South China Morning Post*, March 10, 2015, https://www.scmp.com/lifestyle/arts-culture/article/1733513/k11-founder-adrian-cheng-bringing-six-exhibitions-art-basel.

21. In 2024, Cheng stepped down as CEO of New World Development, the family-owned property development company behind K11, following a year of losses, reflecting a shifting market in the post-pandemic era. See Peggy Sito and Cheryl Arcibal, "Adrian Cheng to Step Down as New World CEO, Likely to Be Replaced by COO Eric Ma: Sources," *South China Morning Post*, September 25, 2024, https://www.scmp.com/business/companies/article/3279929/adrian-cheng-step-down-new-worlds-ceo-take-non-executive-role-sources-say.

22. As a historical hub for international trade, Hong Kong is a business-friendly city. Even within the political system, its Chief Executive is elected by a committee of members and professionals from different sectors of industry. Businesses and business leaders are given power as part of the 1,200-member Election Committee, but not individuals or the general public.

23. Wong Ka Ying of the Hong Kong Artist Union recognizes the challenges posed because Hong Kong doesn't readily recognize artists or self-employed workers. During the COVID-19 pandemic, the Hong Kong Art Development Council's governmental handout defines the artist as one who has received grants or presented in a government-funded venue in the past year. See https://www.labour.gov.hk/eng/public/wcp/SelfEmployedPerson.pdf.

24. *Xu Zhen: A MadeIn Company Production*, exhibition catalogue.

25. *Xu Zhen: A MadeIn Company Production*, exhibition catalogue.

26. Zhen, *Corporate*, 68.

27. Jacques Rancière, *The Politics of Aesthetics: The Distribution of the Sensible* (London: Continuum International Publishing Group, 2004), 13.

28. Rancière, *The Politics of Aesthetics*, 22.

29. See Sotheby's, "Experience the Art of Emptiness with XUZHEN SUPERMARKET," Hong Kong Autumn Auctions, September 7, 2018, https://www.sothebys.com/en/articles/experience-the-art-of-emptiness-with-xuzhen-supermarket.

30. Adam Arvidsson, "Brands," *Journal of Consumer Culture* 5, no. 2 (2016), https://doi.org/10.1177/1469540505053093.

31. Lury, "Brand as Assemblage," 74.

32. Zhen, *Corporate*, 78.

33. Joseph Beuys, *What Is Money?: A Discussion Featuring Joseph Beuys* (Forest Row, UK: Clairview Books, 2010), 57.

34. Ulrich Rösch, *We Are the Revolution!: Rudolf Steiner, Joseph Beuys, and the Threefold Social Impulse* (Forest Row, UK: Temple Lodge Publishing, 2013), 20.

35. Within organization and entrepreneurship studies, there has been much discussion on the different ways in which aesthetics and politics interact with organizational practice. What may be called the "organizational turn" in art can be found in artists such as Theaster Gates who is initiating projects that create cultural infrastructures in impoverished communities in Chicago's South Side. This art trend brings an artistic and cultural perspective to entrepreneurship, where organizing has agency in developing and sustaining the arts through engagements with forms of enterprise. See Holm and Beyes, "How Art Becomes Organization"; Carine Farias et al., "Organizational Entrepreneurship, Politics and the Political," *Entrepreneurship and Regional Development* 31, no. 7–8 (2019): 555–566, https://doi.org/10.1080/08985626.2019.1599186.

36. James Temperton, "Design Collective teamLab Wants to Turn the World into a Work of Art," *Wired*, October 13, 2017, https://www.wired.co.uk/article/teamlab-tokyo-head-office-design-art-experiment-invention.

37. Naoko Aono, "The Vision of Toshiyuki Inoko, a Founder of teamLab," *Pen*, August 29, 2018, https://pen-online.com/arts/the-vision-of-toshiyuki-inoko-a-founder-of-teamlab/?scrolled=0.

38. Takashi Kudo (@serpentineuk), "Did You Miss Our LIVE with @teamLab?," Instagram, July 10, 2020, https://www.instagram.com/p/CCddBxCHZtz/.

39. Kudo, "Did You Miss Our LIVE with @teamLab?"

40. As of 2024, teamLab's biography states: "In order to understand the world around them, people separate it into independent entities with perceived boundaries between them. teamLab seeks to transcend these boundaries in our perceptions of the world, of the relationship between the self and the world, and of the continuity of time. Everything exists in a long, fragile yet miraculous, borderless continuity."

41. Whachul Oh, "Understanding of Self: Buddhism and Psychoanalysis," *Journal of Religion and Health* 61, no. 6 (December 2022), https://doi.org/10.1007/s10943-021-01437-w.

42. Temperton, "Design Collective teamLab."

43. Temperton, "Design Collective teamLab."

44. Fran Kuzui, "Japan's teamLab Transcends Borders of Art and Business," *Nikkei Asian Review*, September 15, 2018, https://asia.nikkei.com/Life-Arts/Arts/Japan-s-teamLab-transcends-borders-of-art-and-business.

45. Kuzui, "Japan's teamLab."

46. Holacracy is a method of nonhierarchical management created by entrepreneur Brian Robertson that encourages peer-to-peer collaboration and a system for decision-making by democratic consensus. However, in the case of the company

Zappos, which adopted this method, it was revealed as an extremely hierarchical, bureaucratic, and restrictive form of management. This reflects the appropriation of values into corporate management structures that appear ideal on the surface, but rather reinforce existing top-down structures. See Steve Denning, "Making Sense of Zappos and Holacracy," *Forbes*, January 15, 2014, https://www.forbes.com/sites/steveden-ning/2014/01/15/making-sense-of-zappos-and-holacracy/#71c7a6b93207.

47. Yunyi Lau, "An Interview with teamLab," *Artling*, May 16, 2016, https://theartling.com/en/artzine/interview-teamlab/.

48. Murakami announced in July 2020 that KaiKai KiKi was on the verge of bankruptcy owing to overspending on his animated films, competition, and the COVID-19 pandemic. See https://news.artnet.com/art-world/takashi-murakami-bankruptcy-video-1891602.

49. Kuzui, "Japan's teamLab."

50. Kudo, "Did you miss our LIVE with @teamLab?"

51. Joseph Pine and James Gilmore have written about the experience economy in which the consumer's time and attention become commodities. Corporations are incorporating experiential design in the marketing and branding products through immersive experiences and cultural events. teamLab's work participates in an experience economy through the creation of unique museum and amusement park-like experiences, which also contribute value to their corporate sponsors including Epson, Microsoft, and Sony, among others. See Joseph B. Pine and James H. Gilmore, *The Experience Economy* (Boston: Harvard Business Review Press, 2011).

52. *Dreamspace V* was a large-scale inflatable installation made of brightly colored PVC (polyvinyl chloride) material which audiences could enter and explore. As the work toured in the United Kingdom in Durham in 2006, a tragic accident occurred when part of the installation became dislodged and flew into the air, killing two people inside. See https://publicdelivery.org/maurice-agis-dreamspace.

53. See https://www.teamlab.art/w/teamlabball. Jonah Asher, "Art Goes Digital: Japan's teamLab Breaks New Ground," *WIPO Magazine*, 2013, https://www.wipo.int/wipo_magazine/en/2013/01/article_0003.html.

54. The shape that constitutes our logo is a rhombic dodecahedron, which is an emergent form that naturally occurs within nature formed by bees as they collectively push against and build the walls of their hives.

55. See https://metaobjects.org/work/samson-young-venice-biennale.

56. Wiebe E. Bijker, *Of Bicycles, Bakelites, and Bulbs: Toward a Theory of Sociotechnical Change* (Cambridge, MA: MIT Press, 1995).

57. Danielle Child, *Working Aesthetics: Labour, Art and Capitalism*, Radical Aesthetics–Radical Art series. (London: Bloomsbury Academic, 2019).

58. Stiegler, *For a New Critique*.

59. Rosi Braidotti, "Posthuman Critical Theory," in *Critical Posthumanism and Planetary Futures*, ed. Debashish Banerji and Makarand R Paranjape (New Delhi: Springer India, 2016), 27.

60. Several Hong Kong–based studios, such as yucolab, IOIO Creative, Ware, and XCEED, also engage with forms of experiential design in this way.
61. Brian Massumi, *99 Theses on the Revaluation of Value: A Postcapitalist Manifesto* (Minneapolis: University of Minnesota Press, 2018), 68.
62. Zhen, *Corporate*, 78–79.

CHAPTER 6

1. For further reading on labs, see Darren S. Wershler-Henry, Lori Emerson, and Jussi Parikka, *The Lab Book: Situated Practices in Media Studies* (Minneapolis: University of Minnesota Press, 2021).
2. For further reading on how cultural collaborations involving art, technology, and science provide benefits for corporations as organizations, see Claudia Schnugg, *Creating Artscience Collaboration: Bringing Value to Organizations*, ed. Samantha Warren and Steven S. Taylor (Cham: Springer International Publishing, 2019).
3. Such initiatives may include artist residencies in universities like this one at Hong Kong Baptist University: https://ava.hkbu.edu.hk/en/academy/artist-in-residence.
4. André Malraux, *Museum without Walls* (London: Secker & Warburg, [1949] 1967).
5. This perspective of the iterative artwork is also present in our work with Lu Yang, which has been discussed in this journal article: Ashley L. Wong, "Cyclic Existence, Iteration, and Digital Transcendence: Lu Yang's Live Motion Capture Performances," *Screen Bodies* 7, no. 1 (2022):): 128–145, https://doi.org/10:3167/screen.2022.070108.
6. Jonathan Kemp, "Practical Ethics v3.0: Version Control," *Kunst und Material: Konzepte, Prozesse, Arbeitsteilungen* 12 (2022), https://doi.org/https://doi.org/10.11588/arthistoricum.1047.c14538.
7. Hanna B. Hölling considers a "temporal materiality of artworks" in her work on archiving computer-based artworks, where change and variation are inherent to the existence of the work. She calls for a rethinking of traditional conservation toward more open interpretation and re-creation of artworks, acknowledging the work of conservators, curators, and technicians in the creation of the work. See Hanna B. Hölling, "The Archival Turn: Toward New Ways of Conceptualising Changeable Artworks," in *Data Drift: Archiving Media and Data Art in the 21st Century*, ed. Rasa Smite, Lev Manovich, and Smits Raitis (Riga: RIXC and Liepaja's University Art Research Lab, 2015), 75.
8. Ensembl was presented as part of the DAOWO Sessions: Artworld Prototypes (2021) presented by Goethe Institut London, Further Field, and Serpentine Galleries. It was also featured in Catlow and Rafferty, *Radical Friends: Decentralised Autonomous Organisations and the Arts*.
9. "Forking" in open-source software development is when developers take a copy of source code from one project and develop this copy independently, creating a distinct piece of software for a new project and direction.

10. Claire Bishop, *Artificial Hells: Participatory Art and the Politics of Spectatorship* (London: Verso, 2012).
11. See onformative, "AI Sculpting: Co-creation in the Age of Artificial Intelligence," 2022, https://onformative.com/work/ai-sculpting/.
12. Yuk Hui, "ChatGPT, or the Eschatology of Machines," *e-flux Journal*, no. 137 (2023), https://www.e-flux.com/journal/137/544816/chatgpt-or-the-eschatology-of-machines/.
13. See Maria Farrell and Robin Berjon, "We Need to Rewild the Internet," Noema, April 16, 2024. https://www.noemamag.com/we-need-to-rewild-the-internet/.
14. Yuk Hui, "Cosmotechnics as Cosmopolitics," *e-flux Journal*, no. 86 (2017), https://www.e-flux.com/journal/86/161887/cosmotechnics-as-cosmopolitics/.
15. Yuk Hui, *The Question Concerning Technology in China: An Essay in Cosmotechnics* (Falmouth: Urbanomic, 2016).
16. Ien Ang has developed the notion of "cultural research" in contradistinction to "cultural studies," in which she recognizes the failure of cultural studies to engage with social reality. See Ien Ang, "From Cultural Studies to Cultural Research: Engaged Scholarship in the Twenty-first Century," *Cultural Studies Review* 12, no. 2 (2006): 194.

BIBLIOGRAPHY

Abbing, Hans. *Why Are Artists Poor? The Exceptional Economy of the Arts*. Amsterdam: Amsterdam University Press, 2002.

Ang, Ien. "From Cultural Studies to Cultural Research: Engaged Scholarship in the Twenty-First Century." *Cultural Studies Review* 12, no. 2 (2006): 183–197.

Appadurai, Arjun. *The Social Life of Things: Commodities in Cultural Perspective*. Cambridge, UK: Cambridge University Press, 1986.

Arvidsson, Adam. "Brands." *Journal of Consumer Culture* 5, no. 2 (2016): 235–258. https://doi.org/10.1177/1469540505053093.

Balsom, Erika. *Exhibiting Cinema in Contemporary Art*. Amsterdam: Amsterdam University Press, 2013.

Barad, Karen. *Meeting the Universe Halfway: Quantum Physics and the Entanglement of Matter and Meaning*. Durham, NC: Duke University Press, 2007.

Barbrook, Richard, and Andy Cameron. "The Californian Ideology." *Mute* 1, no. 3 (September 1 1995). http://www.metamute.org/editorial/articles/californian-ideology.

Barry, Andrew, and Don Slater. "Introduction: The Technological Economy." *Economy and Society* 31, no. 2 (2002): 175–193. https://doi.org/10.1080/03085140220123117.

Baudrillard, Jean. *The Consumer Society: Myths and Structures*. London: Sage Publications, [1970] 1998.

Bauman, Zygmunt. *Liquid Modernity*. Cambridge, UK: Polity Press, 2000.

Bauwens, Michel, Vasilis Kostakis, and Alex Pazaitis. *Peer to Peer: The Commons Manifesto*. London: University of Westminster Press, 2019.

Becker, Gary S. *Human Capital: A Theoretical and Empirical Analysis, with Special Reference to Education*. 3rd ed. Chicago: University of Chicago Press, 1993.

Beech, Dave. *Art and Value: Art's Economic Exceptionalism in Classical, Neoclassical and Marxist Economics.* Boston: BRILL, 2015.

Bennett, Drew. "Drew Bennett on Using Art to Build Community." *If So What*. April 11, 2018. https://www.ifsowhat.com/isw/2018/4/11/drew-bennett-on-using-art-to-build-community.

Bergh, Sissel M. "Notes on Artists, Workers and Cooperation in Norway." *Art Production in Restriction. Possibilities of Transformative Art Production and Coalition-Building*, 2015. http://transformativeartproduction.net/notes-on-artists-workers-and-cooperation-in-norway/.

Beuys, Joseph. *What Is Money?: A Discussion Featuring Joseph Beuys*. Forest Row, UK: Clairview Books, 2010.

Bijker, Wiebe E. *Of Bicycles, Bakelites, and Bulbs: Toward a Theory of Sociotechnical Change*. Cambridge, MA: MIT Press, 1995.

Bourriaud, Nicolas. *Relational Aesthetics*. Dijon: Les Presses du réel, 2002.

Braidotti, Rosi. "Nomadic Ethics." *Deleuze Studies* 7, no. 3 (2013): 342–359.

Braidotti, Rosi. "Posthuman Critical Theory." In *Critical Posthumanism and Planetary Futures*. Edited by Debashish Banerji and Makarand R Paranjape, 13–32. New Delhi: Springer India, 2016.

Buskirk, Martha. *Creative Enterprise: Contemporary Art between Museum and Marketplace*. International Texts in Critical Media Aesthetics. Edited by Francisco J Ricardo. New York: The Continuum International Publishing Group, 2012.

Catlow, Ruth, and Penny Rafferty, eds. *Radical Friends: Decentralised Autonomous Organisations and the Arts*. Lancaster: Torque Editions, 2022.

Child, Danielle. *Working Aesthetics: Labour, Art and Capitalism*. Radical Aesthetics–Radical Art series. London: Bloomsbury Academic, 2019.

Chow, Vivienne. "A Group of Collectors Is Suing Sotheby's over Its 'Misleading' Marketing of Bored Ape Yacht Club Nfts." *Art Net*, August 15, 2023. https://news.artnet.com/art-world/collectors-sue-sothebys-bored-ape-yacht-club-nfts-2349974.

"Corporate Aesthetics: Ingrid Baxter of N.E. Thing Co." *Art in America*, April 8, 2014. https://www.artnews.com/art-in-america/interviews/corporate-aesthetics-ingrid-baxter-of-ne-thing-co-56388/.

Cramer, Florian. "What Is 'Post-Digital'?" *A Peer-Reviewed Journal About* 3, no. 1 (2014): Post-digital Research. https://aprja.net/article/view/116068.

Crawford, Niamh, and Sabina Dewfield. *A Design Sprint for the Creative Industries Sector Vision: Maximising the Spillover Value of the Creative Industries to the Wider Economy*. Design Council UK, London, 2022. https://assets.publishing.service.gov.uk/media/62e10b63e90e0766b251ab73/Creative_Industries_Sector_Vision_Report_FINAL.pdf.

Culture Projects. *Second Cultural Citizenship Survey*. Report No. 2, 2018. https://www.pradagroup.com/pradagroupjournal/e4f74ca298b9eeaeb23436599fa34f63/wp-content/uploads/2019/02/Press-release_Culture-Projects-Cultural-Citizenship-Report-Issue-2.-pdf-1.pdf.

Davis, Aeron. *Promotional Cultures: The Rise and Spread of Advertising, Public Relations, Marketing and Branding*. Cambridge, UK: Polity, 2013.

Davis, Douglas. "The Work of Art in the Age of Digital Reproduction (An Evolving Thesis: 1991–1995)." *Leonardo* 28, no. 5 (1995): 381–386.

de Certeau, Michel. *The Practice of Everyday Life*. Translated by Steven Rendall. Berkeley: University of California Press, 1984.

De Marchi, Neil, and Hans J. Van Miegroet. "The History of Art Markets." In *Handbook of the Economics of Art and Culture*. Edited by Victor A. Ginsburgh and David Throsby, 69–122. Amsterdam: Elsevier B.V., 2006.

Dekker, Annet, and Gabriella Giannachi, eds. *Documentation as Art: Expanded Digital Practices*. Abingdon: Routledge, 2023.

Deleuze, Gilles. *Bergsonism*. Translated by Hugh Tomlinson and Barbara Habberjam. New York: Zone Books, 1991.

Deresiewicz, William. *The Death of the Artist: How Creators Are Struggling to Survive in the Age of Billionaires and Big Tech*. New York: Henry Holt and Co., 2020.

Diederichsen, Diedrich. *On (Surplus) Value in Art*. Vol. 1, Reflections. Rotterdam: Sternberg Press, 2008.

Eppink, Jason. "A Brief History of the GIF (So Far)." *Journal of Visual Culture* 13, no. 3 (2014): 298–306. https://doi.org/10.1177/1470412914553365.

Farias, Carine, Pablo Fernandez, Daniel Hjorth, and Robin Holt. "Organizational Entrepreneurship, Politics and the Political." *Entrepreneurship and Regional Development* 31, no. 7–8 (2019): 555–566. https://doi.org/10.1080/08985626.2019.1599186.

Fowler, Martin, "Three Pillars," May 11, 2011. https://martinfowler.com/bliki/ThreePillars.html.

Fuchs, Christian. "The Digital Labour Theory of Value and Karl Marx in the Age of Facebook, Youtube, Twitter, and Weibo." In *Reconsidering Value and Labour in the Digital Age*. Edited by Eran Fisher and Christian Fuchs. Dynamics of Virtual Work series, 26–41. Berlin: Springer, 2015.

Fuller, Matthew, and Olga Goriunova. *Bleak Joys: Aesthetics of Ecology and Impossibility*. Vol. 53, Posthumanities. Minneapolis: University of Minnesota Press, 2019.

Gandini, Alessandro. *The Reputation Economy: Understanding Knowledge Work in Digital Society*. London: Palgrave Macmillan, 2016.

Gaonkar, Dilip Parameshwar, and Elizabeth A. Povinelli. "Technologies of Public Forms: Circulation, Transfiguration, Recognition." *Public Culture* 15, no. 3 (2003): 385–397.

Gerber, Alison. *The Work of Art: Value in Creative Careers*. Palo Alto, CA: Stanford University Press, 2017.

Gibson-Graham, J. K. "Diverse Economies: Performative Practices for 'Other Worlds.'" *Progress in Human Geography* 32, no. 5 (2008): 613–632. https://doi.org/10.1177/0309132508090821.

Gork, Jacqueline Kiyomi. Interview by Ashley L. Wong. November 13, 2019.

Graw, Isabelle. *High Price: Art between the Market and Celebrity Culture*. Berlin: Sternberg Press, 2009.

Greffe, Xavier. *The Artist–Enterprise in the Digital Age*. Tokyo: Springer Japan, 2017.

Gronlund, Melissa. *Contemporary Art and Digital Culture*. Abingdon: Routledge, 2017.

Groys, Boris. *In the Flow*. London: Verso, 2016.

Guggenheim. "The Variable Media Initiative." n.d., accessed March 28, 2020, https://www.guggenheim.org/conservation/the-variable-media-initiative.

Han, Byung-Chul. *Shanzhai: Deconstruction in Chinese*. Translated by Philippa Hurd. Boston, MA: MIT Press, 2017.

Heikkinen, Merja. *The Nordic Model for Supporting Artists*. The Arts Council of Finland, Helsinki, 2003. https://www.taike.fi/en/file-download/download/public/235.

Hinkis, Tali. Interview by Ashley L. Wong. March 22, 2022.

Hjorth, Daniel, Robin Holt, and Chris Steyaert. "Entrepreneurship and Process Studies." *International Small Business Journal* 33, no. 6 (2015): 599–611. https://doi.org/10.1177/0266242615583566.

Hölling, Hanna B. "The Archival Turn: Toward New Ways of Conceptualising Changeable Artworks." In *Data Drift: Archiving Media and Data Art in the 21st Century*. Edited by Rasa Smite, Lev Manovich, and Smits Raitis, 73–89. Riga: RIXC and Liepaja's University Art Research Lab, 2015.

Holm, Ditte Vilstrup, and Timon Beyes. "How Art Becomes Organization: Reimagining Aesthetics, Sites and Politics of Entrepreneurship." *Organization Studies* 43, no. 2 (2022): 227–245. https://doi.org/10.1177/0170840621998571.

Horowitz, Noah. *Art of the Deal: Contemporary Art in a Global Financial Market*. Princeton, NJ: Princeton University Press, 2011.

Hui, Yuk. *Art and Cosmotechnics*. Minneapolis: University of Minnesota Press, 2020.

Hui, Yuk. "ChatGPT, or the Eschatology of Machines." *e-flux Journal*, no. 137 (2023). https://www.e-flux.com/journal/137/544816/chatgpt-or-the-eschatology-of-machines/.

Hui, Yuk. "Cosmotechnics as Cosmopolitics." *e-flux Journal*, no. 86 (2017). https://www.e-flux.com/journal/86/161887/cosmotechnics-as-cosmopolitics/.

Hui, Yuk. *On the Existence of Digital Objects*. Minneapolis: University of Minnesota Press, 2016.

Hui, Yuk. *The Question Concerning Technology in China: An Essay in Cosmotechnics*. Falmouth: Urbanomic, 2016.

Hui, Yuk. "What Is a Digital Object?" *Metaphilosophy* 43, no. 4 (2012): 380–395. https://doi.org/10.1111/j.1467-9973.2012.01761.x.

Hui, Yuk, and Ashley Wong. "Reclaiming Culture and Creativity from Industry and the UK Creative Economy: Towards New Configurations of the Artistic System." *Societies in Crisis, European Congress on Aesthetics* (2011): 472–477.

Ivanova, Victoria, Alana Kushnir, and Jasper Salomonsz. *Legal Lab Report 1: Art + Tech/Science Collaborations*. Serpentine Galleries (London: 2021). https://d37zoqglehb907.cloudfront.net/uploads/2021/07/Serpentine-Legal-Lab-Report-Final_V3.pdf.

Josefsson, Kira. "Corporate Aesthetics: The GCC at MOMA PS1." *Art in America*, April 24, 2014. https://www.artnews.com/art-in-america/interviews/corporate-aesthetics-the-gcc-at-moma-ps1-56393/.

Jullien, François. *From Being to Living: A Euro-Chinese Lexicon of Thought*. Translated by Michael Richardson and Krzysztof Fijalkowski. London: SAGE Publications Ltd, 2020.

Kemp, Jonathan. "Practical Ethics v3.0: Version Control." *Kunst und Material: Konzepte, Prozesse, Arbeitsteilungen* 12 (2022): 209–226. https://doi.org/https://doi.org/10.11588/arthistoricum.1047.c14538.

Kiefer, Cedric. Interview by Ashley L. Wong. May 31, 2019.

Klein, Naomi. *No Logo: Taking Aim at the Brand Bullies*. New York: Picador, 2000.

Krauss, Rosalind. *A Voyage on Art in the Age of the North Sea: Post-Medium Condition*. New York: Thames & Hudson, 1999.

Kuo, Michelle. "To Avoid the Waste of a Cultural Revolution: Experiments in Art and Technology." Doctoral dissertation, Harvard University, 2018.

Latour, Bruno. "Why Has Critique Run out of Steam? From Matters of Fact to Matters of Concern." *Critical Inquiry* 30, no. 2 (2004): 225–248.

Law, John, and Vicky Singleton. "Object Lessons." (July 2, 2004). http://www.heterogeneities.net/publications/LawSingleton2004ObjectLessons.pdf.

Lee, Benjamin, and Edward LiPuma. "Cultures of Circulation: The Imaginations of Modernity." *Public Culture* 14, no. 1 (2002): 191–213.

Lemmey, Huw. "Mission Creep: K-Hole and Trend Forecasting as Creative Practice." *Rhizome*, March 26, 2013. https://rhizome.org/editorial/2013/mar/26/mission-creep/.

Lessig, Lawrence. *Free Culture: The Nature and Future of Creativity*. Edited by Lawrence Lessig. New York: Penguin Books, 2005.

Leung, Desmond. "Personal Interview." By Ashley L. Wong. June 19, 2019.

Lippard, Lucy R. *Six Years: The Dematerialization of the Art Object from 1966 to 1972*. Edited by Lucy R. Lippard. Los Angeles: University of California Press, [1973] 1997.

Lorusso, Silvio. *Entreprecariat: Everyone Is an Entrepreneur. Nobody Is Safe*. Eindhoven, NL: Onomatopee, 2019.

Lury, Celia. "Brand as Assemblage: Assembling Culture." *Journal of Cultural Economy* 2, no. 1–2 (2009): 67–82. https://doi.org/10.1080/17530350903064022.

Lütticken, Sven. "Legal Forms, Value-Forms, Forms of Resistance." *The Online Journal of Contour Biennale* (2017). http://hearings.contour8.be/2017/01/12/legal-forms-value-forms-forms-of-resistance/.

Malraux, André. *Museum without Walls*. London: Secker & Warburg, [1949] 1967.

Manovich, Lev. "Post-Media Aesthetics." 2001. http://manovich.net/index.php/projects/post-media-aesthetics.

Marx, Karl. *Capital: A Critique of Political Economy*, vol. 1. Translated by Ben Fowkes. London: Penguin Books, [1867] 1976.

Massumi, Brian. *99 Theses on the Revaluation of Value: A Postcapitalist Manifesto*. Minneapolis: University of Minnesota Press, 2018.

McAndrew, Clare. *Fine Art and High Finance: Expert Advice on the Economics of Ownership*. New York: Bloomberg Press, 2010.

McClean, Daniel. "The Artist's Contract / from the Contract of Aesthetics to the Aesthetics of the Contract." *Mousse Magazine*, 2010. http://moussemagazine.it/daniel-mcclean-the-artists-contract-2010/.

McGoey, Linsey. *No Such Thing as a Free Gift: The Gates Foundation and the Price of Philanthropy*. London; New York: Verso, 2015.

McLuhan, Marshall. *Understanding Media: The Extensions of Man*. Cambridge, MA: MIT Press, 1994.

McQuilten, Grace, and Anthony White. *Art as Enterprise: Social and Economic Engagement in Contemporary Art*. London; New York: I. B. Tauris & Co. Ltd., 2016.

McWilliams, Andrew. "Interview by Ashley L. Wong. 2018.

Mellor, Alexia. "Professional Parody: An Examination of Artist Practices Parodying and Disrupting Business Models to New Ends." *Organizational Aesthetics* 4, no. 1 (January 19, 2015): 92–107. https://oa.journals.publicknowledgeproject.org/index.php/oa/article/view/50.

MetaObjects. "Experiments in Distribution of Time-Based Media Artworks," Medium, July 10, 2018. https://medium.com/@metaobjects/experiments-in-distribution-of-time-based-media-artworks-716c601d653c.

Metz, Cade. "The Amazing Murals Created by Facebook's Artist-in-Residence." *Wired*, November 24, 2014. https://www.wired.com/2014/11/take-tour-facebooks-giant-corporate-art-lab/.

Mill, John Stuart. *Principles of Political Economy*. Edited by J. Laurence Laughlin. New York: D. Appleton, 1884.

Mills, Lorna. Interview by Ashley L. Wong. April 13, 2022.

Mills, Lorna. Interview by Ashley L. Wong. May 3, 2019.

Mills, Simon. *Gilbert Simondon: Information, Technology and Media*. Lanham, MD: Rowman & Littlefield International, 2016.

Miranda, Francisco. *Systems Theory: Perspectives, Applications and Developments*. Systems Science series. New York: Nova Publishers, 2014.

Mitchell, William J. *The Reconfigured Eye: Visual Truth in the Post-Photographic Era*. Cambridge, MA: MIT Press, 1992.

Moore, Chris, ed. *Xu Zhen*. Berlin: Distanz, 2014.

Nate, Cohan. "Corporate Aesthetics: Shanzhai Biennial." *Art in America*, April 30, 2014. https://www.artnews.com/art-in-america/interviews/corporate-aesthetics-shanzhai-biennial-56395/.

O'Doherty, Brian. *Inside the White Cube: The Ideology of the Gallery Space*. Santa Monica, CA: Lapis Press, 1976.

O'Dwyer, Rachel. "Limited Edition: Producing Artificial Scarcity for Digital Art on the Blockchain and Its Implications for the Cultural Industries." *Convergence: The International Journal of Research into New Media Technologies* (2018). https://doi.org/10.1177/1354856518795097.

Oh, Whachul. "Understanding of Self: Buddhism and Psychoanalysis." *Journal of Religion and Health* 61, no. 6 (December 2022): 4696–4707. https://doi.org/10.1007/s10943-021-01437-w.

Olson, Marisa. "Postinternet: Art after the Internet." *Foam Magazine*, no. 29 (2011): 59–63.

Ono, Yoko. *Instruction Paintings*. New York: Weatherhill, 1995.

Osborne, Peter. *The Postconceptual Condition: Critical Essays*. London: Verso, 2018.

Paul, Christiane. *New Media in the White Cube and Beyond: Curatorial Models for Digital Art*. Berkeley: University of California Press, 2008.

Pearlman, Ellen. Interview by Ashley L. Wong. 2018.

Pine, Joseph B., and James H. Gilmore. *The Experience Economy*. Boston: Harvard Business Review Press, 2011.

Pollack, Barbara. "Risky Business." *ARTnews*, March 29, 2012. https://www.artnews.com/art-news/artists/risky-business-524/.

Pop, Susa, Tanya Toft, Nerea Calvillo, and Mark Wright. *What Urban Media Art Can Do: Why When Where & How*. Stuttgart: Avedition, 2016.

Pyke, Matt. "Universal Everything on Art Collecting in the Digital Age." Edited by Sedition, Vimeo, 2014. https://vimeo.com/98913293.

Rancière, Jacques. *The Politics of Aesthetics: The Distribution of the Sensible*. London: Continuum International Publishing Group, 2004.

Renwald, Kathy. "US$2.3-Million Bid on Canadian Nissan NFT Fails, Art Sells for US$220,000." *Driving*, 2021. https://driving.ca/auto-news/entertainment/us2-3-million-bid-on-canadian-nissan-nft-fails-art-sells-for-us220000.

Rösch, Ulrich. *We Are the Revolution!: Rudolf Steiner, Joseph Beuys, and the Threefold Social Impulse*. Forest Row, UK: Temple Lodge Publishing, 2013.

Sabiescu, Amalia, and Katerina Charatzopoulou. "The Museum as Ecosystem and Museums in Learning Ecosystems." In *Museum Experience Design*. Edited by Arnold Vermeeren, Licia Calvi, and Amalia Sabiescu, 325–345. Springer Series on Cultural Computing, Switzerland: Springer International Publishing AG, 2018.

Schnugg, Claudia. *Creating Artscience Collaboration: Bringing Value to Organizations*. Edited by Samantha Warren and Steven S. Taylor. Cham: Springer International Publishing, 2019.

Scholz, Trebor, ed. *Digital Labour: The Internet as Playground and Factory*. New York: Routledge, 2012.

Scholz, Trebor. *Uberworked and Underpaid*. Oxford: Polity Press, 2016.

Scholz, Trebor, and Nathan Schneider. *Ours to Hack and to Own: The Rise of Platform Cooperativism, a New Vision for the Future of Work and a Fairer Internet*. Edited by Trebor Scholz and Nathan Schneider. New York: OR Books, 2016. https://doi.org/10.2307/j.ctv62hfq7.

Servais, Alain. "Video Art Market: The Right Time to Rethink the Structure." *Texte zur Welt*, no. 19 (2016).

Shanken, Edward A. "Art in the Information Age: Technology and Conceptual Art." *Leonardo* 35, no. 4 (2002): 433–438.

Shanken, Edward A. "Artists in Industry and the Academy: Collaborative Research, Interdisciplinary Scholarship and the Creation and Interpretation of Hybrid Forms." *Leonardo* 38, no. 5 (2005): 415–418.

Shanken, Edward A. "Contemporary Art and New Media: Digital Divide or Hybrid Discourse." *In a Companion to Digital Art*, edited by Christiane Paul. Blackwell Companions to Art History. Chichester: John Wiley & Sons, 2016.

Shiller, Robert J. *Irrational Exuberance*. Princeton, NJ: Princeton University Press, 2000.

Shirky, Clay. *Here Come Everybody*. London: Penguin Books, 2008.

Sholette, Gregory. *Dark Matter: Art and Politics in the Age of Enterprise Culture*. London: Pluto Press, 2011.

Siciliano, Michael L. *Creative Control: The Ambivalence of Work in the Culture Industries*. New York: Columbia University Press, 2021.

Siegelaub, Seth, and Robert Projansky. *The Artist's Reserved Rights Transfer and Sale Agreement*, [1971] 2012, accessed October 19, 2019, http://www.primaryinformation.org/product/siegelaub-the-artists-reserved-rights-transfer-and-sale-agreement/.

Sito, Peggy, and Cheryl Arcibal. "Adrian Cheng to Step Down as New World CEO, Likely to Be Replaced by COO Eric Ma: Sources." *South China Morning Post*, September 25, 2024. https://www.scmp.com/business/companies/article/3279929/adrian-cheng-step-down-new-worlds-ceo-take-non-executive-role-sources-say.

Stengers, Isabelle. "Introductory Notes on an Ecology of Practices." *Cultural Studies Review* 11, no. 1 (2005): 183–196.

Steward, Julian. “The Concept and Method of Cultural Ecology.” In *The Environment in Anthropology: A Reader in Ecology, Culture, and Sustainable Living*. Edited by Nora Haenn and Richard Wils, 12–17. New York: New York University Press, 2020.

Steyerl, Hito. “In Defense of the Poor Image.” *e-flux Journal* 10 (2009). https://www.e-flux.com/journal/10/61362/in-defense-of-the-poor-image/.

Stiegler, Bernard. *For a New Critique of Political Economy*. Cambridge, UK: Polity Press, 2010.

Stiegler, Bernard. “Too Late? The Final Warning.” In *Work Marathon 2018*. Edited by Serpentine Galleries, YouTube, 2018. accessed August 16, 2021. https://youtu.be/EsGVN7UEopw.

Stiegler, Bernard. *What Makes Life Worth Living: On Pharmacology*. Translated by Daniel Ross. Cambridge, UK: Polity Press, 2013.

Stone, Eric Golo. “Legal Implications: Cameron Rowland’s Rental Contract.” *October 164*, 2018, 89–112.

Svendsen, Lars. *Fashion: A Philosophy*. Translated by John Irons. London: Reaktion Books, 2006.

Terranova, Tiziana. “Free Labor: Producing Culture for the Digital Economy.” *Social Text* 18, no. 2 (2000): 33–58. https://doi.org/10.1215/01642472-18-2_63-33.

Throsby, David. *Economics and Culture*. Cambridge, UK: Cambridge University Press, 2001.

Throsby, David. “The Production and Consumption of the Arts: A View of Cultural Economics.” *Journal of Economic Literature* 32, no. 1 (1994): 1–29. http://www.jstor.org/stable/2728421.

Tokumitsu, Miya. *Do What You Love: And Other Lies About Success and Happiness*. New York: Regan Arts, 2015.

Tribe, Mark, Reena Jana, and Uta Grosenick, eds. *New Media Art*. Cologne: Taschen, 2006.

Tsui, Enid. “How New World Heir Adrian Cheng Combines His Passion for Art with Entrepreneurship.” *South China Morning Post*, March 10, 2015. https://www.scmp.com/lifestyle/arts-culture/article/1733513/k11-founder-adrian-cheng-bringing-six-exhibitions-art-basel.

Velthuis, Olav. “Symbolic Meanings of Prices: Constructing the Value of Contemporary Art in Amsterdam and New York Galleries.” *Theory and Society* 32 (2003): 181–215.

Velthuis, Olav. *Talking Prices: Symbolic Meanings of Prices on the Market for Contemporary Art*. Princeton, NJ: Princeton University Press, 2005.

Vierkant, Artie. “The Image Object Post-Internet.” 2010. http://jstchillin.org/artie/pdf/The_Image_Object_Post-Internet_a4.pdf.

Wark, Mckenzie. “My Collectible Ass.” *e-flux* 85 (2017). http://www.e-flux.com/journal/85/156418/my-collectible-ass/.

Weibel, Peter. "The Post-Media Condition." Mute, March 19, 2012. http://www.metamute.org/editorial/lab/post-media-condition.

Wernick, Andrew. *Promotional Culture: Advertising, Ideology and Symbolic Expression*. London: Sage Publications, 1991.

Wershler-Henry, Darren S., Lori Emerson, and Jussi Parikka. *The Lab Book: Situated Practices in Media Studies*. Minneapolis: University of Minnesota Press, 2021.

Whatmore, Sarah. *Hybrid Geographies*. London: Sage Publications, 2002.

Wong, Ashley L. "Artists in the Creative Economy: Inoperative Modes of Resistance." *A Peer-Reviewed Journal About* 7, no. 1 (2018): Research Values. https://doi.org/10.7146/aprja.v7i1.116059.

Wong, Ashley L. "Beyond Ownership: Sustaining Art as Practices and Processes." Forthcoming in *Curating Superintelligences: A Reader on AI and Future Curating*, DATA browser 10. Edited by Joasia Krysa and Magdalena Tyżlik-Carver. London: Open Humanities Press, 2024.

Wong, Ashley L. "Comment se confronter au marché: les nouveaux édias face au marché de l'art." *Marges*, no. 28 (2019): 98–112. https://doi.org/https://doi.org/10.4000/marges.1760.

Wong, Ashley L. "Cyclic Existence, Iteration, and Digital Transcendence: Lu Yang's Live Motion Capture Performances." *Screen Bodies* 7, no. 1 (2022): 128–145. https://doi.org/10:3167/screen.2022.070108.

Wong, Ashley L. "NFTs and Digital Collectibles: Creating Systems of Ownership for Digital Objects." *Visual Culture Studies*, no. 3 (2022): 211–237.

Wong, Ashley L. "Paolo Cirio, Political Aesthetics of the Art Market." *Clot Magazine*, August 4, 2020. https://www.clotmag.com/interviews/paolo-cirio-political-aesthetics-of-the-art-market.

Wong, Ashley L. "Thoughtworks Arts Residency: Leveraging Corporate Resources for Art & Social Change." *Clot Magazine*, September 27, 2018, https://www.clotmag.com/biomedia/thoughtworks-arts-residency-leveraging-corporate-resources-for-art-social-change-by-ashley-lee-wong.

Wu, Chin-tao. *Privatising Culture: Corporate Art Intervention since the 1980s*. London: Verso, 2002.

Xu Zhen: A MadeIn Company Production. Exhibition catalogue. Beijing: Ullens Center for Contemporary Art, 2014.

Xu Zhen. *Corporate*. Produced by MadeIn Company. Edited by Katrin Bucher Trantow and Peter Pakesch. Translated by Andrew Horsfield. Vienna: Verlag für Moderne Kunst, 2015.

Zelizer, Viviana A. Rotman. *Economic Lives: How Culture Shapes the Economy*. Princeton, NJ: Princeton University Press, 2011.

INDEX